Algonquin Park

EXCURSIONS WITH A PHOTOGRAPHER

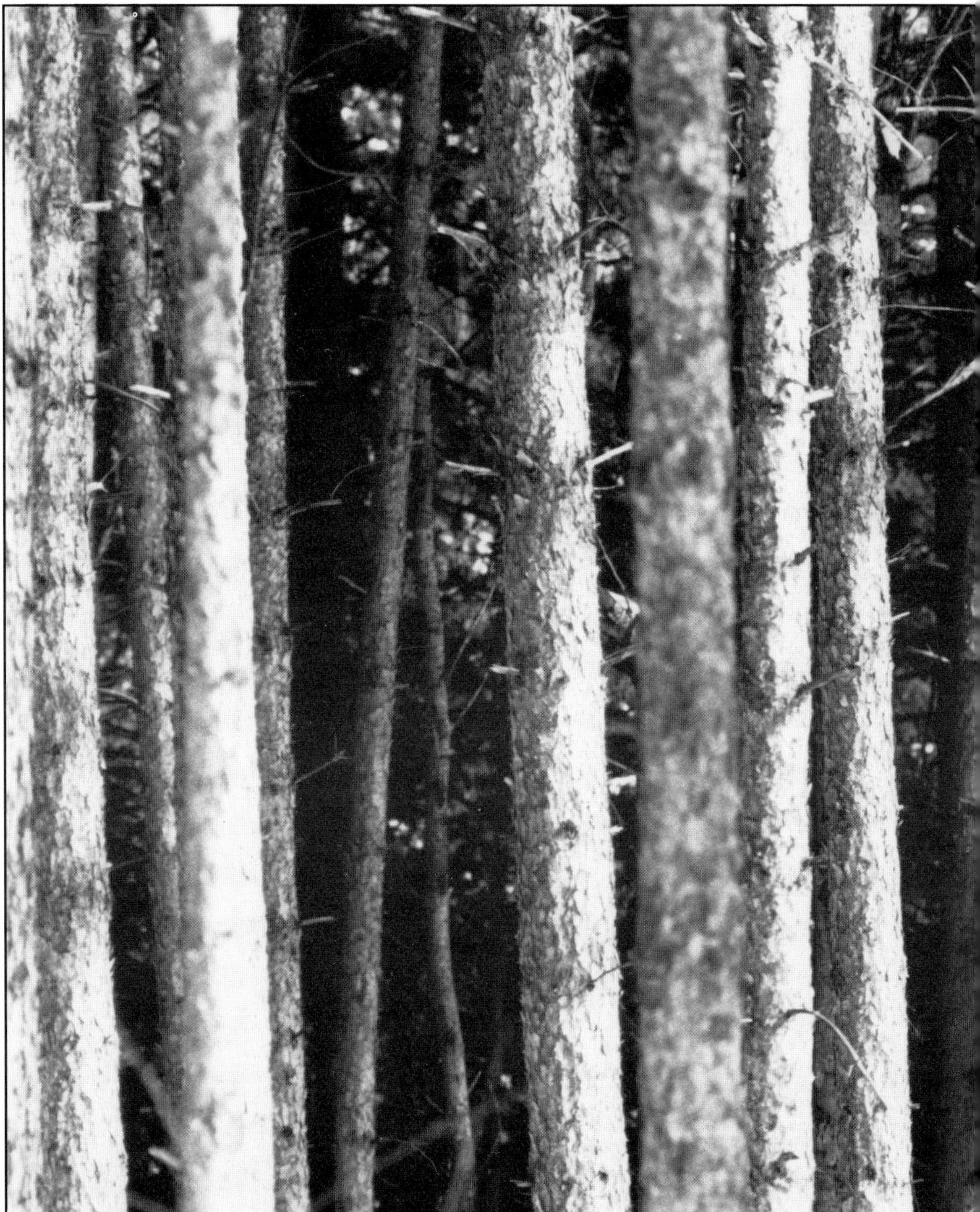

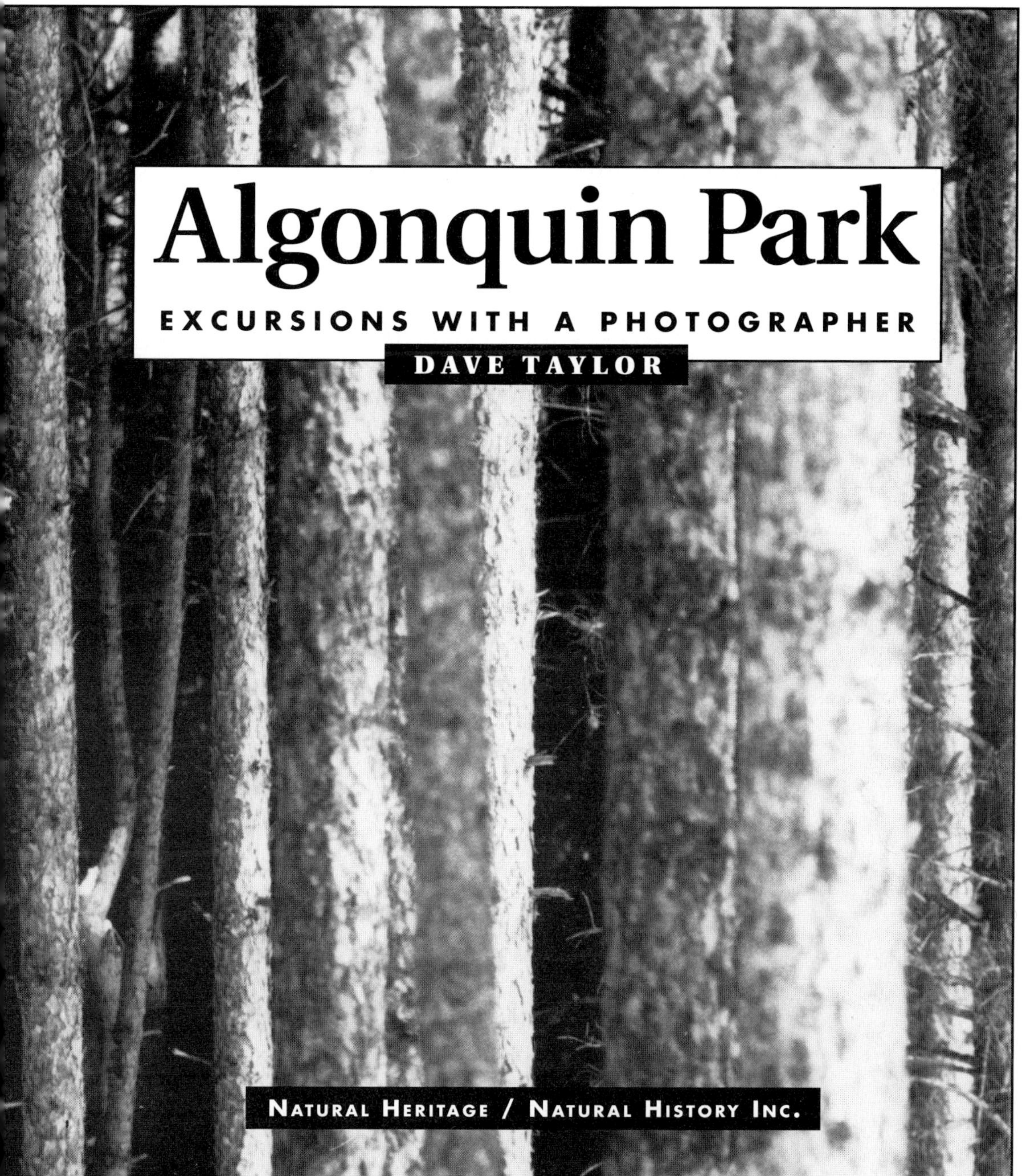

Algonquin Park

EXCURSIONS WITH A PHOTOGRAPHER

DAVE TAYLOR

Natural Heritage / Natural History Inc.

Algonquin Park: Excursions with a Photographer
by Dave Taylor

Published by Natural Heritage / Natural History Inc.
P.O. Box 95, Station "O", Toronto, Ontario M4A 2M8

Design and typesetting: Robin Brass Studio
Printed and bound in Canada by Hignell Printing Limited, Winnipeg, Manitoba

Canadian Cataloguing in Publication Data

Taylor, Dave, 1948–
Algonquin Park: Excursions with a Photographer

ISBN 0-920474-88-8

1. Algonquin Provincial Park (Ont.) – Pictorial works. 2. Algonquin Provincial Park (Ont.) – Description and travel. 3. Natural History – Ontario – Algonquin Provincial Park – Pictorial works. 5. Nature photography. I. Title

FC3065.A4T38 1994 508.713'147 C94-930434-4
F1059.A4T38 1994

Natural Heritage / Natural History Inc. gratefully acknowledges the assistance of the Canada Council, the Ontario Arts Council, and the Government of Ontario through the Ministry of Culture, Tourism and Recreation.

For my Mom and Dad, who gave up Wasaga Beach for South Tea Lake. We had some great times there.

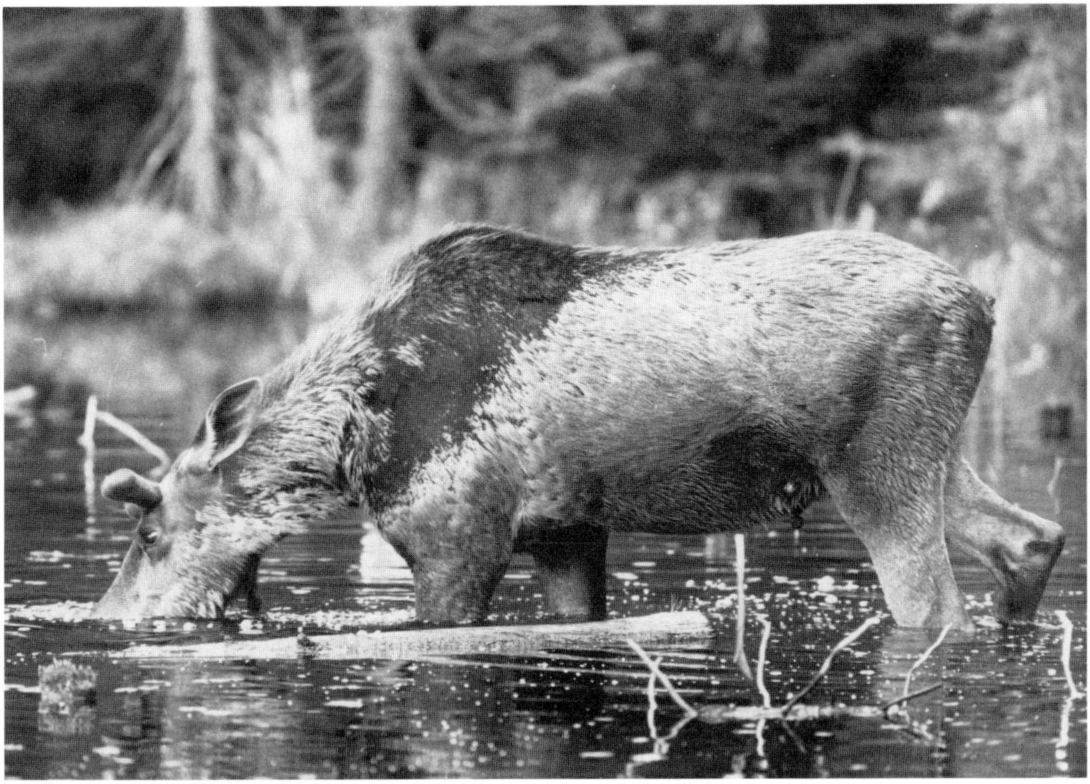

In the spring, visitors come from miles around to see moose like this young bull. The moose are drawn to the salt-rich mud and water that collects along Highway 60. (300mm 2.8L auto-focus)

Contents

Introduction

Let's be honest, Algonquin Provincial Park is not the best place in the world to photograph wildlife. Banff National Park in Alberta or Wyoming's Yellowstone National Park offer a greater diversity of animal life and better opportunities. Even these pale when compared to Kenya's spectacular Masai Mara Game Reserve and its huge herds of wildebeest and zebra and attendant predators.

As a professional wildlife photographer and writer, I've visited these places and many more besides. Yet, for all their wonders and photographic opportunities, it is Ontario's Algonquin Park that looms largest in my affection and memories.

True, there are better places to see wild animals and scenery but there is no place like Algonquin. There is no other park like it within a half day's drive of five million people. Residents of Toronto, Buffalo, Montreal or Ottawa (and places in between) can be home from work on a Friday evening by five and be in the park by midnight.

Extend the range to a full day's drive and there are countless millions more who can make it to the park's borders.

I am one of those who make this trek. Algonquin is a three-hour drive for me. It's a short drive, a mild inconvenience really, that is easily compensated for by Algonquin's potential bounty. I can leave home on a Saturday morning and be photographing moose by ten. And, if I choose, I can be home in time for supper that night.

I can also, if I want, be paddling a canoe into a wilderness where I will encounter few if any people.

I said "potential bounty" because I've found Algonquin to be, at times, both a generous and a stingy host. My notes contain accounts of days when wolves, bears and moose were all encountered on a single trip. On the other hand, there are accounts of days when the only life sighted was a forlorn robin flying rapidly into the woods. I've shot fifteen rolls of film in a day. I have also shot fewer than fifteen photographs over a weekend!

That is the way Algonquin is. As you read this book or any other on the park, remember that the photographs were taken over a period of weeks, if not years. Do not go to the park expecting to see everything in one day, one week or one month. Patience and tenacity are rewarded here.

I hope to accomplish many things with this book. First, I want it to be an honest book. None of the photographs that illustrate this book were taken outside the Algonquin ecosystem. Note that I said "ecosystem" and not "park." There are a few special places I will direct you to that are outside the park's boundaries but well within its ecosystem.

As you read the book, it will be come apparent why I selected this criteria for this book.

I also want to share with you "typical days." As I prepared to write this book, I made several trips to the park, many trips only a day long. The purpose of these trips was to provide a snapshot of a given day in a given season so that you can have some inkling of what to expect. Some days were diamonds, some were not, but all were learning experiences for me. You will find these excursions sprinkled throughout the first section of the book.

I also want this book to be more than a "how-to" book about nature photography. There are plenty of these and you will find some of the best listed in the bibliography. In the second section, I will share my ideas about cameras, lenses and films but this I do more as background so that you can understand how my equipment and thoughts colour my approach to photographing Algonquin.

I deliberately deal with these matters last so that we can get quickly to the meat of the book: the Algonquin ecosystem. Through recent projects, I found myself using my cameras to record more than just portraits of plants and animals. I was recording their "ecosystems."

An ecosystem is a complex set of relationships that make up the living world. Algonquin's ecosystem is a worthy study for it encompasses predators and prey, seasonal changes, varying northern environments and the influence of human beings. By studying it, you can learn a great deal about how such things work. This knowledge can be then applied to other spots: Florida's Everglades, Africa's savannas or the alpine tundra.

I approach the subject this way because of the "global" nature of this project. The techniques I use can be applied in Ontario or Kenya. The understanding of ecosystems I seek to portray in the resulting images and text reflects concepts that are valid globally as well.

This book sets out to explore Algonquin's ecosystem with a camera, but I hope you the reader will also learn something of the park's wonder and its complexity. However, this is not a book about ecosystems (Algonquin's or any place else's). It is a book about visiting a place and coming to an understanding of its nature through the medium of photography.

It is this approach, or bias if you prefer, that determines the layout of this book. The chapters contain information about the particular features of this part of the ecosystem or that one: this is intended as background information that I used in setting out to record on film what I was seeing and studying.

It is my hope that the combination of these two elements will encourage and help you to record your own version of Algonquin Park.

As you read the text about Algonquin's ecosystem, you will find frequent references to photographic techniques and equipment. If your primary interest is photography, you might want to consider reading the second section on photographic equipment before reading the first chapters on exploring the park with a camera.

Looking back over my years visiting the park, I can recall many special moments. It was there I saw my first moose. It was there I learned first hand about the power and majesty of the black bear.

And it was there that I found myself surrounded by a pack of wolves one night. Of this last incident, there are no photographs except those that live in my memory. And that, perhaps, is the best place for all Algonquin's images to live.

Enjoy your visit.

DAVE TAYLOR

A WORD ABOUT THE CAPTIONS

All captions for photographs are followed by the type of lens used to take the picture. Its focal length is given first, then the aperture stop, then the type of lens – an "L" after the f-stop indicates that it is a high-quality colour-corrected lens; if no "L" appears, it is a standard lens. Auto-focus indicates that it was not a manual-focus lens

PART 1

EXPLORING THE ALGONQUIN ECOSYSTEM WITH A CAMERA

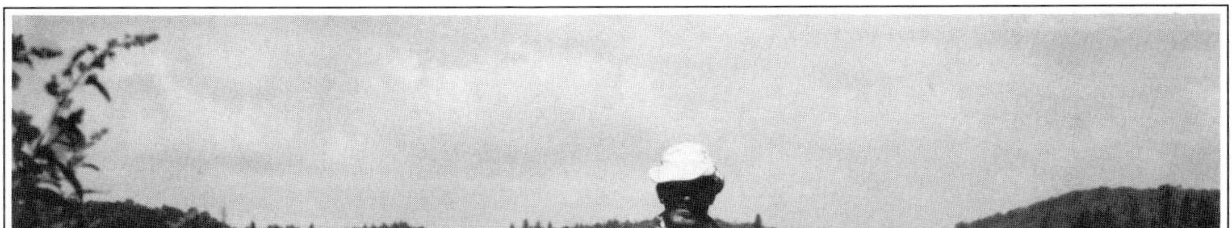

All set for a trip in the park. I've got my camera, canoe and good weather. (Bob Bowyer, 200mm 2.8L auto-focus)

Excursion 1

Saturday, February 27

I left Mississauga around eight in the morning and headed north. It was one of those rare February Saturdays when the weather fully cooperated: no snow squalls, no wind, no clouds. This perfect day for photography was the first of several such excursions to the park I planned in order to update material for this book.

My purpose in making these trips was to share with you, the readers, what a photographic trip to the park might be like. I hope that through reading about these excursions you will get a feeling for what you can see and photograph throughout the year. Remember that there are no guarantees. Some days will be "diamonds" and others will be "fool's gold." The excursions in this book are presented the way they unfolded.

With dry roads and little traffic, I arrived in the park by 10:45. My first stop was at the west gate. I had two reasons for this. The first was to purchase a day pass. The money supports the park and I do not begrudge the fee.

It is possible to drive through the park without getting a pass, especially now that the west gate is beside and not on the new entrance road. I am certain many people are tempted to ignore picking one up, however all picnic areas, campgrounds and facilities have signs clearly marking them as areas where a pass is required. The fine for not having one is $25, and I know of several people who have been ticketed for not having a permit on display.

The other reason I stopped at the gate was to ask about wildlife sightings along the road. Some gate attendants have greater knowledge about wildlife than others due to personal or academic interests. It pays to ask very specific questions. Today it proved a valuable stop. A few moose had been seen but not in any one location, but there were, I was told, bird feeders at Minnesing Trail head and up Opeongo Road where the park naturalists were doing some research on grey jays. The birds should be easy to find.

This latter piece of information was revealed when I asked about feeders. I try to picture the day unfolding and to visualize what I want to get from it, knowing, because of my late arrival and planned early departure, that moose would not be a guaranteed species. I also knew that winter birds would be

Whiskey jacks will come readily to you for food in winter because they are nesting or soon will be and they need the food. (28mm 2.8L auto-focus)

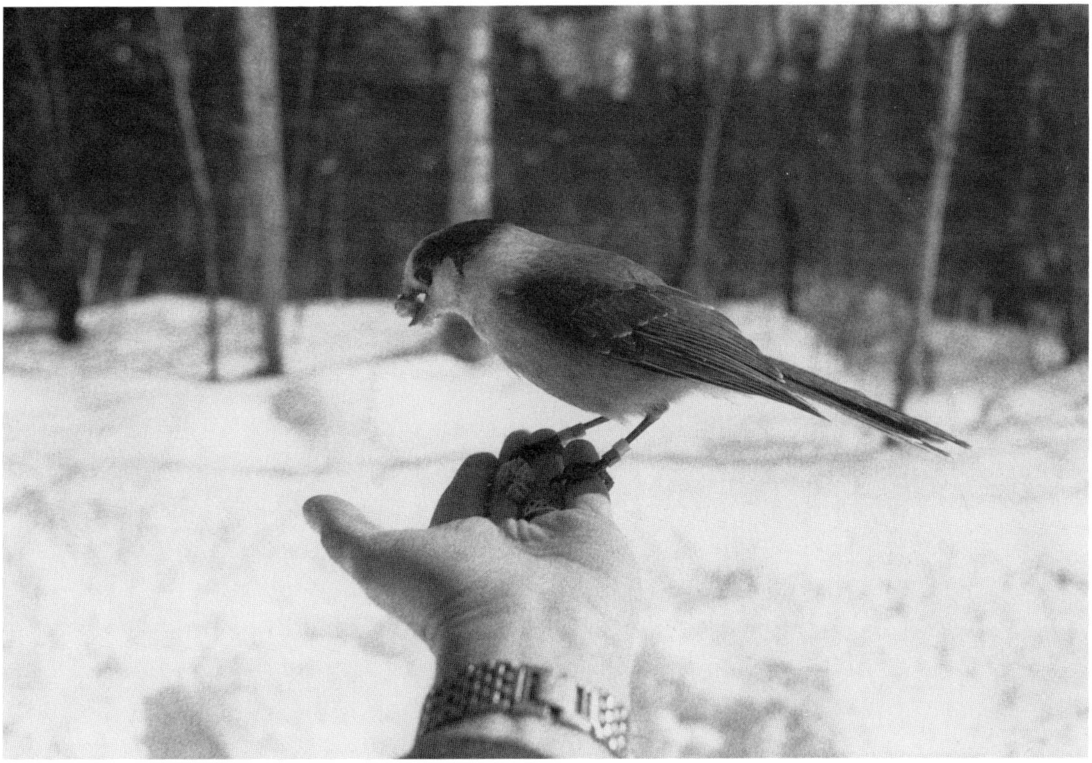

hungry and visiting feeders at this time of year. What I didn't know was whether there were any feeders set up in the park.

Armed with this information, I set off down the road. Moose tracks were everywhere through the metre-deep snow. I also spotted wolf, otter and fox tracks as I drove along. I stopped to photograph many of these tracks using both black and white film and slide film.

I had one camera with a 300mm f/4 lens coupled to a 1.4 tele (which gave me 420mm 5.6) and the other with an 80-200mm f/2.8 zoom on it. Of the two, the zoom lens was best for tracks but I soon switched to a 28mm f/2.8 wide angle. I just wasn't pleased with the images I saw through the zoom lens.

I drove through the park slowly, checking for moose. I've learned through years of doing this that you don't look for moose standing by the side of the road in winter. Instead you look in behind the pine trees. Moose are very tolerant of the cold but prefer the protection these trees give them from the wind, for it is wind chill rather than freezing temperatures that causes moose discomfort.

They are very hard to see hidden in the woods and I am sure that I drove by at least one or two lying within a few metres of the highway.

In any case, I didn't see a living thing: just one den near the road by Smoke Lake that was obviously being used. The tracks looked like wolf tracks but I doubt they were. I thought they might be fisher, but no one could identify them later from the shots I took.

It was getting on for twelve when I arrived at the snow barricade that closes off the top half of Opeongo Road. If there were bird feeders about, I didn't see them but I fully expected that the birds would find me. They did. I made a show of slamming the car door a couple of times and before long two grey shadows glided in.

I don't make a habit of baiting or feeding animals but with these camp robbers I make an exception. I had some granola bars, which I broke up and began tossing for the jays. These birds are among the first Ontario birds to nest doing so in late winter. Since there were only two I assumed that one was the adult bird and the second last year's offspring. The other parent was probably sitting on the nest by now. On the other hand, it was possible they were adult birds intent on getting an extra bit of food before they nested.

Grey jays have a fascinating life history. Although they lay three or four eggs, only one youngster survives. If any of the hatchlings are males the parents usually select to feed the strongest of them. The rest starve to death. Only when there are no males will a female survive and be fed.

This seems a strange habit but it works very well for Algonquin's grey jays. The entire park ecosystem has all the pairs of jays it can support. There is literally no room for expansion. By having only one youngster survive each year, the parent birds ensure that the year's population losses will be replaced. Even with this limited number of surviving hatchlings, more young birds survive than are needed.

The parent birds feed their offspring until the end of summer when they begin to hoard food for next winter. They go to great pains to make certain that their offspring doesn't know where their food is cached, for if the yearling knew where it was, it would be stolen! Nesting in February demands that the birds have enough food stored to feed both themselves and their next hatchling for there is no other food available to them at this time of year.

So by feeding them I was helping the birds through tough times, so tough, in fact, that the yearling bird will try to destroy the new nest and kill that year's hatchlings so that his parents will feed him instead of the chicks. If he (or she) succeeds, survival is guaranteed. If he or she fails, death is likely.

Given this background, it is not surprising that grey jays will readily land on your hand to take food. Survival may well depend on it! It makes a good "photo-op" too. Armed with a wide-angle lens, I couldn't resist taking a few shots.

I spent about half an hour with these birds and then pushed on to the East Gate, where I stopped to photograph birds coming into a feeder full of sunflower seeds. The birds were going to the shady side of the feeder so I set up my tripod and 600mm lens to photograph them in the trees. Naturally, by the time I was set up, all the birds had vanished but a few minutes of patient waiting was all it took before they returned. I photographed red- and white-breasted nuthatches, evening grosbeaks, purple finches and a distant blue jay. Then I moved on.

I didn't actually see the moose: I saw its legs. It was standing still but the shape of them gave it away. Trees taper upward, not downward. I turned the car around and made a second pass. Yes, it was a moose, but it was buried in conifers and very hard to see. I would have to go in after it. I put the zoom back on one camera and grabbed the 420 too. Then I quietly but hastily opened the trunk and put on my snowshoes. The moose was still there!

Unfortunately the straps on the snowshoes were not properly done up and I pitched forward into the deep snow. (Hint: Always double-check your snowshoe straps!) Mumbling under my breath and doing everything I could to keep my cameras from plunging into the snow, I extricated myself, certain by now that the moose was well and truly gone.

She wasn't, so I crouched down and "maaaaaaaed" like a calf. It is an excellent idea to learn how to imitate various moose calls and today provided me with further proof of that advice. The cow actually walked towards me, and then she produced a loud sound somewhere between a bark and the huff of a steam engine. It was then that I saw that she had a real calf. By now I was shooting as often as I dared. I moved the camera very slowly and tried to look at her only through the view finder.

I took a few more shots and she trotted away. I called, and again she returned. I took a few more shots. Finally she made up her mind that I was not her baby and trotted off driving her yearling calf ahead of her. I followed but aside from hearing that wonderful bark of her's, I never saw her or her calf again.

My next stop was the Minnesing Trail head where I found, as promised, the bird feeder. Once again there were two grey

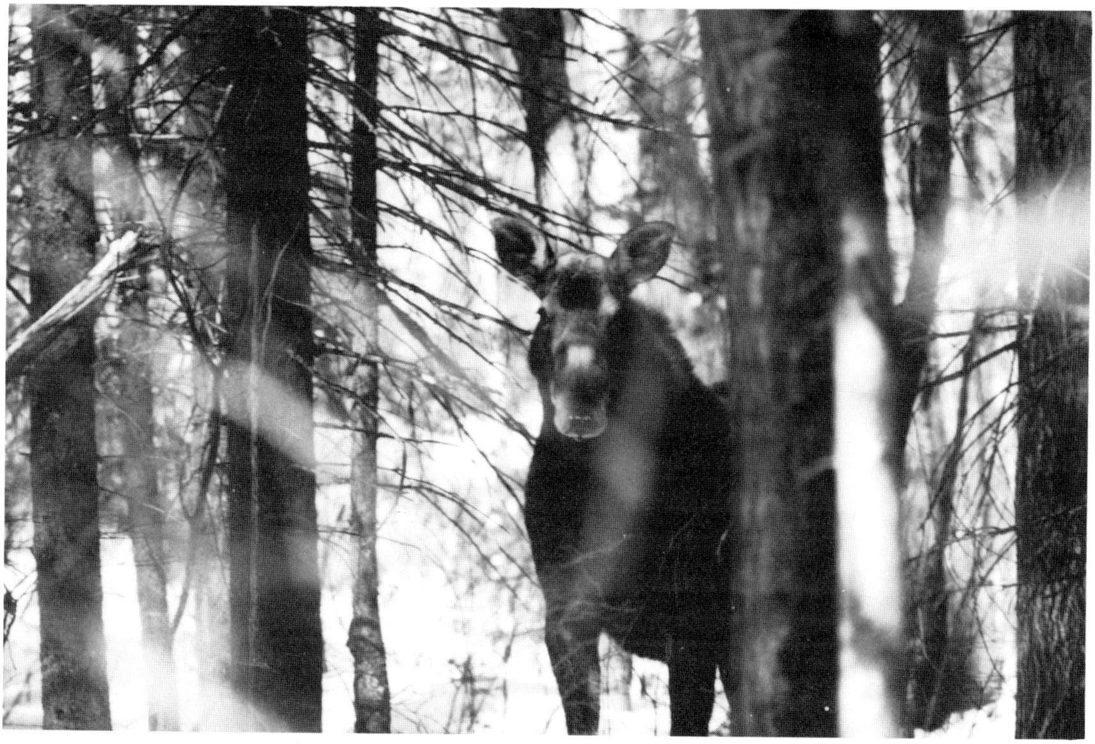

jays there and the usual chickadees. I photographed both for about twenty minutes and then moved on.

It was 2:30 and I had one more stop to make before I headed home. I knew where I'd find some deer.

When I reached Dwight, I took Highway 35 south towards Dorset and soon I found the snowy hills on either side of the road lined with deer tracks. This area is a deer yard (a place where deer group to spend the winter) and it is unusual not to see any deer during January and February. Some resident cottagers even feed them, so I took the time to investigate a few of the cottage roads to see if any deer were being fed within good camera range. Luck was with me. I saw about twenty deer and got some good shots. All the bucks had dropped their antlers but still looked handsome.

By four I was on my way back to Mississauga. A good day all in all. Nine species photographed and some good scenics were what I had to show for my effort. It had been worth the drive.

This cow moose came to my imitation of a calf moose. Note the raised ears and hackles. She is not really sure about me. (300mm 4L autofocus)

CHAPTER 1

The Land

To truly capture the Algonquin ecosystem on film it is first necessary to come to an understanding of the land that underlies it. In fact, to understand the ecology of an area you must first have some understanding of the land, for it is the land that determines which plants will grow and which will not. It is the land and its location and altitude that determine the climate: and it is the land that gives a place a sense of history and permanency.

Most of us virtually ignore all but the most spectacular mountains, volcanoes or sea shores when we visit an area. No matter where you go try asking yourself some simple questions.

Why do I find these particular plants here?

What was this place like one hundred years ago? A thousand? Ten thousand? A million? A billion?

Why is there so much (or so little) water?

How did this place come to be?

How can I capture these things on film?

Let's begin with a crash course in Algonquin's geology. Algonquin lies on the southern edge of the Canadian Shield. Historians will tell you that this mantle of rock "created" Canada and gave the country much of its character. People can't farm on it very well, they haven't built huge cities here, and for much of the year most people find it uninhabitable.

The shield has three seasons: cold, buggy and pleasant. The cold season lasts six to seven months. The buggy season lasts two to three months, and what's left is bearable.

It is cold because it lies well to the north. There is a good reason why there are no Miami Beaches here. Ice and snow claim the land for much of the year so even though there are sandy beaches that run for kilometres, there are few resorts built on them.

It is buggy because when all that ice and snow melt, the rocky land refuses to let much of it drain away. Pot holes, swamps, muskeg and bogs abound here, thanks to the underlying rocks, and these still waterholes provide the perfect places for insects, especially mosquitoes, to breed. Where the water does run off, the rapids and fast-flowing streams provide perfect habitats for blackflies to reproduce. Neither insect provides much joy for visitors.

NEITHER FISH NOR FOWL

If you doubt the truth of this, take a good look at a map of Canada. Most Canadians live well south of the shield where the climate and the insects are more hospitable. It is because of the cold and insects that Canada's population has grown more slowly compared to our southern neighbour's. It is also

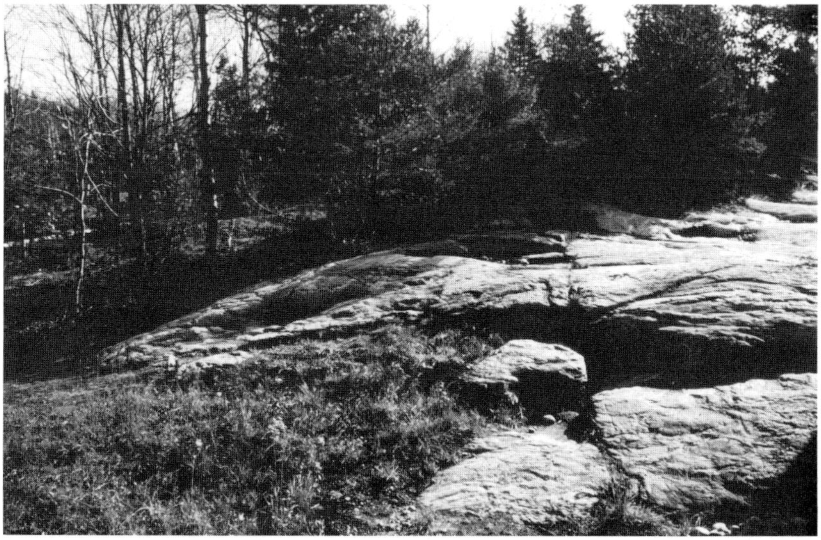

The rocks along the side of Rock Lake Road clearly show the gouges left by the glaciers. (200mm 2.8L zoom autofocus)

thanks to these two factors that much of the country remains wild.

Algonquin, however, lies at the southern end of the shield and its climate is much more pleasant than most of this region's. It is also closer to populated areas and for many people the accessibility of the park and its surrounding areas create the impression that this must be what the Canadian Shield looks like.

To a large extent, this impression is wrong. Algonquin is very much a mixture of both the southern environments and more northern ones. It is neither fish nor fowl, which is to say it is unique. Where the more typical regions of the shield have moose and caribou, Algonquin has moose and white-tailed deer. Algonquin has pines and beech trees instead of spruce trees. Ecologists call this mixing a transition zone.

But where Algonquin is closest to the truth about the Canadian shield is in its rocks. And it is with these rocks that we shall begin our photographic discovery of the park.

Two types of rocks form the base of Algonquin's ecology: metamorphic gneisses and grey or pink igneous granites. The gneiss rock was originally sea-bottom sediments 1.5 billion years ago. Much of what we now call North America was

Metamorphic rocks were created by the tremendous geological forces that shaped the Canadian Shield half a billion years ago or more. If you look closely you can see the layers of compressed sediments. (200mm 2.8L zoom auto-focus)

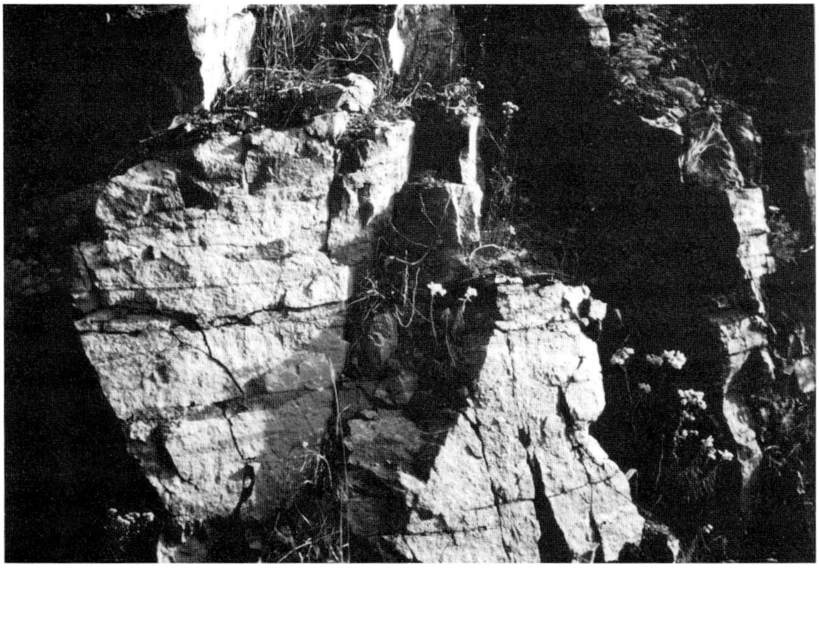

at that time covered by a shallow sea in which year after year, eon after eon, the eroded sediments from the surrounding land were laid down. However, there is more to the story than that.

Sedimentary rocks, such as the sandstone and shale deposits found in southern Ontario, have the same sea-bed origins as much of Algonquin's gneisses. They are found in layers too, but they are much "softer" rocks, easily broken apart. These rocks date back about 450 million years.

Something happened to the much older sediments in the area we know as the Canadian Shield to greatly alter them from sedimentary into metamorphic rocks.

HOT TIMES LONG GONE

Their present layered appearance dates from a little over one billion years ago when they lay twenty to thirty kilometres below the Earth's surface. Here they were subjected to intense heat and pressure that "plasticized" and squeezed them. The layers of sedimentary rocks were compressed and hardened. Volcanic rock pushed and intruded its way through cracks and faults much the way mud oozes between your toes. Finally they were extruded, pushed up above the surface, into their final alignments as part of the mountain-building process that went on during that period. Looking at them, it is easy to see their layered sedimentary look mixed with the contrasting lines of volcanic rock.

The mountain range that once rose over Algonquin rivalled the Rockies. The rocks we see throughout the park were essentially the bases of these mountains, but the peaks have been eroded by a billion years of wind, rain and glaciers. I can't help but wonder what incredible animals walked that long vanished terrain. Dinosaurs? Almost certainly, but any evidence of their presence has long ago been scraped away.

A sample of these metamorphic rocks may be see along Highway 60 about a kilometre past the west gate. In fact, for the first twenty-five kilometres of the park road, most of the roadside rock formations are of this type. These sedimentary gneisses, once muddy sandstone, now appear grey, green, black, brown or pink. A careful look will reveal quartz, feldspar and other intrusive rocks.

TAKING ROCK FOR GRANITE

Much of the rock visible along the highway is granite. This rock resulted from similar geological forces except this was originally molten magma, and its form reflects its fluid origins. Granite does not appear in a layered state.

During the active mountain-building period of Algonquin's geological history, the molten rock often broke through the gneisses layers and flowed over the land. As it cooled, the rock often separated into bands of quartz and other minerals, giving this rock its marble-cake appearance.

Many of the rock cuts along the eastern portions of the park highway are through this type of rock.

These rock cuts offer a good place to see the structure of Algonquin's Canadian Shield but are not my favourite places to photograph the shield. I prefer the rocks where they are exposed through more natural forces rather than the hand of man.

One of the best ways to photograph Algonquin's Precambrian ancestry is from a canoe. Many of the lakes in the park have fairly steep sides, having been gouged out by the recent ice ages, and although most of the rock has been covered by soil and vegetation for centuries the wave action of the lakes keeps the shoreline barren and exposed.

Pay some attention to the time of day you visit the rocks. Too much shadow or too bright a sun can alter their appearance. Overcast days with even lighting will give you the most detail. If your purpose is to record the rocks for a more scientific discussion, consider placing a common object in the photo to give the audience something to which to compare their size. A favourite and appropriate choice for this object is the Canadian dollar coin, the loonie.

I find a wide-angle lens works best for shots taken from

the canoe. After all, rocks are big and they don't run off at your approach. Focus is less of a concern with wide-angle lenses as well, because they have a much better depth of field than does a telephoto lens at the same aperture.

"Depth of field" refers to the part of the photograph that is sharp. It varies with the aperture setting of the lens. The more open or wider the aperture is, the less the depth of field will be. The smaller the opening, the greater the depth. Understanding how this works is crucial to the creative use of a camera. Even an auto-focus camera cannot "think" about the effect opening or closing the aperture will have on your photo. In the course of this book, we will refer to a variety of tricks and techniques employing knowledge of the depth of field.

It is important that you, as a photographer, understand what it is and the advantages and limitations it places on your abilities. Wide-angle lenses offer the greatest range of depth while telephotos have the least. (I should point out that technically, that last statement is wrong. All things being equal tests have shown that when a wide-angle photograph is blown up so that its central image is the same size as a telephoto's central image, the depth of field is about the same: not greater or lesser. However, we will assume my statement about the depth of field is true because it "appears to be so" to our eyes unless we go to the trouble of extreme blow-ups. Trust me on this and don't worry about it too much!)

My 28mm lens can, at its smallest aperture opening (f/22), offer a depth of field for an object anywhere between half a metre from the lens and infinity. My 600mm can – with luck, a similar aperture opening and a subject at a reasonable distance – offer a depth of maybe two metres or one metre on either side of the subject.

Of course, the lower (smaller) the aperture setting the lower the shutter speed must be. The "exposure" of light on film is a balance between the lens opening and the shutter speed. The wider the opening, the faster the shutter speed can be. The smaller the opening, the longer the shutter speed. This fact has a bearing on why I prefer the wide-angle over a telephoto for scenics taken from a canoe. Under good conditions, the average person can hand-hold a lens as long as the shutter speed is close to the length of the lens. For example I can confidently hand-hold my 200mm lens at speeds over 180th of a second while my 300mm requires at least a 250th and a 500mm a 500th and so on. A wide-angle can therefore be hand-held at much lower shutter speeds than a telephoto which allows you to get a greater depth of field.

TIPPY CANOE AND TAYLOR TOO

A canoe seldom falls into the category of "good conditions" when it comes to using a telephoto lens. Not only that – it is impractical to use a telephoto lens from a canoe when you are close to the subject.

Photographing rocks and cliffs from a canoe is a wonderful creative experience when compared to photographing rock faces along the highway. First there is the challenge of manoeuvring your craft into position and keeping it there. Then there are all the other "objects" usually found around such rocks: roots, fallen trees, moss, pollen lines, cracks and clefts, the rock's textures and, of course, the water itself. Most of these elements are absent from the more staid and uncluttered highway "cuts."

The creative part comes in when you try to compose the photograph so that these things form a pleasing image to your eye. Tilting the camera up gives you a sense of height, straight on can give you a "flat" photo that with proper light can come alive, while moving the viewfinder a little this way or that can result in new images that can surprise you.

Always consider the location and quality of your light source when you are shooting. Sunlight falling directly on your subject can create a bland appearance. Shooting rocks when they are side-lit can offer a greater feeling of depth because the shadows give the image a three-dimensional quality. Low-angle (early or late day) sunlight can also enrich the colours of your picture.

Shooting on an overcast day can bring out more saturated colours and tones than a sunny day can.

Frankly, I cheat a little in the creative department. I have a well-stocked library and frequently browse through the work of other photographers to see what it is they "see." If I like it, I try to capture similar images. I remember a high school art teacher telling me that copying somebody else's style was lazy and a kind of cheating. That is bunk. The best artists I've met, as well as the best photographers, all began by trying to capture someone's style and technique. That is why art courses teach about the "masters." That is why photography courses taught by the "pros" are well attended. People want to learn the "secrets" so that they can try them out themselves.

I expect that the readers of this book will look at my work and say to themselves "I like that shot" or "Taylor missed with that image" or "Boy, I wish I'd seen that!." I hope that they will then go out and try their hand at matching and improving upon my work.

This really isn't cheating. It is learning to "see" what a camera "sees." It is a talent that can be nurtured by studying the work of other photographers and deciding what images you like best. You will find that no single photographer will constantly produce images that you like. Nor will your work con-

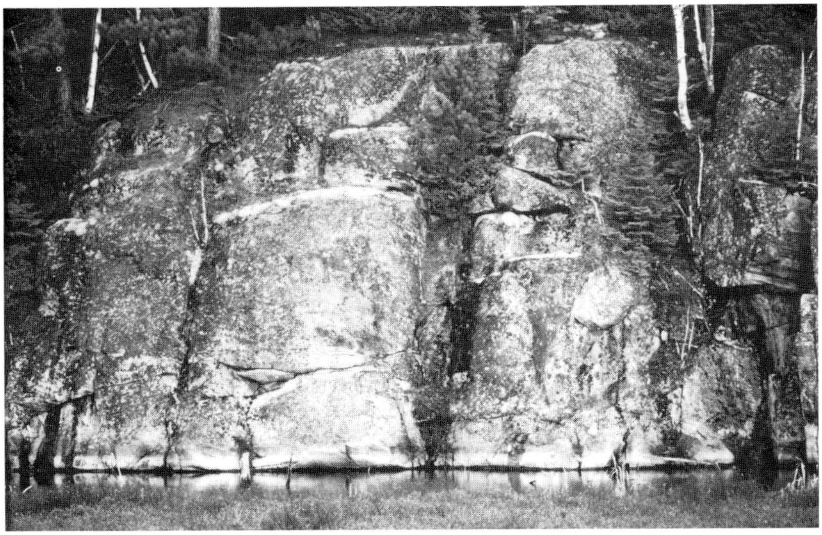

This granite cliff face was gouged and scoured by the most recent glacial period; a mere 11,000 years ago. (200mm 2.8L auto-focus zoom)

sistently meet the approval of your critics (usually your spouse and close friends) even when you personally select your favourite shots. Sometimes your best shot is overlooked by everyone while a picture you nearly tossed out is met with what you feel is undue praise.

Studying the work of others is helpful but that alone won't develop your talent. Taking pictures, lots of them, and editing them carefully will begin to develop your own talent and style.

"Why is this picture more pleasing to me than that one?"

"What did I do right here that gives this one such a nice feel?"

"What sort of lighting did I take this one in?"

"If I could re-shoot this rock, how could I improve on it?"

"Does this picture capture what I set out to capture?"

"How would so and so have done this?"

Photographing rocks from a canoe is only one method of capturing Algonquin's geology. Another is to look for places where the bare rock has been exposed by erosion or fire. The road to Rock Lake has many such places on it. Here, once again, we are selecting an area where the hand of man has had a less than obvious impact on the land.

Hiking around on these flat rocks you will find opportunities to set up a camera on a tripod or to lie flat on the rocks and get different angles. While you are here, look for the "scratch" marks left by the ancient glaciers.

GREAT SHEETS OF ICE

Twelve thousand years ago, Algonquin was covered by the continental ice sheet. It was over two kilometres thick here (imagine standing at the base of the CN Tower and looking up an ice cliff six times that height to get a picture of how tall that wall of ice was!) and it was flowing more or less south. As it did so, it pushed ahead of it great mounds of rock and soil, scraping away a billion years of geological history and laying bare the Precambrian rocks below. These rocks were too hard and too thick to be worn completely away but they were scratched and gouged by the ice and the boulders it carried with it.

It was the repeated bulldozing of several glacial periods that removed the evidence of dinosaurs and other long gone beasts from the fossil record here. It was also these ice sheets that created much of what we see in the park today.

The Rock Lake area is a good place to find other evidence of this recent glaciation. As you drive towards Rock Lake Road from the west, you will begin to climb up a fairly steep hill. At the top of the hill is the Look Out Trail, which leads you to a spectacular view of the countryside. Continuing on in your car, you then descend the hill and arrive at the road to Rock Lake. Like the Look Out Trail this road parallels the cliffs, which are ancient faults in the earth that have been polished and ground by the glaciers.

Highway 60 follows a "cross fault" that runs perpendicular to the north-south faults the trail and Rock Lake Road follow. The "hill" you climbed in your car peaks at the trail entrance. It is made up of sand, gravel and clay deposited there by the glaciers. This glacial till can be photographed along the road in several places.

As for the cliffs, the best photography can be had a kilometre or two down the Rock Lake Road. Pull your car off well to the side in a straight section as logging trucks and fast drivers sometimes barrel by.

The Rock Lake cliff is my favourite, and it is one well suited for both a wide-angle and a telephoto lens. A wide-angle, especially when held low to the ground, captures the sweep and breadth of the canyon's wall. The telephoto on the other hand, can isolate specific features such as cracks or trees growing along its face.

The wide-angle lens is best for horizontal shots because it can take in much of the length of the cliff. The telephoto performs better when held vertically and produces images that capture the height of the cliff.

This cliff face is the most easily reached of all Algonquin's many cliffs but it is not the most spectacular. That honour is held by the Barron Canyon, which can be reached by going into the park through Petawawa. The Barron Canyon is a two-kilometre-long gash in the park's topography that is well worth the one-and-a-half-kilometre walk along a clearly defined trail.

Once there, you emerge from the forest to stand on top of a one-hundred-metre-high cliff overlooking the Barron River. This cleft in the earth owes its origins to the glaciers as well, but here the creative force was not the power of a slow-moving ice field but a surging river about a thousand times more powerful than Niagara Falls!

The melting ice field 10,000 years ago created huge lakes that were emptied by raging rivers. These rivers in turn carried the ground-up granite and bedrock and deposited them as sand beds throughout the park. The beach at Lake of Two Rivers is one such alluvial beach.

It is on the east side of the park that the true extent and power of these ancient rivers can be seen. Much of this side was covered by these rivers draining away the meltwater from the glacial Lake Algonquin (the remains of which are the comparatively smaller lakes we know as lakes Huron and Michigan). These rivers drained into the Champlain Sea (now the Saint Lawrence and Ottawa valleys), where it deposited incredible amounts of sand and other fine particles now known as "outwash plains."

Here on the east side of the park the huge beds of sand deposited by the glacial rivers do not trap moisture, creating a drier soil. Trees that prefer this soil type include pines and poplars, which explains their abundance on this side of the park.

But what of the west side? Why do we find beech and maple trees there instead of pines and poplars? We will explore the answer to these questions when our photographic safari looks at Algonquin's forests in more detail.

So how has all of this affected the Algonquin we know today? It is no understatement to say that all this pushing and shoving of earth and ice not only affected but virtually created the Algonquin ecosystem.

For example, although the mountains created by these geological pressures have been eroded away through the eons and have more recently been ground down by the glacier, they still continue to affect Algonquin. The hills on the west side are up to 500 metres above sea level. The hills on the east side are not nearly so high, cresting at about 200 metres. Both are higher than the surrounding countryside.

The result of this height difference affects Algonquin's climate, making the west side cooler and damper than the east side. The west has an average of only eighty-four frost-free days compared to one hundred and five days on the east side. The altitude also affects precipitation. The west averages 100 cm (33% of which is snow) a year compared to the east side's 90 cm (26% as snow).

So the land form affects climate in a very real sense. Anyone who has ever camped in the park in the summer has no doubt heard it jokingly referred to as the Algonquin Rain Forest.

All that rock and sand we've been discussing also have a direct effect on the ecosystem. Both granite and gneiss rocks are extremely hard and possess low amounts of potassium, phosphorus and calcium, nutrients that are important for the health of a variety of plants and animals. This lack of naturally occurring salts limits the numbers of certain plants and animals and helps explain the presence of moose on the roads after spring melts. They come out to the roadside pot holes seeking the precious nutrients that have collected there after a winter of road maintenance.

The bedrock is very hard (non-porous) so that little moisture is absorbed into soil but instead collects in depressions and lakes. The lakes on

Just south of Highway 60, on the Rock Lake Road, there are good views of this cliff. The road follows an ancient river valley that dates back to the last glacial period. A few years ago a great horned owl nested here. Its a place I still check out regularly. (28mm 2.8L)

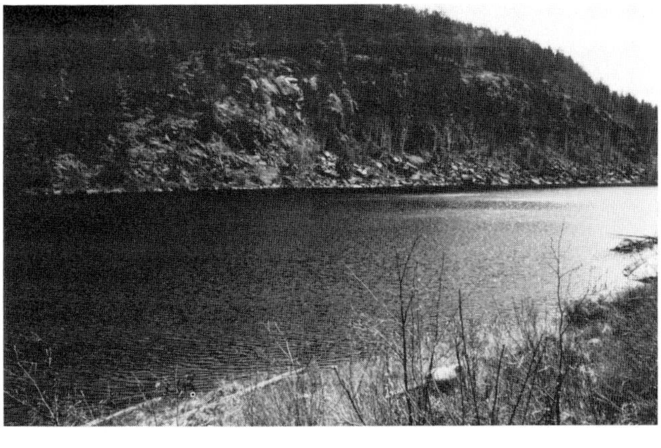

the park's west side are generally low in algae and plankton growth thanks to a combination of two factors. First there is little nutrient value in the run off water which feeds them thanks to the underlying rocks. Another reason for the clear appearance of many of Algonquin's lakes is the killing effect of acid rain. The "poison" from the sky has its origins in the continent's big industrial areas. To the south of the park, the acidity is reduced by the limestone bedrock found there. Limestone is basic and neutralizes the acid rain. Algonquin lacks limestone and its lakes suffer as a result.

All this leads to a lack of microorganisms, which in turn limits the number of game fish in the park's lakes. The lakes based on limestone to the south of the park, in the Kawarthas, produce much greater numbers of insect larva, minnows and ultimately game fish than do Algonquin's undernourished lakes.

However, Algonquin's lakes are cold, thanks in part to their glacial origins and the park's altitude and latitude. Cold-water lakes are rich in oxygen, which makes them suitable for trout, a fish that loves cold water. Indeed, lake trout and brook trout are found in over 1,500 lakes here as are other cold-water-loving fish, including burbot and lake whitefish. Almost completely missing from most of the park are the warm-water fish such as sturgeon, walleye and muskellunge. Some are found in the lower reaches of the Petawawa River on the east side. These fish are common south of the park, however.

(Facing page) Setting off on our daughters' first canoe trip, Bob Bowyer and I looked forward to showing the girls the wildlife and scenery of the park. (35mm 3.5)

Not satisfied with nature's scheme, smallmouth bass were introduced in many of the park's lakes at the turn of the century by mankind.

As you photograph the park, keep in mind the land. I find that knowing what I now know about this subject brings a whole new way of "seeing" my photographs. When I look back over my images of moose and beaver, loons and jays, I now view them in the context of the park's geology.

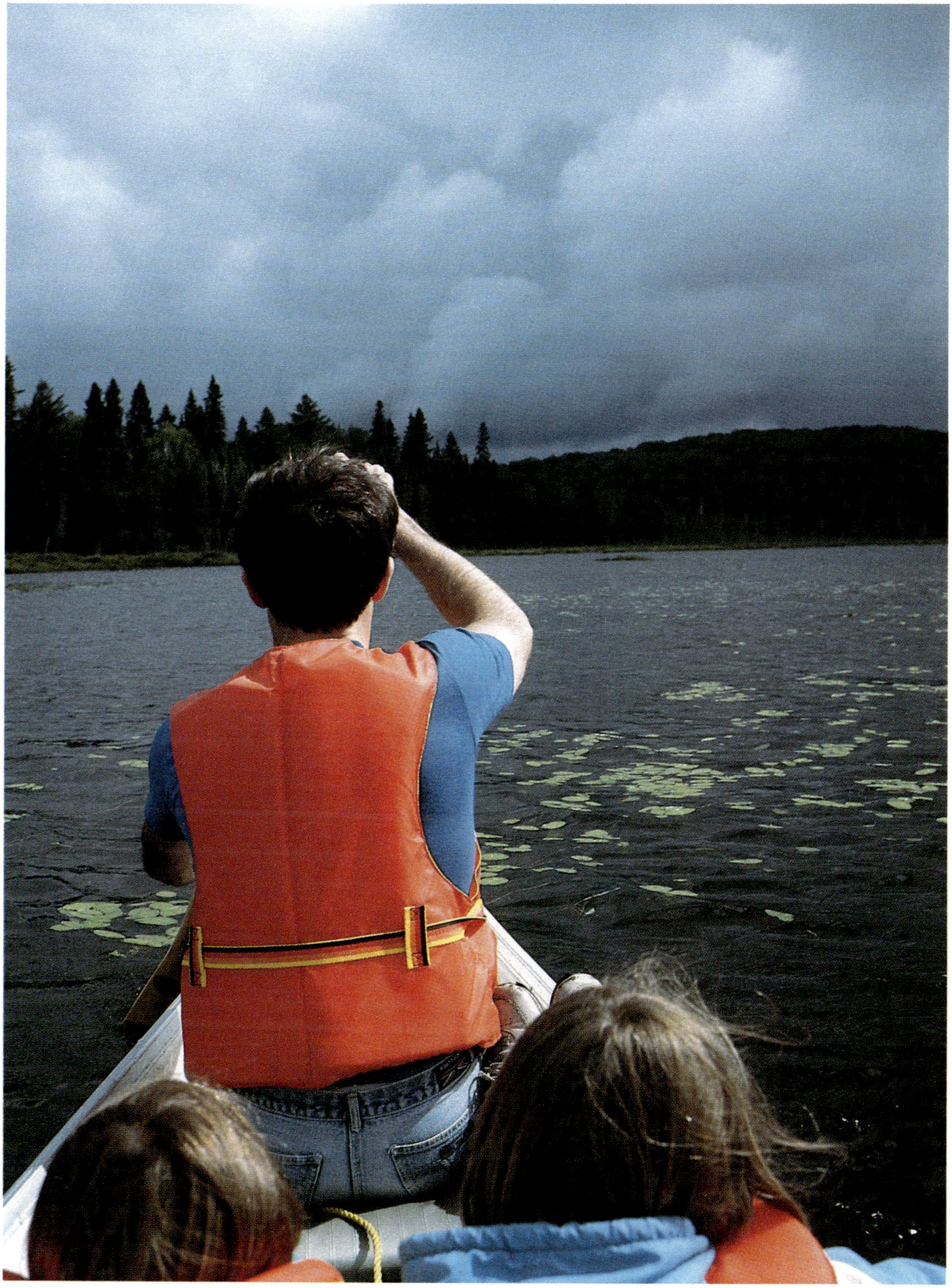

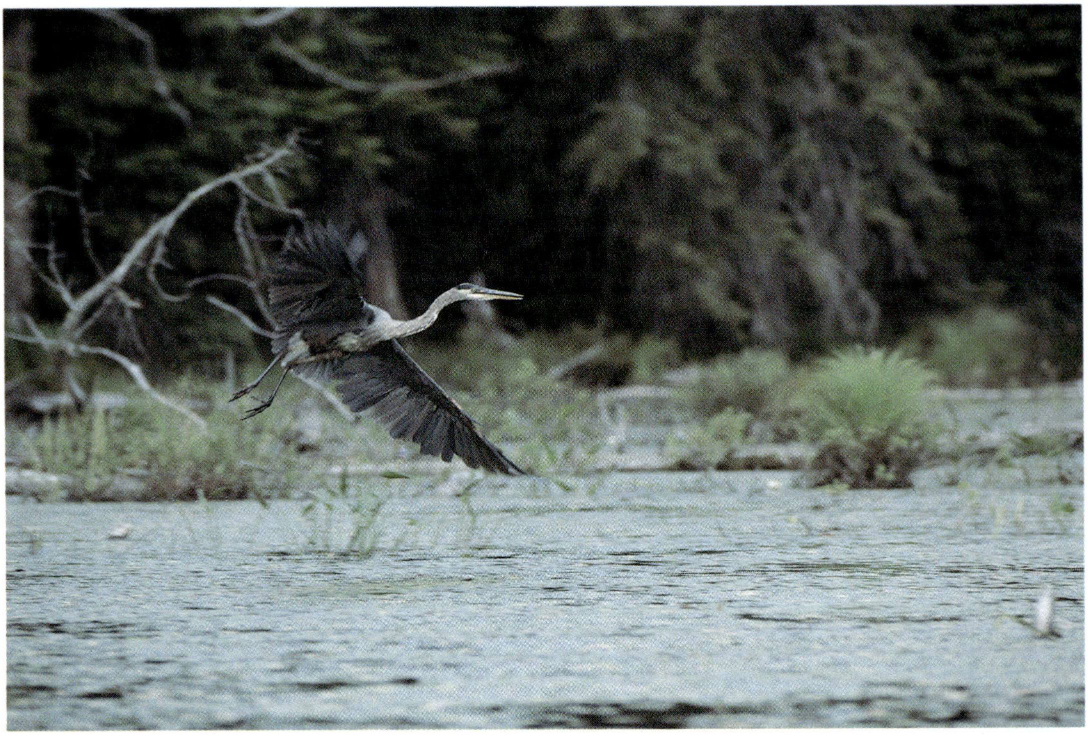

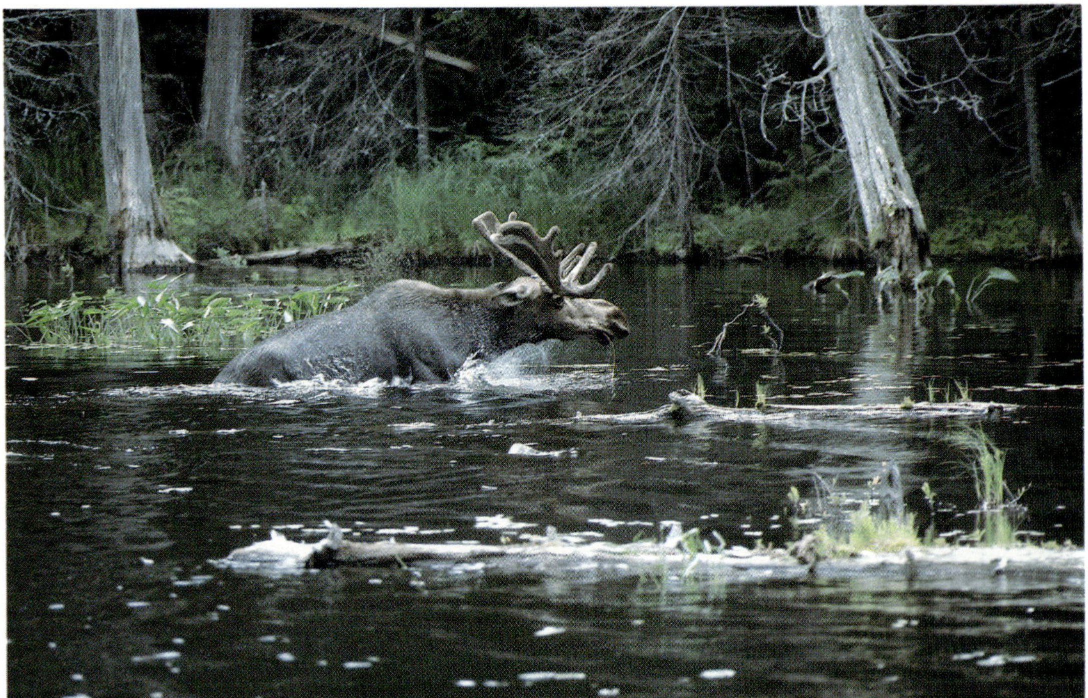

The Northern Lights are rare in Algonquin in the summer. (50mm 1.4)

(Below) Tamaracks glean what nourishment comes their way with the help of fungi that grow along their roots. They are found in more open areas of the bog. (200mm 2.8L auto-focus)

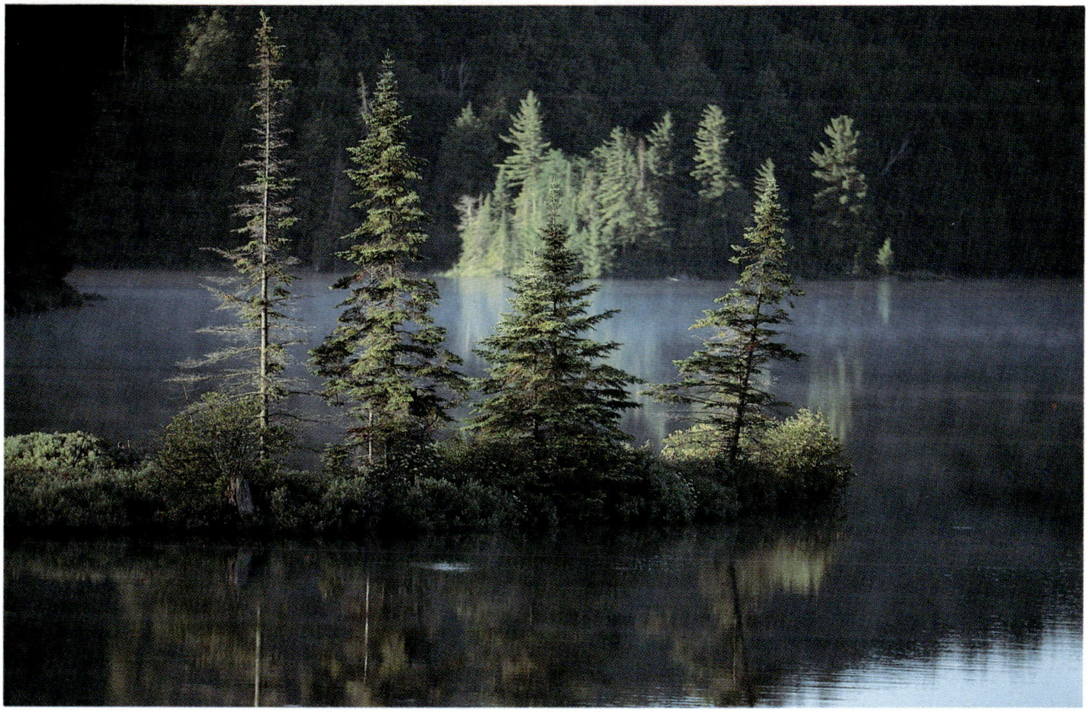

(Facing page, top) Great blue herons are a common sight along Algonquin's waterways. Most are wary and flush at your approach. (300mm 4L)

(Bottom) Flies are a moose's constant companions in summer but remain invisible for the most part until the moose submerges or shakes himself. (300mm 4L)

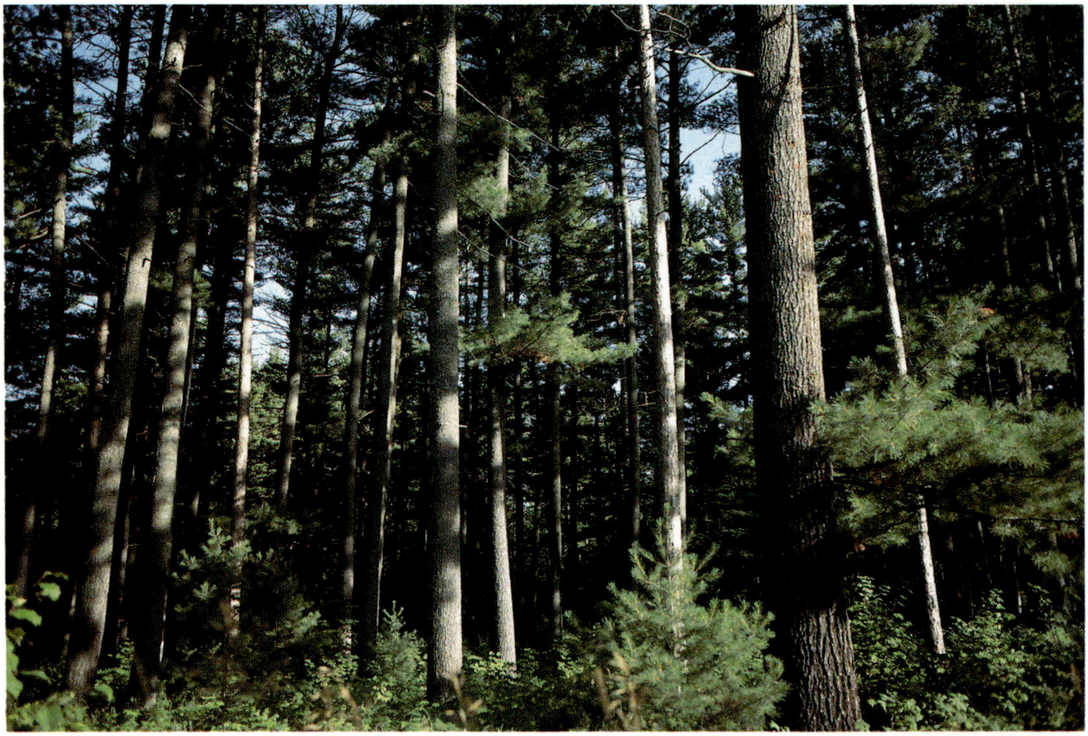

(Above) Hundred-year-old white pines can be seen in Achray. These are the largest such trees that can be easily reached by the park's road system. (28mm 2.8L auto-focus)

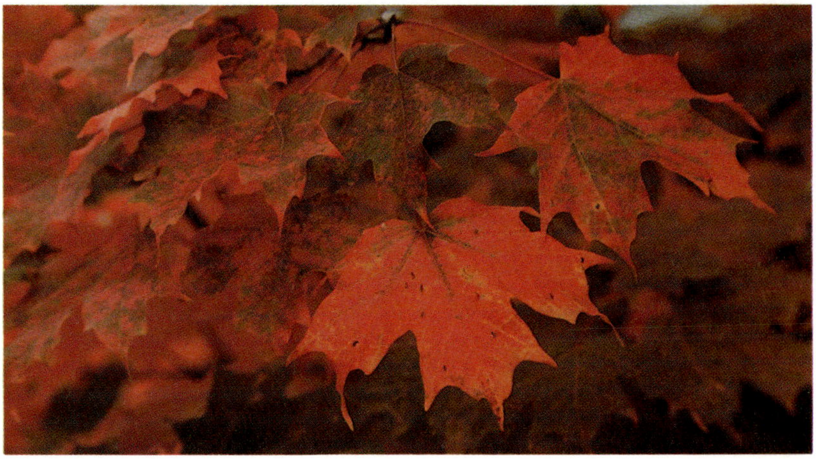

(Right) Red maple trees are known for their bright red leaves in fall but did you know that the red leaves are from male trees? Females have yellow leaves. (200 2.8L auto-focus)

(Facing page, top) The layering in this metamorphic rock is the compressed sediments laid down by eons of erosion and volcanic activity in the distant past. These ancient rocks are among the oldest on earth. (200mm 2.8L auto-focus zoom)

(Bottom) British soldier lichen, named after the bright red caps, is a common sight along the road's rocky cuts. (200mm 4. macro)

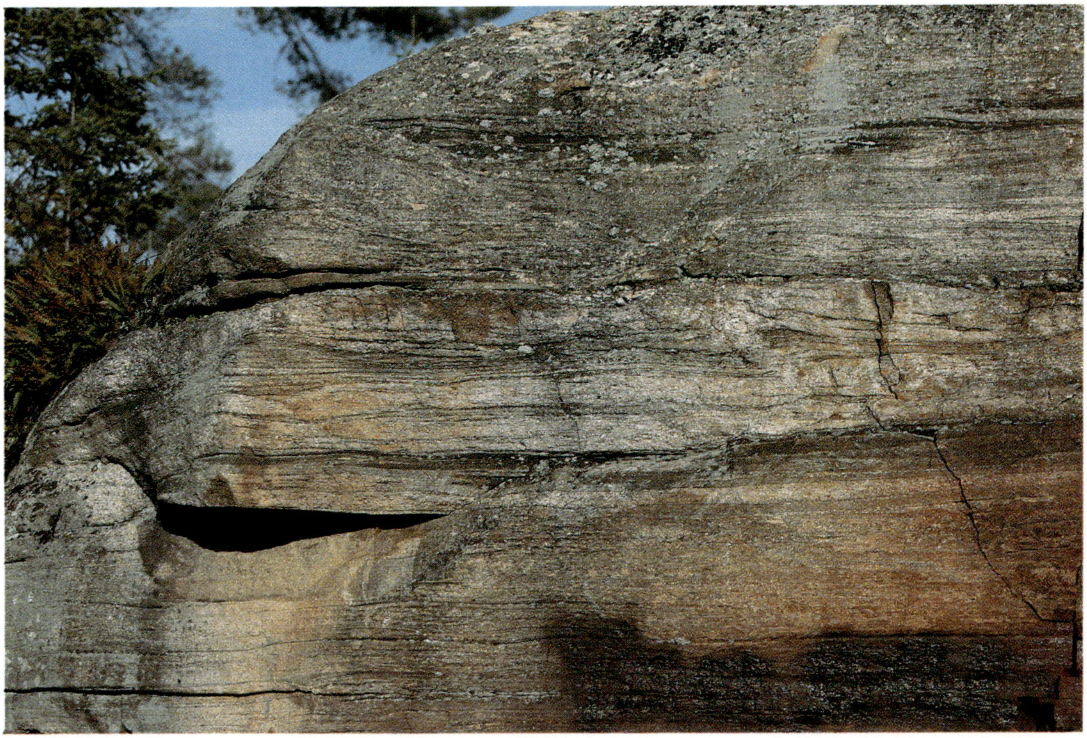

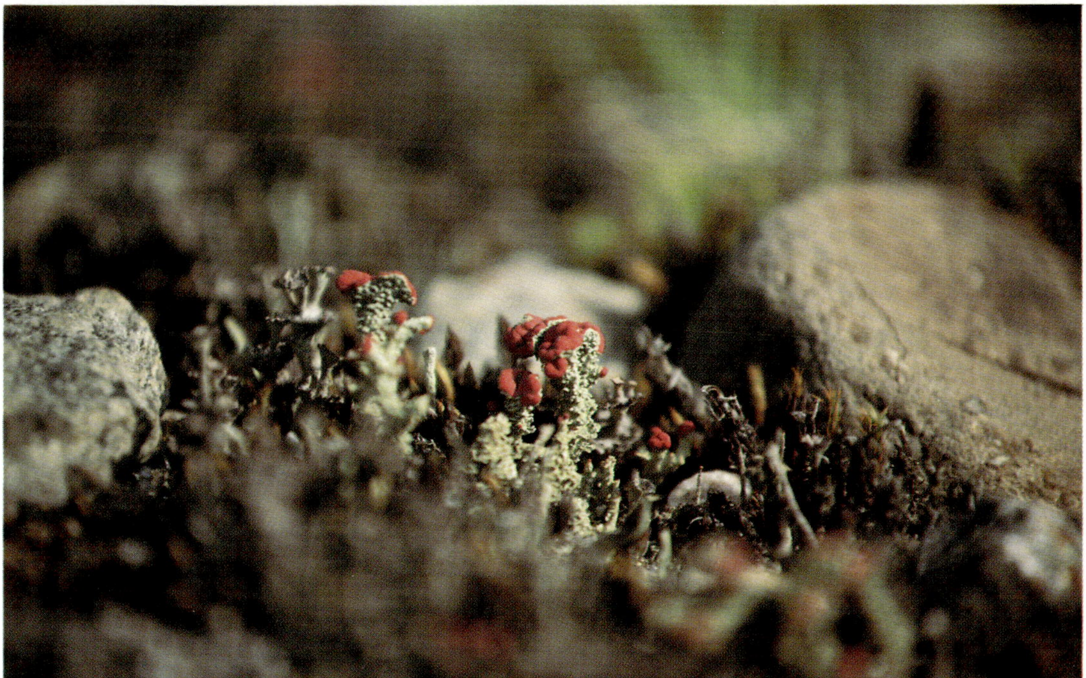

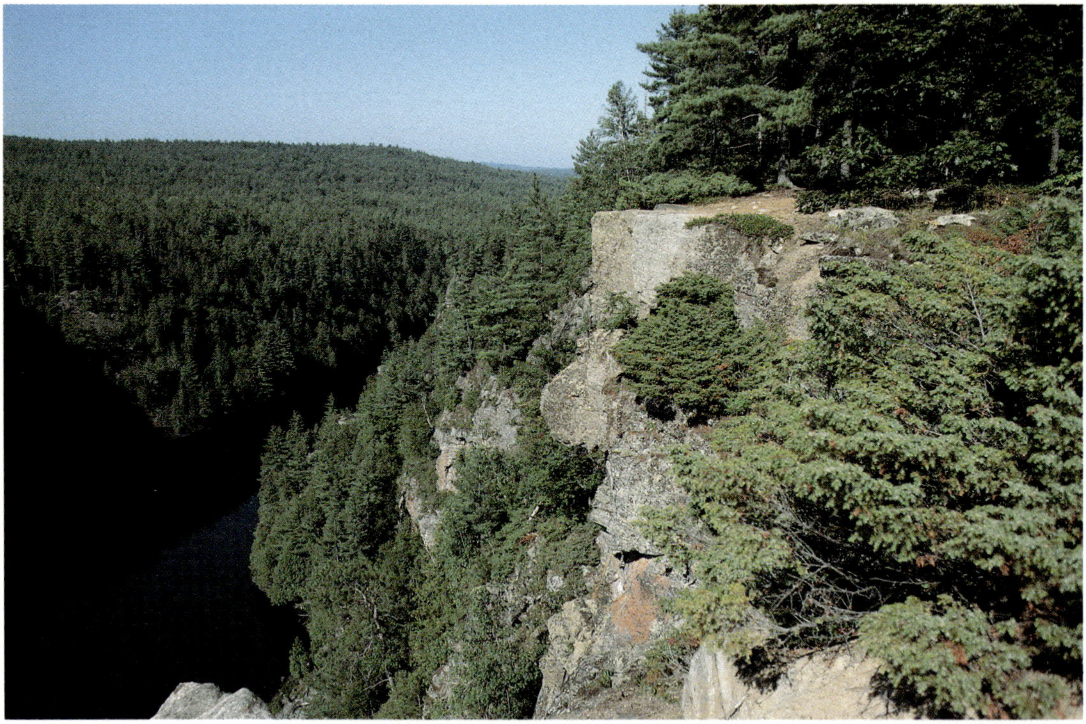

The Barron Canyon (above) is accessible from the Achray Road by a moderate hiking trail. It is well worth the 1.6 kilometre walk but you should be aware that there are no protective railings here. (200mm 2.8L zoom)

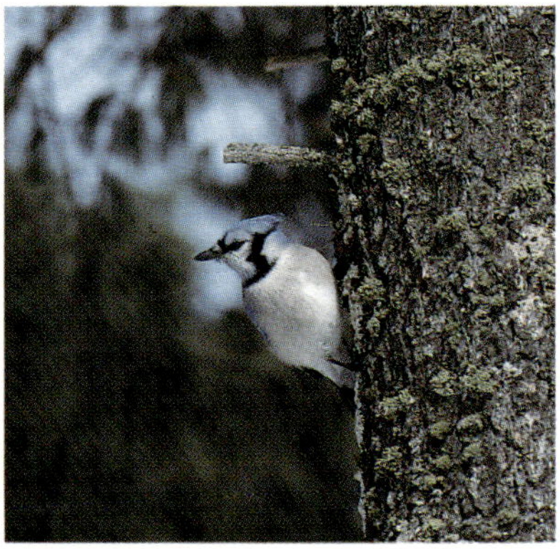

Blue jays are often heard in the forest. Their best-known cry sounds like "thief ... thief" and sounds a warning that something has disturbed the bird. (500mm 4.5L)

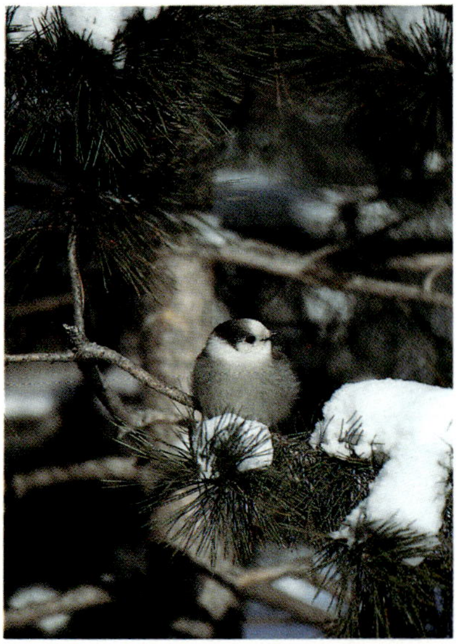

Whiskey jacks and other birds will puff out their feathers to conserve body heat in frigid weather. (300mm 2.8L auto-focus with 2x tele)

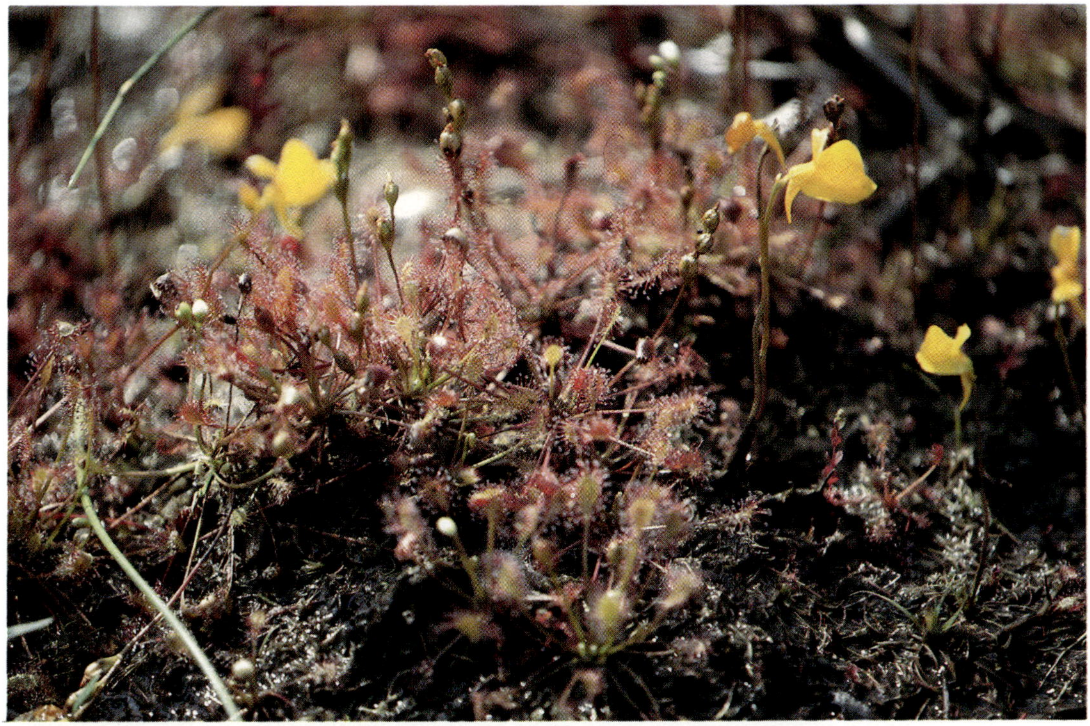

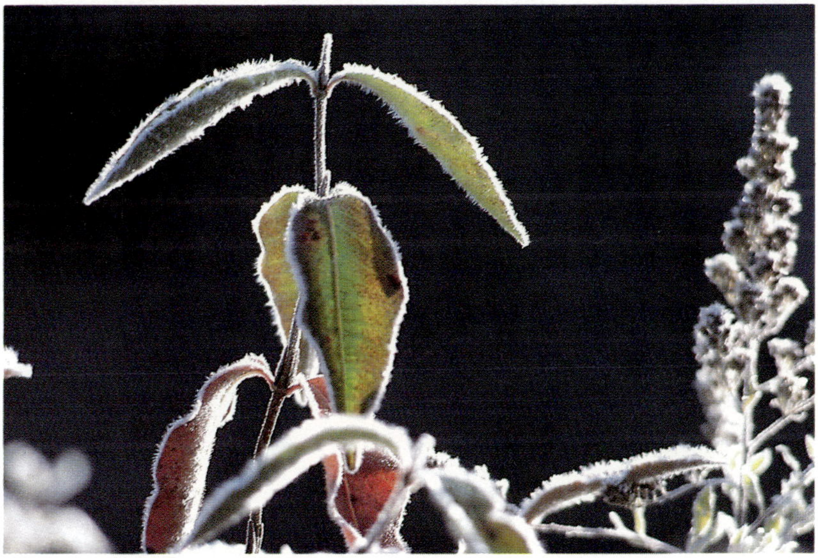

Sundews (above) are truly carnivorous plants that rely on the insects that they trap and digest to give them the proteins needed to survive in the barren world of the bog. (200mm 2.8L auto-focus)

Back-lit frost crystals outline the leaves of a plant in late August. Cold temperatures and even snow are not unknown during the last two weeks of this month. On the other hand temperatures can also soar into the 30s. (500mm 4.5L)

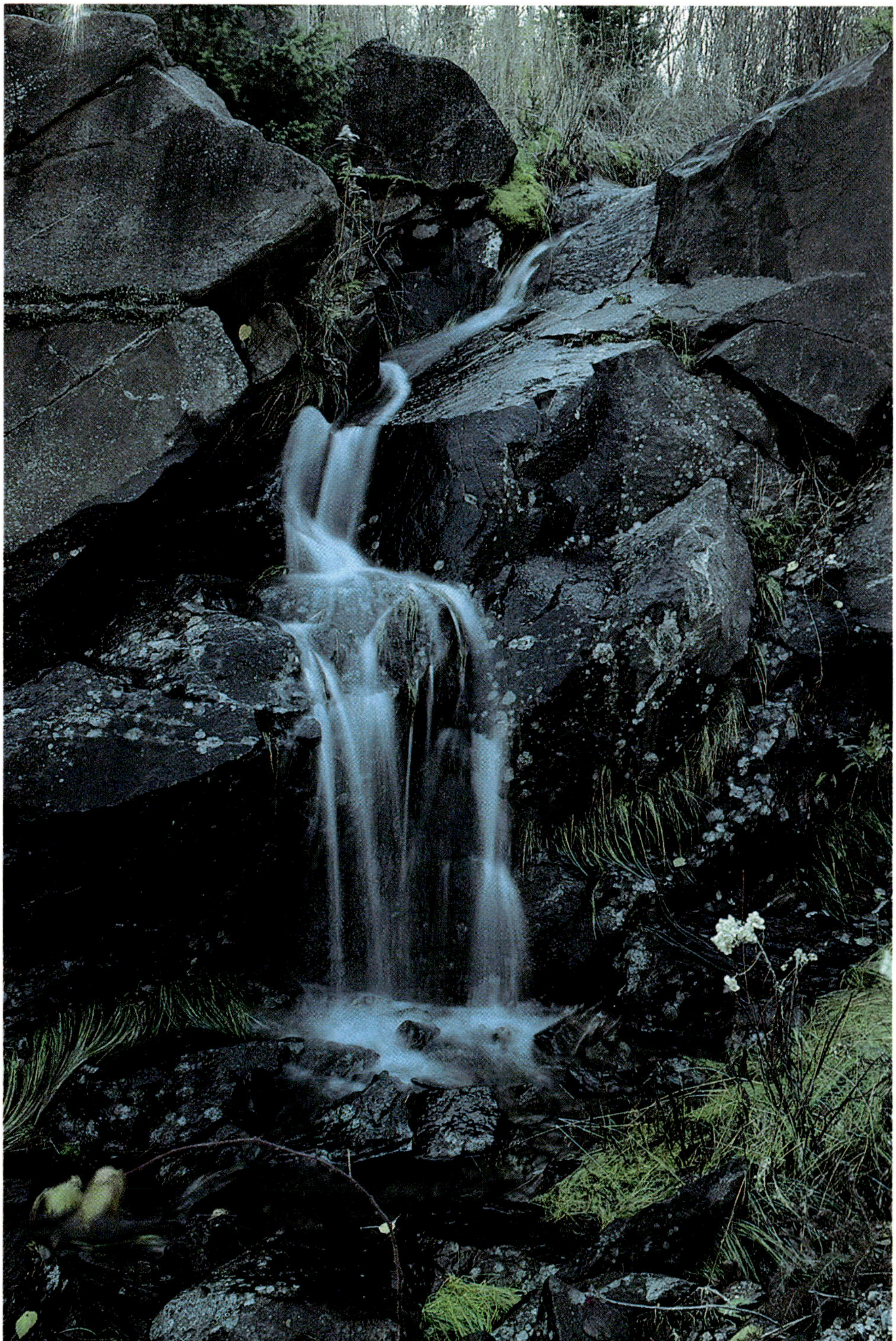

Excursion 2

Saturday April 24

This was to be a very quick visit to the park because my guests and I had to be back in the city by six that night. It was 6:30 before we got away from the Etobicoke mall where we left one of our cars so I wasn't feeling there would be much accomplished by this visit. It seemed too short.

I'd forgotten how good the park can be in April!

Don McClement and his sons Ben (seventeen) and Brendan (fourteen) joined me for the drive north. Don drove, which was just as well as I had been out late the night before and could barely keep awake at times let alone carry on an intelligent conversation. Fortunately, by the time we were in Algonquin, the park itself roused me out of my stupor and it was only on the drive there and back that I felt myself drifting.

Don and I have been friends for over twenty years and we both share a love of nature. He too is a photographer but prefers to specialize in black and white and underwater photography. We have shared many adventures in the wild but precious few of them have been in Algonquin. I looked forward with pleasure to this visit to the park with him and his boys.

We arrived in the park by 10:00 and within minutes I managed to find them a moose. I say "find" because quite literally that is what I did. The cow moose was in a spot that kept her

(Facing page) A small stream flowing over the granite rocks by the park highway becomes a translucent waterfall when photographed at a slow shutter speed of 2 seconds. (35mm 3.5 auto-focus)

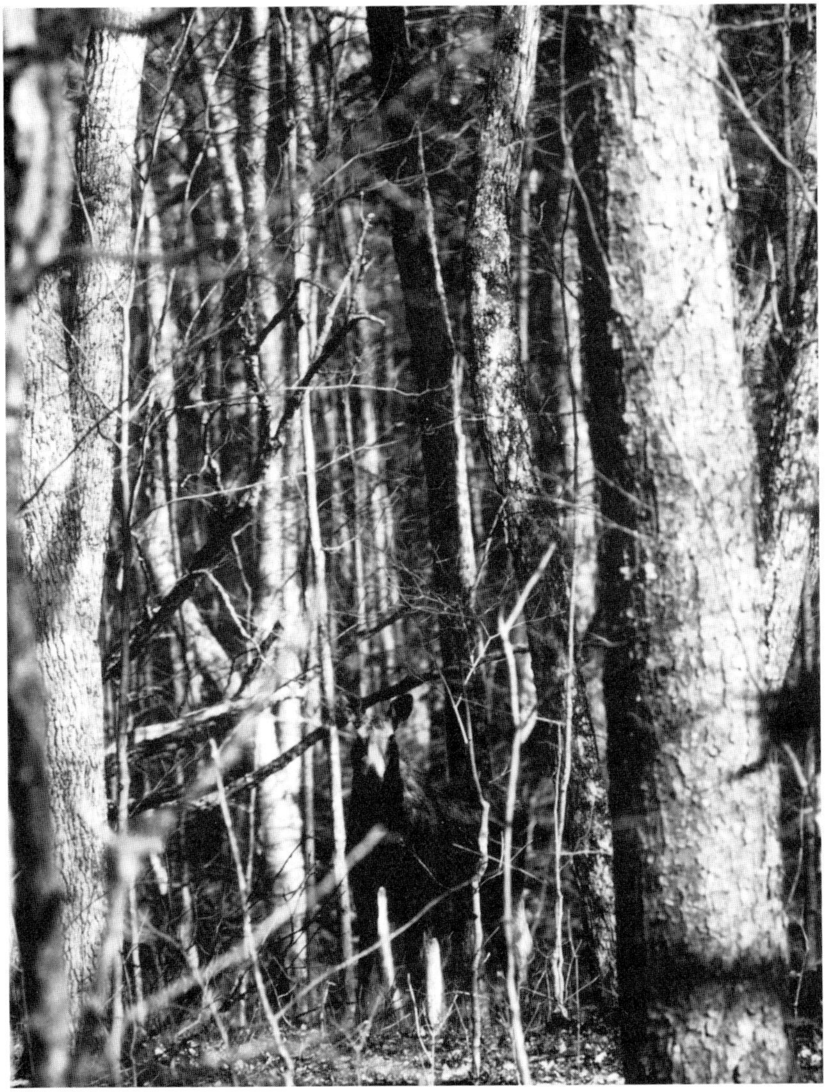

Sometimes a vertical shot works best. I like this one because it captures the cow's size with respect to the forest she lives in. (300mm 2.8 autofocus 2x tele converter)

totally hidden from the road. Someone who didn't know where to look would never have found her. Fortunately, I knew from past trips about this spot, so I sent Ben over to check out the hidden gully. No one was more shocked than I when he came back and said there actually was a moose there! I pretended that this was not pure luck but success based on scientific research and an understanding of moose behaviour.

Everyone knew this was pure nonsense. Just how much

luck had been involved became evident a little later when, after searching countless other similar locations, we came up with a grand total of no moose. It was clear they were using the muddy mineral licks by the side of the road. Tracks were everywhere but there were no moose to be seen.

We drove the highway a couple of times and then decided to take a break and do a little hiking. We drove into Mew Lake where we found an empty campsite and parked. There was still snow on the ground, and nearby we saw the remains of "igloos" made by winter campers. We guessed that within a week the last snow would be gone and with it the last vestiges of these snow huts.

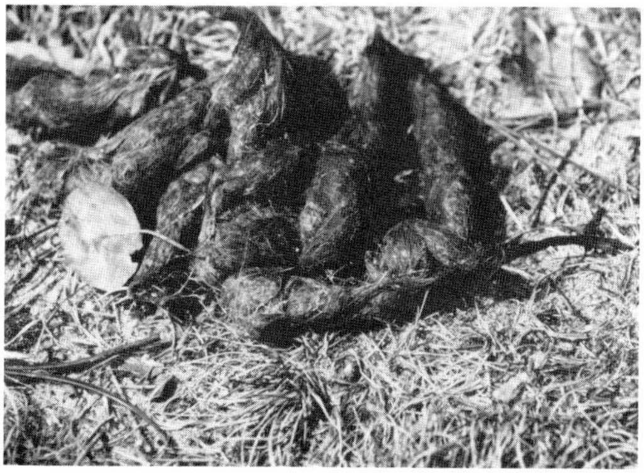

Wolf scat is not common but it can turn up anywhere. This large dropping was photographed near Mew Lake Campground in the early spring. I thought I could see moose hair in it, but it takes a microscopic analysis to know for certain. (200mm 2.8L zoom auto-focus)

At the back of Mew Lake Campground is the old airport landing field. It is built on the sandy deposits of an ancient glacial river bed and is quite flat. It is also an excellent place to look for wildlife and their tracks. We needed a break from sitting in a car and this was just the spot. We all hoped to see a moose or two but that was not to be.

It wasn't long, however, before we saw signs of moose activity, including droppings, tracks and bitten-off twigs. We also found the tracks of a deer, porcupine, fox and a wolf. Our most exciting discovery was the large wolf scat, which we bent over with interest. Don and I pointed out to the boys the long guard hairs of a moose that made up the bulk of the stool and pronounced with certainty that this wolf had fed recently on one of the long-legged members of the deer family. (Note of caution: Never handle wolf scat without wearing gloves and a face mask as the scat could contain bacteria harmful to your health.)

We followed a path that led away from the old runway to the Upland Hiking Trail. The trail was wet with meltwater and it wasn't long until we heard the roar of water flowing over rocks. We hiked out to the small waterfalls where I switched to a wide-angle lens in order to photograph the falls. Then it was back to the car and the picnic site for lunch.

What was left of the winter's snow had dwindled fast even in the short time we were gone. The day was becoming noticeably warmer when we left a half hour later. It was getting on for 1:30 and we were already beginning our journey back to the city. I had a hunch that a moose or two would turn up on our drive and slow us down a bit and I was right.

Just before Cache Lake, there are two ponds on the south side of the road where I've seen moose a number of times, and sure enough we discovered two moose there – a cow and a calf. Actually, we found them by watching where other traffic had stopped and then looking where the other people were looking. It may be cheating a bit but it works!

The cow and the calf were a fair distance out. She was feeding on the first shoots of water lilies while the calf looked on. I had enough time to set up my 600mm lens on the tripod to shoot them before they wandered into the forest again.

Not bad but I was disappointed that Don's sons had seen moose either running away or at a fair distance. I'd hoped for a more intimate (and exciting) experience for them but it appeared we were out of luck.

We hadn't driven 200 metres up the road when Don spotted something in the forest. We backed up and took a good look.

It was a bull moose.

We decided to "stalk" it and this time the moose did not run off but continued to feed. Both Ben and Brendan got quite close to the bull, so close at one time that Ben and I had to look up to watch the bull feeding on twigs just a few metres in front of us. We stood quietly, not wanting to scare off the moose, which clearly knew we were there but chose to ignore us.

This encounter lasted about thirty minutes before the animal moved into a swamp where we chose not to follow. That ended our day and we saw no more moose or any other wildlife.

CHAPTER 2

The Elements

As a photographer, I get excited by the living things I see, especially the animals. It is a bias that colours the way I shoot pictures. I've never really done the statistics but I would guess that for every scenic shot or photograph of a flower I've taken, my files include over one hundred wildlife images!

My recent projects concerning ecosystems made me consider what I had overlooked. As I've explained in the preceding chapter, the underlying structure of the land is an important factor and one that is a worthy subject for our creative energies.

But there are other elements of the ecosystem just as photogenic. Perhaps more so.

A word of explanation is in order here. Living ecosystems consist of two basic components. Obviously there are things classed as "living" or more properly, "biotic." Less obvious are those things we call "non-living" or "abiotic." Note that "non-living" in this sense does not mean "dead." It means instead those things that never were, never could be, never will be alive.

So what are they? They are the water, sun, moon, stars, rocks, fire, air, rotation and tilt of the Earth, altitude, latitude. A pretty potent list of things to go about ignoring, isn't it? Also a very difficult list of things to capture on film, but fortunately we can cheat a little and in doing so create some images that will probably rank among the best you will shoot during your visits to the park.

By themselves, the abiotic factors are elusive but in combination, they are often spectacular. Combine them and you get weather, seasons, sunrises and night-time spectaculars along with a host of photographic possibilities.

The source of all energy (well, virtually all energy) on Earth is the Sun. It heats the land, evaporates water and in doing so sets the world's weather patterns in motion. The amount of sunlight falling on a place is directly related to the amount of living things that place can support. "Biomass" is the term used to describe the weight of all living things in an area.

The latitude of a place determines the amount and quality of the sun's energy that strikes it. The rainforest that grows on or near the equator gets the greatest yearly amount of sun. Rainforests have the world's greatest biomass, thanks in part to all the solar energy that falls here. Here there is no winter, no spring, no fall ... just endless summer. Go north or south of that line and you encounter poorer and poorer ecosystems until finally you reach the poles, where virtually no living thing can survive.

Algonquin lies about halfway between these two extremes. Not surprisingly then, it supports about half the biomass of a rainforest.

But lying halfway also means Algonquin experiences seasonal changes. For over half a year, few if any plants grow in Algonquin Park and those that do survive there must cope with the freezing temperatures that are so common. Deprived of growing plants for almost half a year, the animals that rely on them must learn to make do without fresh nourishment to drive their food chain.

Obviously, for the photographer intent on recording Algonquin's ecosystem, the sun takes on a crucial role. The question is how best to capture on film the sun and the weather it generates?

Having done a fair bit a travelling, I can tell you that there are few better places in the world than Algonquin to achieve this photographic goal.

During the summer, you have to be willing to get up early to capture the sun, but it is well worth the effort. Foggy days are common in the park in all seasons except winter. The sun quickly dissipates the fog once it rises above the horizon, but in the time between sunrise and the last wisp of fog, the photographic opportunities are abundant.

THE EARLY BIRD GETS THE SHOT

An early-morning paddle across a quiet lake is a magical experience in the fog. It is cool and still. The lake is dead calm. The haunting cry of a loon and the sound of other early risers starting breakfast are the only things to remind you that you are not alone.

If you are wise, you will have selected your destination, usually some island with an appropriately positioned pine tree that will give a centre of interest for your picture.

You will not be taking a picture of a tree but a picture of the

Richard Stevens puts our canoe into the Tim River while I photograph the "action." Travel in Algonquin Park is bound to expose you to a variety of elements, in this case cold, fog and rain. (35mm 3.5)

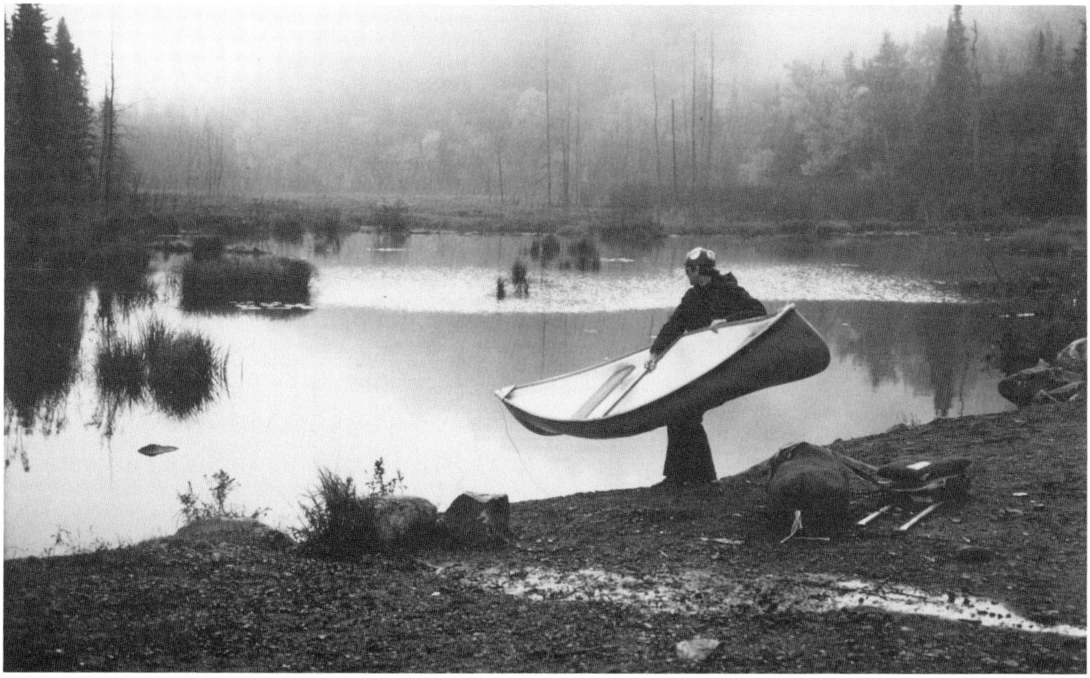

elements. Point your light meter at the tree alone and you find there is not enough light for you to shoot, but point it towards the fog and there is more than enough. Use this reading for your exposure. The resulting photograph will show the tree silhouetted against the foggy backdrop of sky and lake.

This formula works and is often copied. The creativity comes from the way the sun, the tree and the other elements in the picture are positioned by the photographer. Shift location several times, make several exposures and spend as much time as you need. The scene will change as the sun heats the air and the fog dissipates. Do not be in too much of a hurry to rush back to camp for a warming cup of coffee.

There are many places along the park highway where similar shots may be taken. A popular one is a picnic site by Smoke Lake but its accessibility is its drawback too. It has been photographed time and time again. Better to find a spot to call your own.

The setting sun is equally popular but Algonquin's sunsets are not very spectacular. Sunsets in the northwest section of the park are the most beautiful thanks to the pollution in the air from North Bay and not-too-distant Sudbury. The airborne pollutants give the evening sky its colour as the sun's rays bounce off them.

No matter where you are in the park shots of the sun at dusk or dawn are always worth a try. Sometimes the film's own colour balance or exposure time will result in a colour shift that you failed to see.

To take a foggy-sunrise picture, the best lens is likely the wide-angle or a short telephoto. A setting sun can be photographed with these lenses but I find they fail to do it justice. Try, instead, a long telephoto. By using the long lens, you increase the size of the sun in the picture, enhancing its importance.

A tripod mount is essential in order to hold the lens steady. Wait until the sun is just above the horizon and then take your picture. If the sun is high, you should not look at it directly through your lens (or even with the naked eye), but a setting sun is safe enough because its light intensity is weakened by the atmosphere.

If you can include in your image the sun's light shimmering off a lake, then do so.

I do not recommend including the sun in pictures other than at dawn and dusk. First, there is the possibility of damaging your eye and there is a real chance of doing some damage to your camera or lens as well. I make an exception to this "rule" if the midday sun is covered by something. A particularly attractive cloud bank that allows the sun to appear as a bright-looking ball when viewed through the haze can make for an interesting shot. Sometimes shooting the sun as it plays peek-a-boo through the branches of tall trees can work well too.

Weather and the seasons are a direct result of the variance in the sun's energy heating the Earth. Both are easier to record with a camera then the sun itself.

Let's begin with a look at the seasonal changes in the park and the effect they have on its ecosystem. Winter is a time of immense beauty in the park, but it is also the most stressful of the seasons on all life forms. As noted above, only those animal species prepared to go for prolonged periods without fresh plant material in their diets can survive in the park. Trees and many plants go into a dormant state, storing energy in their roots or bulbs below the soil.

SURVIVING WINTER'S RAVAGES

Deer and moose must exist on bark and twigs, neither of which are very nourishing. To compensate for this poor diet, these animals slow down their metabolism during the worst winter months, January and February, and doze the winter away.

Mice and voles must survive either on what they have stored or the little they can collect beneath the snow. Although they remain active, they shut off their reproductive drive for most of the winter so that no new babies make excessive demands on their limited resources. Seed-eating birds all but vanish from the park and most insect eaters are totally absent. They migrate to warmer southern climates still rich in food sources.

Large predators, both birds of prey and carnivores, make do by feeding on the plant eaters that remain. Their fortunes are tied directly to the plants, too, for if there is little to feed the herbivores their declining numbers mean fewer predators will survive the winter.

The park's largest predator, the black bear, escapes the tough times by going into a deep winter sleep.

We'll explore the life of these animals more fully a little later on in the book but now let's consider photographing winter.

ZEBRA'S STRIPES AND FOREST SHADOWS

Snow is a real challenge to capture. It is a nightmare to photograph because it is white. All light meters are set to produce a "grey" image. That is to say that they handle best the middle tones but fare less well on the extremes – the blacks and whites. Light meters tend to expose both black and white so that they both go grey.

Once you understand this, you can set about to trick your camera into taking a properly exposed picture of snow. (We don't usually want grey snow in our pictures!)

First, remember the "zebra effect." When I was on safari in Kenya, I learned that with zebras you didn't have to play with your exposure at all even though they were black and white. Why? The camera's meter read both and did not have to compensate for either since the blacks and the whites in effect balanced each other off so that they read "grey" to the light meter. I shot exactly what the camera told me to.

Now Algonquin is painfully short on zebras, as you may have noticed but it is rich in places that obey the "zebra effect." On a bright winter day, you will see this wherever you find white snow and black tree trunks. All you need to do is insure that your viewfinder encompasses equal amounts of both and you will get a properly exposed picture.

But wait! Suppose you are taking a picture of a small object (an animal, friend or log) with a background of a snow-covered Algonquin lake. There is no way to find that "balance" between light and dark because out there it doesn't exist.

(Facing page) There is much beauty to be seen along the road in winter and that includes the road itself. This picture combines the pleasing element of the curve in the road with the contrasting light hitting the snow covered trees. A little bit of sky hints at the height of the hill without drawing your eye away from the birch tree in the centre. (200mm 2.8L autofocus zoom)

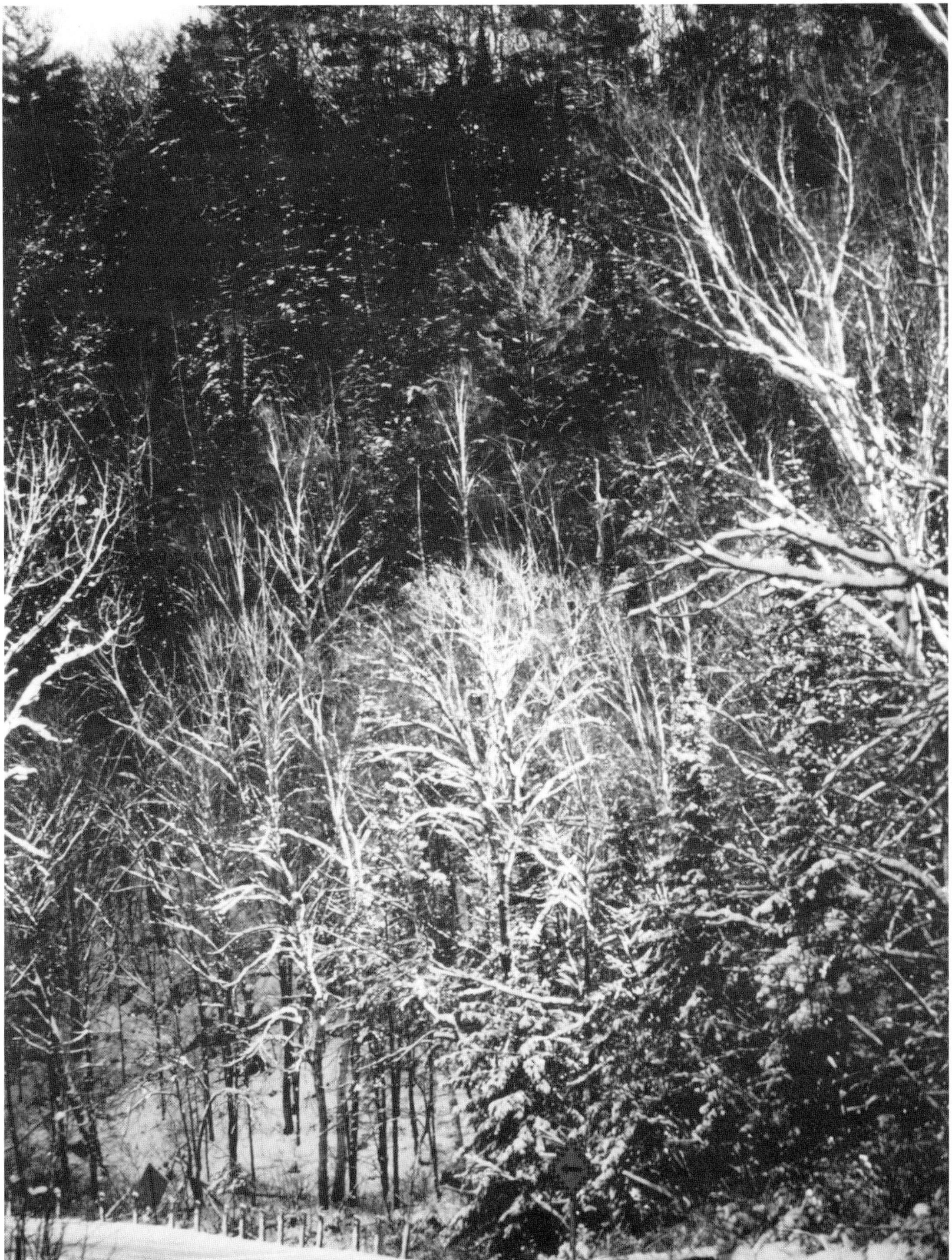

Most of the better cameras now offer the photographer a choice of three automatic exposure settings: spot, centre-weighted and averaging. I normally leave my camera set on the middle one: centre-weighted. On most cameras, this setting exposes for the part of the image that appears in the centre third of your viewfinder. It is a compromise that works for most of the shooting I do and can be the solution for the situation described above provided you have time to play around. It is not ideal for an object – a wolf for example – that is rapidly moving away from you but it will work for scenics and posed shots of your friends.

Hold your hand out in front of the lens so that it occupies something approaching the "zebra effects" balance. In other words, like the zebra, you want to have some "white" to counter balance the "darkness" of your subject. Depress the shutter button halfway, which will (on most cameras) lock the exposure and then focus on your subject.

This will be more difficult with auto-focus cameras because you will have to make a choice to either set the exposure manually and focus automatically or set the focus manually and the exposure automatically. Really good cameras will have an exposure compensation dial that will let you dial up the correct exposure while keeping everything in the "auto" mode. This procedure will vary from model to model, so consult your instruction book and learn how to do it.

Why not take the exposure only from your hand? This works and will give you a properly exposed picture of your subject but I doubt you'll like the results. By not including the snow in your meter reading, the snow will be very washed out and lack any texture or depth even though your subject is correctly exposed.

Always remember that any photograph is an interpretation of reality. You and your audience will bring to it personal expectations, and with snow that usually means a somewhat under-exposed (i.e., darker) main subject and denser looking white snow.

I have no doubt that unless you have taken a lot of winter shots this all sounds slightly crazy to you – and maybe it is.

Still, from my experience with both extremes (white snow and very black bears) this approach works.

Remember too that the type of film you use has a bearing on this. Black and white and colour print film can be played with in the developing stage to correct your exposure errors. If, like me, you shoot slide film, you must exert finer controls when taking the pictures because you cannot correct it later.

What if your subject is running and you don't have time for all this nonsense? Simple. Switch to the spot meter setting on your camera. This one concentrates its attention on the very centre of your viewfinder and will give you a reading of that spot only. It will work fine unless you are very close to your subject. This one has even greater application at other seasons, as we will see.

The third setting, averaging, takes in a roughly figure-eight-shaped range that stretches across the viewfinder, usually the middle third. It is great for more "even lighting" shots, such as the foggy morning picture, and terrible for tricky shots like the snow scene.

KILLING BATTERIES

Photographing winter will be covered in more detail in later chapters, but this is the place to remind you about batteries. Nothing kills a battery more quickly than winter's frigid temperatures. Be prepared for this fact of life and expect your batteries to go dead on you at a critical moment. I used to carry a Canon F1 camera just in case all else failed because I could operate without a battery at all. I no longer worry about this and trust my new cameras to do the job. This confidence comes from knowing the general climate and temperature limitations I will expose my cameras to. Seldom do I work in temperatures below –20 degrees Celsius and I have found that the cameras function to at least that level.

I do, however, carry spare batteries at all times. In the winter, I keep them in a shirt pocket close to my skin. That way my body heat keeps the batteries warm. Even a few minutes in my pockets restores batteries that the cold had seized up.

THE "BLACK LEAVES" OF SUMMER

Summer is just about as tricky as winter to photograph but for the opposite reason. Where winter is mostly white, summer is mostly black – at least it appears to be to your light meter which "sees" everything as a variable of grey. Green forests come across to it as virtually black (or at least very dark grey). Before I understood about the "grey" system, I was at a loss to explain why my summer forest pictures always tended to look washed out. The reason is obvious now. The camera was overexposing to make my dark greens the equivalent of mid-grey greens.

To correct this, take readings from slightly lighter green areas or compensate your exposure reading by closing down your lens a half or full stop by using your exposure compensation dial to let less light in and darken your image. (Note that with snow and white sand, you open up your aperture a half stop or a full one to let more light in.)

For those who do not have cameras with this type of control or for those who feel their cameras are always reading too dark or too light, compensate by resetting the ISO speed on your camera. Check your manual to see if this is possible for your brand.

Spring and fall tend to be the easiest seasons to expose for; there is a good mixture of light colours and dark because things are either filling in (spring) or dropping out (fall).

We'll go into more details about photographing the seasonal changes in plants when we discuss them in the next chapter.

Seasonal change is a fact of life in the north and it gives the land a special kind of variety over the course of a year. On the other hand, weather is a more instant and vastly more variable daily occurrence.

Algonquin's weather can be at times benign and relaxing and at others violent and scary. It can be dull as well. As a youth, I spent several summers camping in the park and I well remember one trip when we had light rain and drizzle every day for three weeks. One of the great lies perpetrated on tourists the world over is the "blue skies" advertising rule of thumb.

I once worked for a stock photo agency that refused to take any scenics unless the skies were blue with few or no clouds.

These pictures, it was explained to me, could be sold to promote tourism or beer because nobody wanted to be associated with any place that had (god forbid) real weather. I note that much of Ontario's current television tourist advertising no longer features "blue skies" but rather red ones, yellow ones or orange ones. These skies are not sunset shots but are provided courtesy of coloured filters. You will observe that you see few if any clouds, no matter the colour of the sky.

Frankly, I do not approve of such "lies." Indeed, as a photographer I rather like "weather." Clouds, especially the white ones (cumulus) and the dark black thunder clouds (cumulonimbus), make for spectacular shots. Grey overcast clouds provide even lighting, which makes determining the proper exposure a cinch: it is whatever the camera says it is!

I prefer a wide-angle for cloud photography because in most cases a telephoto does nothing to enhance the cloud's appearance. A cloud demands room. It needs land and water below it. It needs the sky and space above it. It needs to float. Telephoto shots eliminate these things and result in a bland picture.

CLOUDY DAYS

Clouds also make wonderful backdrops for pictures that are about other things. My favourite shot of an Algonquin thunder cloud features a friend paddling the canoe while the threatening monster towers in the background. The picture is about canoeing, but the story it tells is heightened by the ominous threat of the coming storm.

A photographer is constantly aware of light. If you watch the interplay of light and dark as a heavy storm approaches you will see that the truly black skies appear when there is bright sunlight still making its way through the cloud cover. Once the storm blankets the sky, the dramatic contrast is gone and the sky becomes merely dark grey and much less interesting.

Be on the lookout for that "dramatic" lighting and be prepared to act. In the summer, the best (or worst) storms are usually proceeded by a shift in the wind direction to the north. A drop in temperature may accompany this shift as well as the front approaches.

The first thing I do is get my campsite ready to weather the storm and then I seek a good location from which to shoot. Never try to capture the storm from a canoe or motor boat and always remember to put safety first. A camera struck by lightning is usually ruined – so, for that matter is the photographer holding the camera.

Rain is another fact of life in Algonquin and should be recorded as part of the ecosystem's story. However, it is very difficult to capture unless it is a real downpour. Sometimes a fill-in flash helps to light up the raindrops between the camera and the subject. It is certainly worth a try.

Rain splattering on a pond or other body of water can be an effective way of showing it. Close-ups of water droplets dripping off leaves or branches is another tried and true shot that is worth spending a couple of frames on.

My preference is to photograph the rain as part of the environment. Try for sheets of rain falling on a lake as the wind whips the storm across it. Or try capturing the water rings on a pond as a moose feeds in it.

Large mammals (and in the park moose are the easiest of these to find) make interesting subjects, especially when they are wet. The texture of their coats takes on a rougher character and the moisture imparts a special sheen. Although I've never done it successfully in the park, I have succeeded in capturing rain in Africa by purposely positioning myself so that the animal is backlit.

This is difficult to do in Algonquin because it requires an open area (such as a savannah) and a fairly low sun. Algonquin's forest pretty much eliminates both these factors but keep the technique in mind should the opportunity ever present itself.

Although this next technique likely will not capture the effect of falling rain, it will result in a "soft" rich photograph. It works best when the light is at a minimum at midday thanks to a heavy overcast. Set the camera up on a tripod and set the shutter speed at a 1/60 of a second or less. I've always been pleasantly surprised by the result since the colours the film captures are not those that I remember seeing at the time.

KEEPING DRY IN A WET WORLD

Photographing rain or any precipitation does present the problem of keeping the camera dry. With the new electronic cameras, this becomes a critical issue. A single drop of moisture in the wrong place and your camera may cease functioning. Using an umbrella is one solution – just remember to keep it over the camera and not yourself. Some manufacturers sell "raincoats" for their longer lens. These usually cover the lenses and the camera as well as your head and they are worth the minimal investment. I used this trick recently in Alaska to keep my cameras and lenses dry as I photographed sea lions from a boat in the middle of a storm with three metre swells. I've had better shooting but seldom has any been more interesting.

Shooting from inside your car and using the window as a support works. At times I've even used my hat to shelter my camera.

Keeping your camera dry while you are canoeing or hiking presents a different set of problems. While canoeing I always keep my cameras inside a waterproof container. I have a waterproof carrying case that I use on short trips (it also keeps dust out) but on longer trips I keep my lighter camera bag stored inside a waterproof bag. A sturdy garbage bag will do if you can't find a commercial one made for this purpose.

In a canoe it is not only rain that you need to worry about. A poorly placed paddle can splash or drip on your equipment. Water can collect in the bottom of the canoe or a drinking container could spill. Don't ever take any of these things for granted.

Might as well leave the camera stored, right? Wrong. I keep a camera with a medium telephoto lens mounted on it wrapped up in a waterproof bag in front of me. I usually set the camera and bag on top of an old life preserver, which serves to cushion it and it keeps out any spilled water in the canoe. If something happens or I see a shot I want, it is a simple matter of quickly taking the camera out and snapping the shot, then replacing it in its safe spot between pictures.

Be sure to keep your film dry as well. The plastic case the film comes in will keep it safe in all but a good dunking. I've never yet had a plastic container save a roll of film I've dropped into the water.

Always insure your cameras just in case all this good advice fails or you have an accident. That way at least you can recoup some of your loss.

WATER, WATER EVERYWHERE

Water in all its forms makes an interesting study. We've talked a little about it as rainfall and included lakes in our images of the rocks, but there are other things to consider as well. The next chapter will look at the "watery" environments of the park so let's confine our discussion here to some of the grander displays of water in the park – falls, rapids, lakes, streams and rivers.

Waterfalls and rapids are a joy to photograph. I prefer smaller, gentler waterfalls and rapids as subjects, but the big ones, such as Ragged Falls just outside the park's western boundary, are powerful raging spectacles that can best be captured by remembering what was said about photographing snow – rushing water, like snow, is white.

A popular technique for shooting moving water is to take a time exposure on a still day. This requires a tripod and ideally a remote shutter release to reduce camera shake. Use as long an exposure as you can get for the picture – at least one or two seconds, and longer if possible. A low ISO film is ideal. This is one place where ISO 25 is the perfect choice but ISO 64 or even 100 will work. Avoid faster film if you can.

Compose your picture carefully. Consider your angle. Are you shooting straight on, up at it or down? Take several exposures at different speeds and at different angles. The resulting images will not freeze the water but will smooth it into a glowing ethereal stream that is quite charming to look at. Some shots you will like better than others but it will work. (Note that the longer the exposure, the "smoother" the tumbling water becomes.)

The most difficult thing to manage with this type of photography is the light. Bright days make it difficult to slow your shutter speed down enough, while heavily overcast days may give a

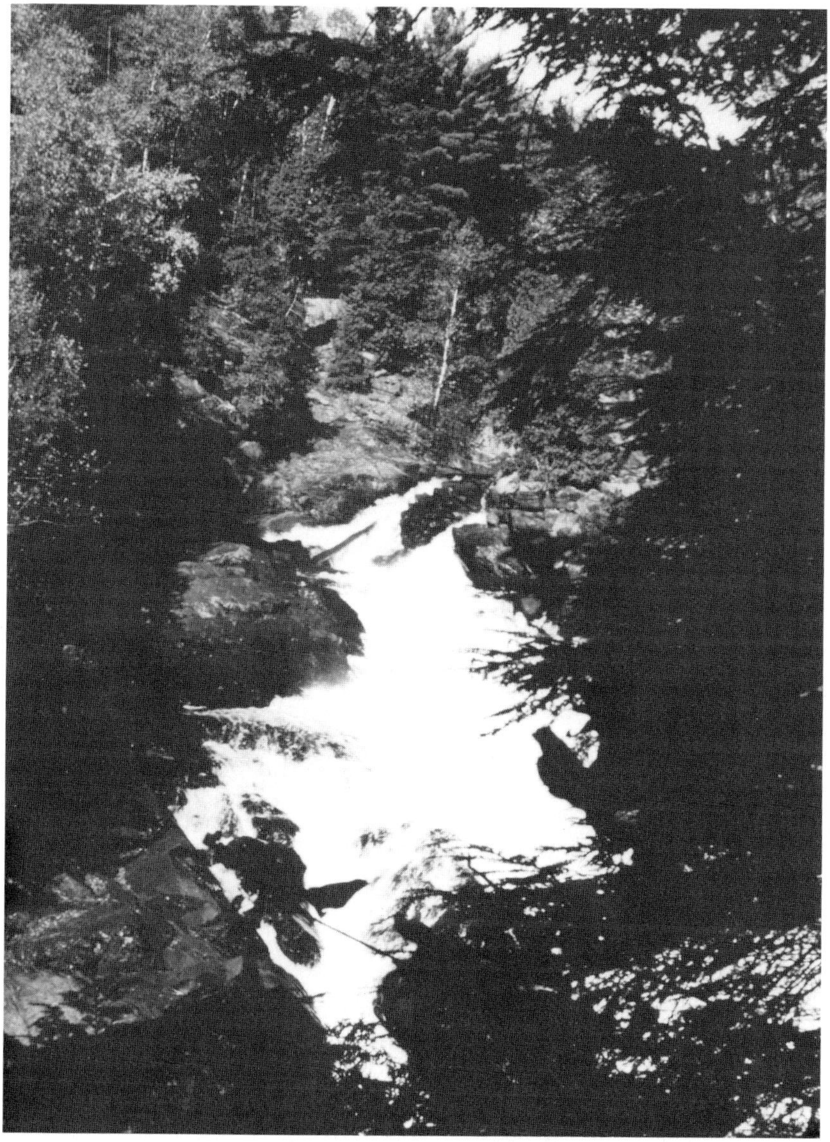

Ragged Falls is easily reached off of highway 60 just west of the park. Here the Oxtongue River rushes over the Canadian Shield in one of the largest waterfalls visible along the park's main road. (35mm 3.5)

grey cast to your photograph. You will learn best while playing with this technique a number of times over a number of trips.

The same technique can be used to capture lightning as well as the aurora borealis, stars and the night sky. (The one exception to capturing night time images is the moon, which can best be photographed by using a telephoto lens.)

A word about lightning before we move on. As of this writing, I have not successfully managed to get a picture of it flashing across Algonquin's skies. My shots of lightning come from visits to Tucson, Arizona, which is one of the best places in the world to capture this phenomena. Each summer the desert heat here draws in moisture from the Gulf of Mexico which cools when it hits the surrounding mountains. The results are spectacular thunderstorms. A time exposure at dusk or later works best but be warned you will waste a lot of film. At least I did.

When it works well, it makes for a very interesting picture but it takes many tries. Where do you think the next flash will be? How long an exposure should you try? Are you close enough or too far away? It is very much a guessing game. You will not know how you fared until you see your results and no doubt there will be some surprises. I found the overall colour shift in the resulting slide to be remarkable – a sort of purple hue to some shots that I did not expect or like.

Remember, if you see a flash through the view finder you missed it. Your reflexes aren't that good.

Now back to other forms of water. Algonquin's rivers and streams are bound to be included in the scenic shots of your trip. The park boasts thousands of them and a few are easily photographed from Highway 60. Good spots to work include the Oxtongue Picnic Grounds, the Tea Lake Dam, Smoke Creek, the Mew Lake–Lake of Two Rivers area and Sunday Creek.

The best shots, however, will come by getting off the road and into the back country. A canoe is the vehicle of choice here since it is ideal for exploring these pathways.

Many lakes can be seen from the road as well but as with rivers and streams, your best photographic opportunities will come by venturing into the interior.

Try capturing the mood of Algonquin's waterways by photographing them in different seasons and weather conditions.

In the next chapter, I'll give you some more specific ideas.

IN THE LONG AND SHORT TERM

Fire is a very important factor in a forest ecosystem but it is one which I have never seen in the park. This is partly due to the park's management policy but it is also due to the amount of logging that has gone on in the park and continues to this day. We will consider this artificial "fire" model in the chapter on human influences.

These factors – both biotic and abiotic – drive Algonquin's ecosystem and a change in any of them affects the cycles of the park. Some years the park will seem wetter than other years. Sometimes fall colours appear early and pass quickly while in other years they seem to linger. If there is anything that is constant in these abiotic factors, it is the angle of the sun's light hitting the land. Although this factor changes from day to day, it is the most predictable factor over the course of several years.

In the last few years, the park's weather has been altered by the El Nino effect, which has been especially strong, resulting in longer winters. El Nino is the name given to a change in global weather patterns created by a warming of Pacific Ocean currents off the coast of South America. This change alters wind and ocean currents worldwide and creates unusual weather fluctuations. Massive flooding may occur in one area while droughts occur in others. Even something so distant from the park has its effects here, reminding us that the Earth itself is one ecosystem.

Volcanoes, too, have had their effect and so has global warming, but through it all, the angle of the sun's rays reaching the earth has gone unchanged.

Why is this important? Although it is the easiest abiotic factor to overlook (and the most difficult to photograph), recent research has suggested that the angle of the sun's rays has a profound effect on living things. Plants buried under snow apparently respond to the sun. The reproductive cycle of deer and moose is turned off and on by it. Sap in trees, not to mention their reproductive cycles, is also effected by it. In a sense, the events of the park year are very much a direct result of this overlooked factor.

Understanding how the angle of light affects things along with an awareness of how other "non-living" factors create the world you are trying to capture on film can open more creative ideas and challenges for you and your camera the way it did for me.

Excursion 3

Saturday, May 7

It had been a late night and I hadn't bothered to set the alarm so my departure for Algonquin was later than planned. Still, I was in the park by 10:15 and I was reasonably well rested. I was alone on this trip as none of my friends or family were able to join me.

My goal this time was to get pictures to illustrate the chapter on the park's geology as well as to add to my files of moose and spring flowers. I had a very definite shooting schedule in mind with locations and shots selected because of past experiences. I knew I'd see moose, but of course I could only guess at their locations so I allowed for extra time to allow some flexibility.

I planned to use only two lenses on this day-long trip: my 28mm and my 80-200 zoom. Although it sounds strange, my plan was to use the zoom lens primarily while photographing the rocks and the 28mm for the moose – exactly the opposite of my usual approach.

I saw a total of nine moose, all of them in or near the muddy ponds where the winter's road salt had washed off and collected. Because I've made so many trips up here at this time of year, I had a fairly good collection of spring moose shots in my collection and I was looking to add some different images to my stock.

That was the reason I felt free to use my wide-angle lens. I had lots of close-ups of moose and I thought I'd try using the 28mm lens to capture the moose in its environment. This meant getting fairly close to the animal so that it wouldn't be a mere speck in the picture, so I knew I'd be taking a few limited risks. Moose are big animals and they can be aggressive.

I chose my moose carefully. I ruled out a cow and twin yearlings because they were nervous to begin with and I knew they wouldn't stay. I tried a young bull but because of his location at the base of a steep ditch, I was unable to get the angle I wanted. After a few shots I moved on.

I passed on one large bull feeding above a rock face and I'm glad I did. As I watched him, a car pulled up and a burly tourist sauntered up the hill to within touching distance of the moose in order to get a close-up with his camera. The moose charged, sending the photographer scurrying for his car.

Should you ever be tempted to try such a stunt ... don't! If you must approach moose or any other large animal, do so slowly. Watch the animal but do not stare at it intently as this will make the animal nervous. Note the position of its ears and hackles. If the ears go down or the hackles go up, back off immediately.

I also make a habit of watching the behaviour of people around large mammals. If I see them doing something likely to cause the animal to react, I back off, fearing that the animal will not differentiate between some foolhardy clown and me. I've tried on occasion to warn people of the danger of such behaviour but they usually ignore me or – worse – they suggest I go do something physically impossible! Most times I just quietly leave.

Finally I found a cooperative moose slurping up muddy water in as good a location as I could have hoped for. He was not put off by the park visitors who stopped to view him and they on their part behaved quietly around the animal. With a little patience, I was able to slowly work my way to a position level with his where I could get the picture I wanted.

With the wide-angle lens, I was able to include the moose, the forest and the mud hole all in the same shot. I left very pleased with my effort and with no doubts whatsoever that I had made the correct choice of lens.

I used the wide-angle lens to photograph some wildflowers as well. This time I held the camera as low as I could and allowed the auto-focusing to work its magic. The results were some pleasing pictures of trilliums.

The rock I had in mind for today's shoot was a glacial erratic that sits off by itself near the bridge where Opeongo Road crosses a stream. I shot almost an entire roll of film on it trying to get the one shot that would "capture" it. I began by shooting from the side of the road, then I walked a well-beaten trail that parallels the stream and found I could frame the rock using the pine trees growing along the trail.

Both lenses worked well with this subject and I constantly found angles that suited one or the other. It was a great exercise.

I cut the day short because the skies clouded over and my shooting light was pretty much done. Never the less when I left the park about three that afternoon and headed home, I was pleased with my results.

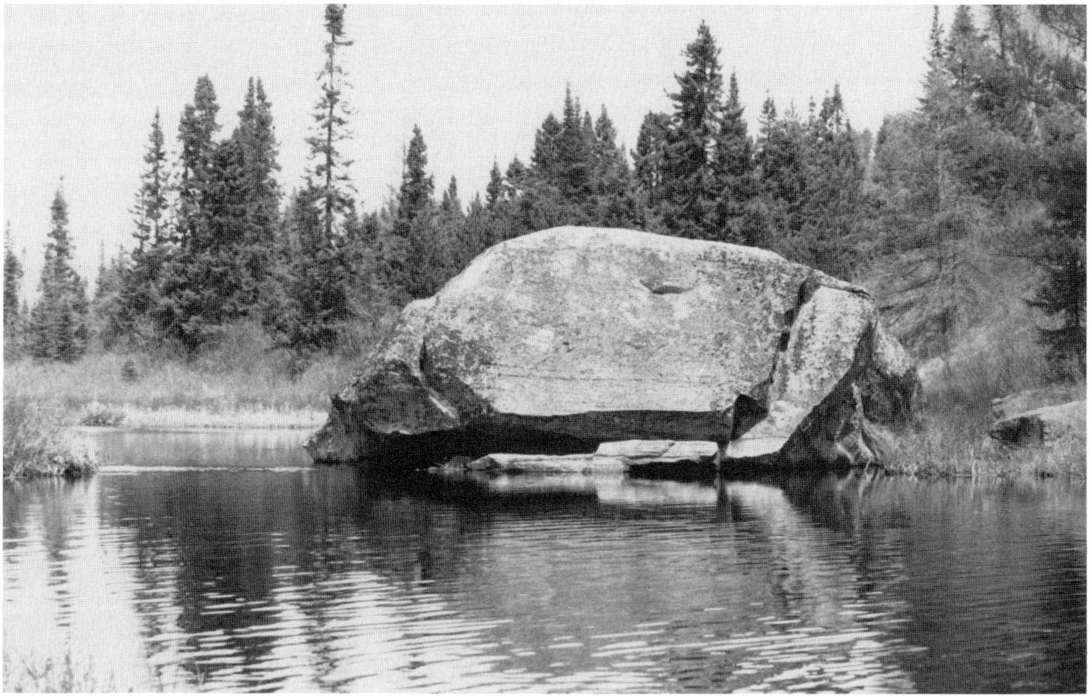

This boulder, a glacial erratic left over from the last ice age, is one of the most familiar rocks in the park. It can be found on the east side of the bridge on Opeongo Road bridge. (200mm 2.8L zoom)

CHAPTER 3

The Waterways

Given the choice of photographing in a forest or on a lake, I'll take the lake every time. Forests are difficult places for a photographer to work in. They are dark, the animals can vanish quickly, and it is not the easiest thing in the world to hike through them with a tripod and a pack full of cameras, especially if there is thick underbrush.

But Algonquin's waterways are not at all like that. They are open and bright with reflected light. Camera equipment can, with care, be easily transported and any life that ventures out usually is fairly approachable. In this chapter, we will pick up on some ideas discussed earlier and apply them to capturing not only the waterways but the life found there.

First, let's consider the variety of water environments found in the park. As noted in the chapter on rocks, Algonquin's lakes and streams are not well endowed with nutrients and are, if anything, rather impoverished environments. That is not to say that they lack life, indeed – given half a chance, life will evolve to fill any under-used place. So it is here that we find some marvellous species with which to work.

Like all visitors to the wilds, I have my favourite "secret places." One of my very favourites lies within an easy day's drive along the park's border. No, I'm not going to tell you where it is exactly because, heaven knows, there are enough people visiting it already. If you know the park well, you may recognize it from my description; and if you don't, a study of the park map will clearly show you several places that could be it.

My secret place, you see, is not unique. It is one of many such places that with a little looking and some luck can be discovered by anyone.

What I like about "my" spot is that it combines in a single day's paddle several types of Algonquin's waterways. It begins with a meandering stream that quickly immerses itself in a bog. The stream flows from the bog into a medium-sized lake, which in turn empties into a large river that is lined in places with an extensive marsh.

Along the shores one encounters rocky faces, sandy beaches and, of course, forests. Tucked in between are other marshes and bogs, islands and trails that all beg to be explored.

It is a place far from the bustle of Highway 60 and well away from the logging areas, yet it is close enough that within four hours of leaving the city, I can be exploring its waters.

This chapter deals with this tiny microcosm of the park's watery worlds. It was with great pleasure that I made a special trip there for this book. Accompanying my daughters and me on this trip were three other dads and their daughters. For three days we shared adventures along this microcosm of the park's waterways.

BOGGED DOWN

The parking lot is barely out of sight when the meandering stream we're following enters a bog. A bog is a by-product of the last glaciation period when the ice fields kept the climate cold.

The Algonquin winter simply renews the relationship and helps keep the water cool year round. It may be 30 degrees Celsius up where my head is but if I dip a foot into the water

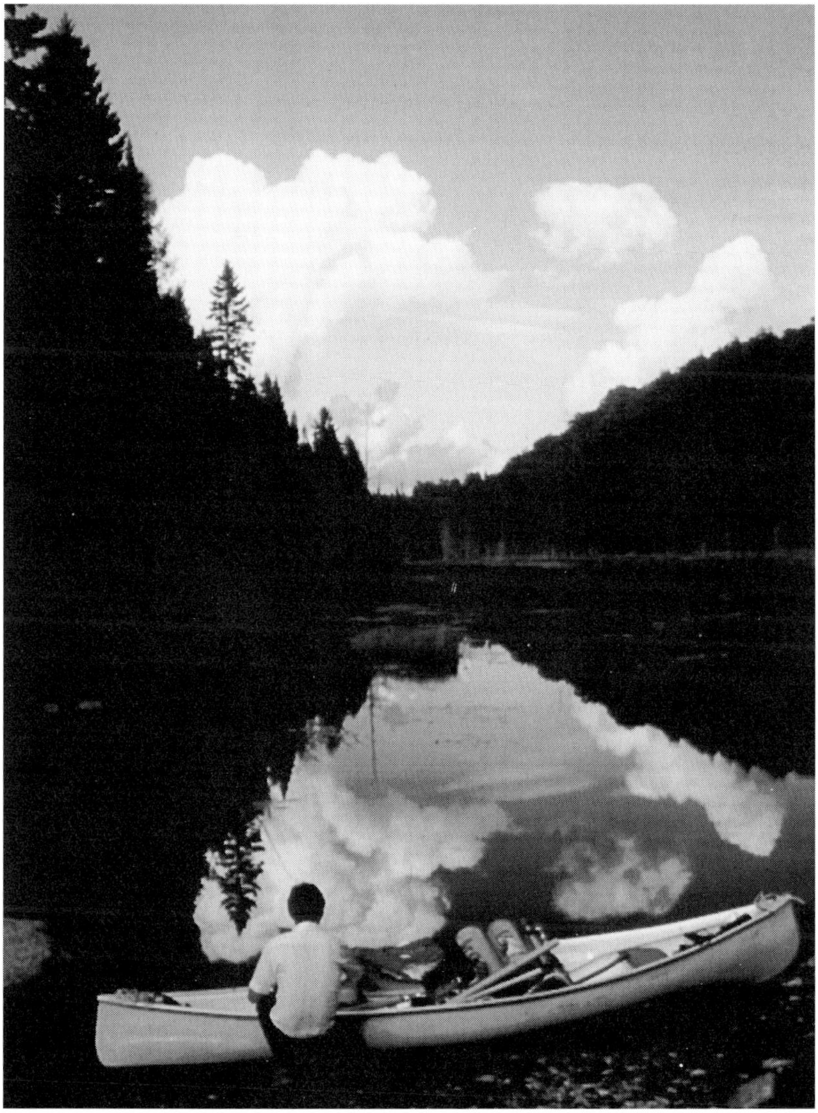

Don McClement checks our gear as we set off for a late day canoe trip in August. We only saw two moose and both were skittish. July seems to be the best time for such sightings. (35mm 3.5)

as I glide along, the temperature beneath the surface barely reaches 10 degrees.

Although many bogs are typically found in depressions left by the glaciers, Algonquin's bogs owe their existence to a series of changes that date back to the end of the glacier period. Where I go the bog, occupies an arm of what was once a much larger lake than the one this stream now leads to. On either side of the stream, I can see the old shorelines for they are steep and emerge from the bog dramatically as rock faces.

As time passed, the water level of this ancient lake lowered and forests claimed the dry land here. Then beavers arrived, perhaps the first coming about 7,000 years ago. These large rodents changed the land. The slow-flowing water was trapped. Once dammed, the water no longer moved and became still. Nutrients already scarce became scarcer as little decomposition could occur in this trapped cold water. The tea-coloured river our group is following is a product of this long, cold, slow "steeping" of rotting vegetation. Lacking nutrients to support more conventional water plants, the slow-moving stream was ideal for the typical bog plants to take over and lay claim to the edges.

Although pines and hardwood species like maple and beech line the rocky shoreline, the trees of the bog are black spruce and tamarack. Both are hardy trees that can survive the rigorous, almost arctic-like conditions of the bog.

Black spruce get by on a lot fewer nutrients than most spruce trees and are able to eke out an existence here. While by no means rare in the park, they are confined to boggy wetlands. If you drive further north away from the park towards Cochrane, they become one of the most common trees of the true Canadian Shield. Take time to photograph these trees with their droopy branches that appear almost to drip moss. They give the bog a spooky feeling and can provide the setting for some dramatic pictures.

Tamarack, on the other hand, are rather cheerful looking trees. These conifers have a lacy green appearance in the summer and look not unlike Christmas trees. By winter they take on a more sombre style as they lack needles entirely. What happened to their needles? Are the trees dead?

Tamarack are unique among conifers because they alone drop their needles after each growing season. With the arrival of fall the needles turn yellow and drop off. Before the needles drop they brighten up the bog and make it a place well worth a return visit for a photographer.

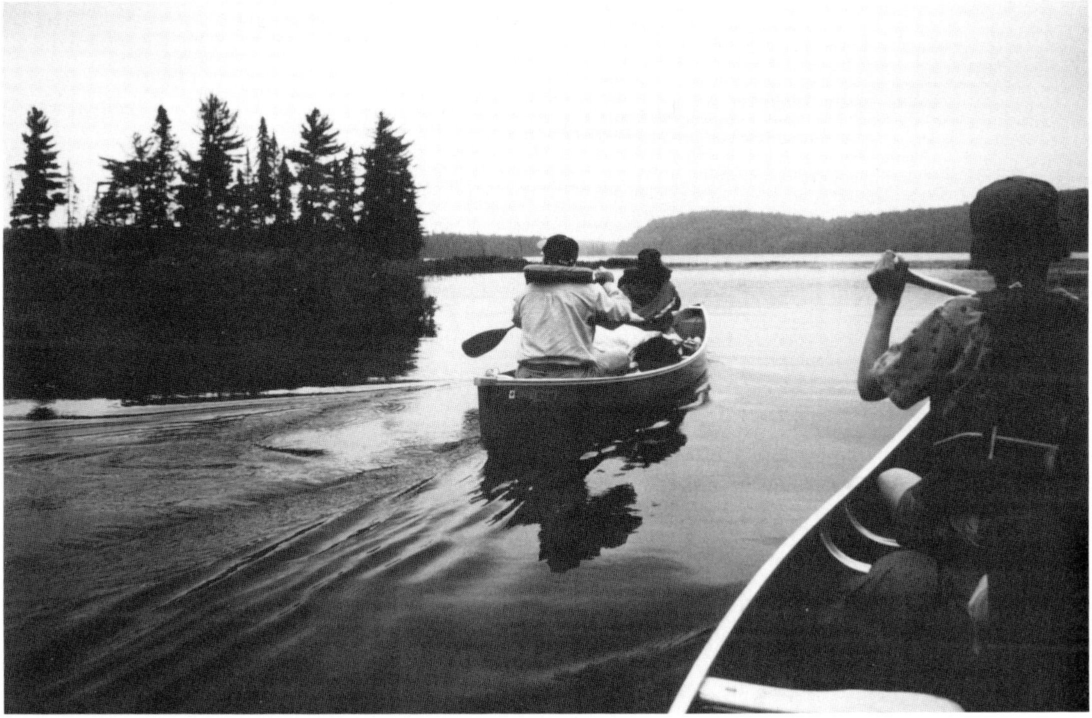

Open water at last! Ian Stanners and his daughter Heather, are the first to reach the lake where we will camp. Liza and Ashley wait patiently while Dad takes his shot. (28mm 2.8 auto-focus)

They lose their needles for the simple reason that they no longer need them. Tamaracks are able to get nutrients from the bog through a complex arrangement that allows the tree's roots to draw nutrients directly from the slow-moving water and from a variety of fungi that surround the rootlets. Losing their needles helps the plant control the need for water in the winter when none is available because the bog is frozen solid.

THE QUAKING LAND

It is important to remember that where you see tamaracks and black spruce growing, there was once open water. Indeed, if you were to step out of a canoe onto the "land" around these trees, you might get very wet.

Under what appears to be the shore on which these trees are growing is a layer of peat (sphagnum) moss. This moss, commonly used in household gardens, has the ability to hold many times its weight of water. So effective is this moss at hanging onto water that virtually no new water flows into it. It is like a saturated sponge. This means that any nutrients that might get washed in from the shore are simply channelled through the main stream and lost forever to the bog itself. As result, anything growing there must be able to adapt to a very poor environment.

One plant that can tolerate this nitrogen – and calcium – poor environment is a shrub called leatherleaf. Its roots are able to extract from the peat moss the nutrients it requires while at the same time forming a mesh with the moss itself which keeps the mossy "ground" stable.

Leatherleaf is a member of the heath family of plants. Other members of this family that can be found living in bogs include the bog laurel and labrador tea. On this particular trip, the bog laurel was in full bloom and I could see its tiny pink flowers all along the stream's course.

All three plants keep their leaves year round. As a result of this, they have had to adapt to almost desert-like conditions when winter winds rob them of their moisture and there is no melted water to replace the loss. In order to keep moisture in, all three species have thick leathery leaves designed to minimize the loss of water in critical months. Many desert plants show this same adaptive trait as well. The needles of the black spruce function the same way.

Other plants thrive here, too. Sheltered by the shrubs and anchored on the floating peat moss, they get their nourishment not from the moss but from the insects that abound here.

KILLER PLANTS

The round-leaved sundew is an insect-eating plant. Like its more famous relative, the Venus flytrap, it captures insects. The sundew's leaves are covered with tiny red bristles which exude a droplet of moisture. This droplet is quite sticky and when an insect lands on it, it's trapped. The leaves then fold over the struggling insect and the plant releases enzymes which digest it. In this way, the plant manages to survive in a barren environment. Pitcher plants, once thought to be carnivorous insect eaters too, have surprised scientists. It was long believed that these common bog plants had to ingest insects in order to get their required amount of nutrients. Then somebody took the time to actually look inside the plant. To his surprise, instead of finding dead insects he found living ones. The pitcher plant is best likened to a living terrarium. The plant requires not dead insects but living ones in order to survive.

The pitcher plant traps insects and then, through photosynthesis, releases oxygen, which allows them to breathe. They in turn enrich the plant through their fertile droppings and the carbon dioxide they release. Apparently the pitcher plant was at one time a carnivorous plant but has since evolved into a more benevolent species, losing in the process the enzymes needed to break down animal matter and instead reverting back to a more typical plant lifestyle.

It's a wonderful world, but how do you go about photographing it? I chose to work from a canoe as opposed to wearing waders or working from the shore. The canoe was a good compromise and allowed me to select individual locations to work from. At this point I enlisted the help of one of the other dads, Ian Stanners; he helped steady the canoe while I fidgeted around with my cameras.

Over the course of our trip I would return to photograph these plants several times. Each time I worked with two lenses, a 28mm and an 80-200mm zoom. Exposure readings were left to the camera since the colour tones of my subjects fell pretty much into the neutral grey area. I was able to shoot both on a sunny day and on an overcast day and found that the overcast day gave me the best results. The colours of the plants appeared more saturated on the grey days than they did against the dark shadows cast on the sunny day's shoot.

I found a location at the edge of the bog that had both pitcher plants and sundews. As this particular trip was in early July, the pitcher plants were in full bloom with their greenish-red flowers poking through the leatherleaf shrubs. To photograph the flower heads I used the zoom lens. I tried to select backgrounds that blended well with the overall tone of the picture I wanted. This meant a fair bit of jockeying the canoe around and I was grateful for Ian's patience.

Since the water was grey-black, I deliberately lined up some shots to include it. I also selected spots that featured the surrounding shrubs. I avoided shooting against the grey sky. (A rule of thumb is never shoot against a grey sky. A second rule of thumb is to break rules of thumb occasionally!)

Having seen in the viewfinder the images I was after, I turned my attention to the bog mat. Here surrounded by the delicate greens of the moss itself the "pitcher" portion of the plant was the largest object to be seen. Beside and in front of it grew the much tinier sundew. Too tiny, I thought, for my lens to record its features clearly.

Don't underestimate what the wide-angle can do for you. A trick many photographers know is that the closest focusing distance is not really the closest focusing distance. Remember the discussion about depth of field we had earlier – well this situation provided a perfect opportunity to employ that knowledge to trick the camera into doing what I needed it to do.

The problem was simple. The sundew was so small that even when I had the lens focus as closely as possible from above I couldn't see the detail I wanted. However, by shooting at the slowest shutter speed at which I could hand-hold the camera, I was able to gain a few extra centimetres to get the image I needed. In effect, I focused beyond the subject and allowed the depth of field gained by the low f-stop to bring the foreground into focus.

The shot I wanted was one taken from water level and this is where I put the auto-focus feature to good use. I selected a pitcher plant and took a reading of the closest focusing distance from above. This number would act as a guide to help me judge whether the camera was focusing where I wanted it to. Because I was photographing from a canoe, I was unable to look through the viewfinder of the camera when I held it at water level. I then leaned over the side of the canoe and held the camera as close to the water as I dared. Keeping it horizontal to the water was tricky and my partner in the stern provided another angle of view to verify that it was indeed level.

Then I allowed the auto-focus feature to take over while I guessed at the area the final image would encompass. I took several shots, hoping to get one that worked. When I did get the processed film back, I was pleased to see that this little trick worked well!

The mat of moss and shrubs did not cover the entire valley thanks to the stream I was exploring. In the spring runoff, the flow of water is strong enough to tear off portions of this mat and stops them meeting in the middle. When our group explored the river, we constantly encountered these torn off chunks of floating bog constantly.

ENCOUNTERS WITH DINOSAURS

Thanks to this open water, there were larger animals for me to train my camera on. A blue heron was flushed out and flew off. These birds nest in colonies wherever they can find sufficient trees to their liking. In Algonquin, these nest colonies are not as large as ones I've encountered further south. This is no doubt a reflection of the smaller number of fish that can survive in the park's nutrient-poor lakes. One colony in the southern part of the province contains over 300 nests but here they average fewer than 35.

In my travels I have met various members of the heron family and have never failed to find them fascinating. In Florida, there are over a dozen varieties of herons and egrets, yet here in Algonquin only two species are found – the great blue heron and the American bittern.

They remind me of dinosaurs, especially when you see them run after their prey (which I admit is a rare sight in Algonquin). I'm one of those amateur "dinosaurologists" who subscribe to the theory that birds and dinosaurs are one and the same, so seeing this predator gives me extra pleasure. It provided a glimpse of a world long gone that I can see only in my imagination.

When you photograph these birds, you'll usually need a long lens. Some of my best shots have come from the waterways along the Opeongo Road where, from time to time, I've come across cooperative herons that continued their hunting while I set up.

The shot I wanted was that moment of the strike and the kill. A tripod helps a lot in such a situation because the heron will stand for long minutes waiting for an unsuspecting fish or frog to swim by. If I try hand-holding the camera, the strike invariably comes when I am too tired to hold the camera up any longer.

I've seen bittern here too. These small herons put a lot of faith in their ability to hide among the reeds, as they stand with bills pointed skyward and freeze. The pattern of their feathers mimics the shading of the reeds and they become all

To capture a fishing blue heron takes patience, a tripod and a bit of luck. (300mm 2.8L auto-focus with a 2x tele)

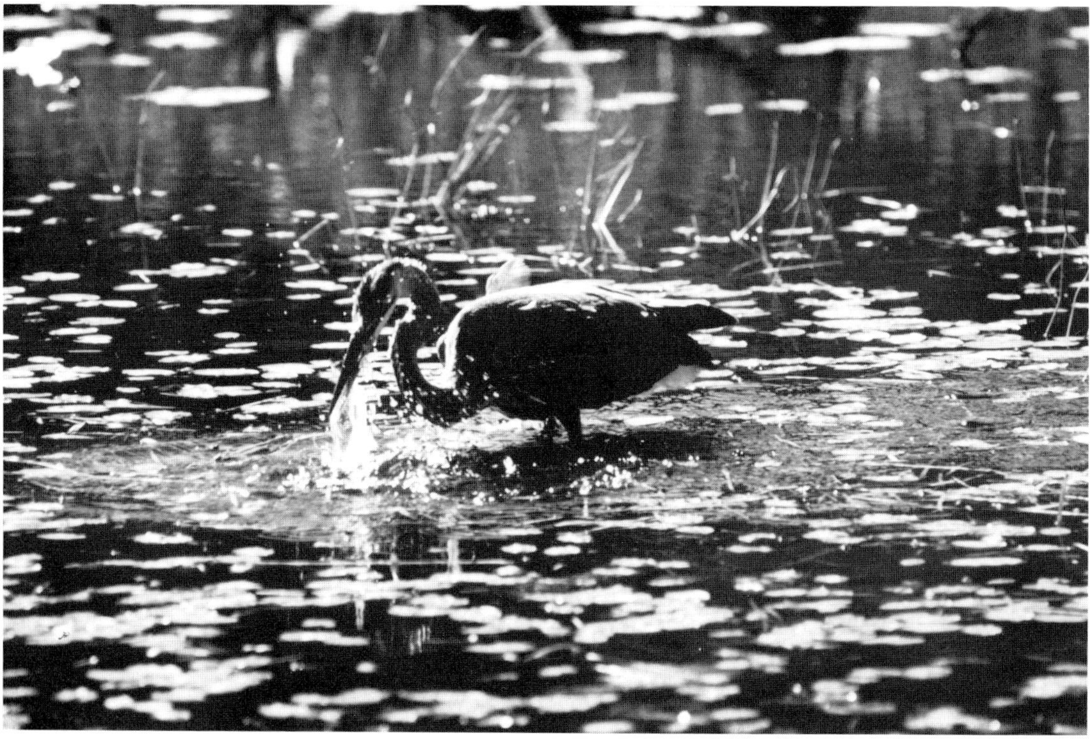

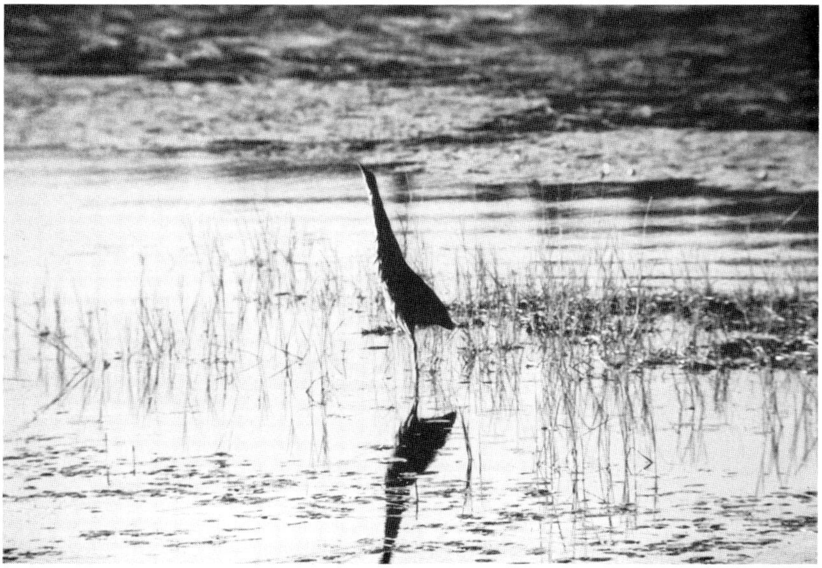

Bittern will stand with their body and beak stretched out and pointed upward so that their feather patterns blend in with the patterns of the marsh weeds. Of course it helps if there are reeds about to hide in. (500mm 4.5L)

but invisible. I once saw a rather naive bittern try this trick in an area where all the reeds had blown down. He stood out like a sore thumb but did not fly away. I took his picture and left him standing there.

When I am canoeing I always try to anticipate what may lie around the next bend. I replaced my 28mm with a 300mm because I was hoping to see a heron or some other wildlife. On this day however, the heron we see is nervous. It offered only a "jump" shot and I managed to get one shot with my 300mm lens before the bird is gone. I was glad I had changed lenses.

A TRUE WORKAHOLIC

It was not long before we began to encounter signs of the bog's true creator, the beaver. Beaver lodges poked their tops through the sphagnum mat and I couldn't help but wonder how these large rodents reach them without exposing themselves to danger. Paddling closer to inspect them revealed a network of well-maintained channels pushed through the bog that allows them to swim unseen to and from their homes.

The bog needs the beavers to dam up the flow of water so that it can continue to exist. Beavers, on the other hand, do not require a bog. Since being trapped virtually to the edge of extinction 150 years ago, the beaver population has rebounded to a point where scientists now believe there are more beaver in North America today than there ever were. It is believed that Ontario alone houses between one and two million beavers.

When you consider that each of those animals will down an average of 200 trees in a year, you can imagine their importance to the ecosystem! I remember once driving along Highway 60 and encountering whole stretches where the small saplings along the road had been chopped down. At first I thought it was the work of road crews but on closer inspection found that it was the work of this industrious rodent.

Beavers live in colonies headed up by an adult female. Young beavers usually leave the colony in order to establish their own groups, leaving the adults to breed again the next year. If there is food enough in an area, the wandering young may not have to travel too far at all.

Beavers are not easy to photograph despite their relative abundance because they are most active during the night. Dusk and dawn are the best times to catch them out and about but a fast lens is required.

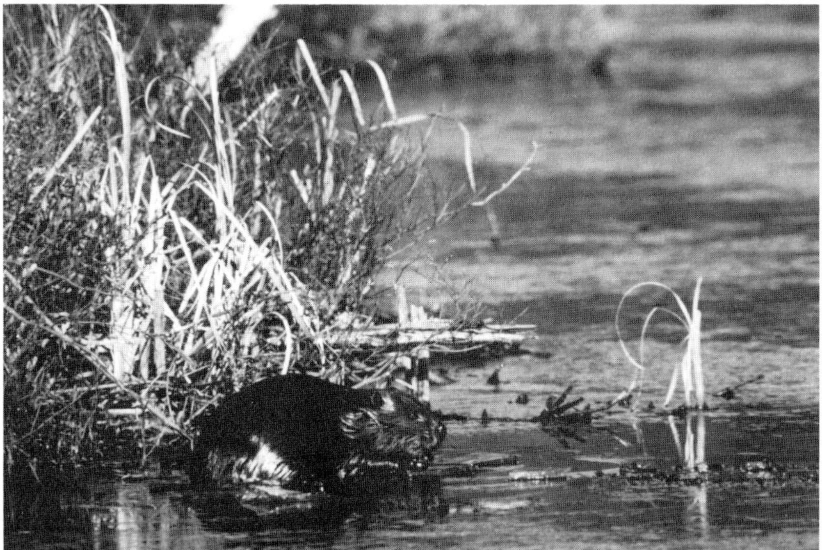

Beaver are quite capable of pushing or gnawing their way through the ice in order to get to a tasty titbit. If they wander far from their "plunge-hole" they are very vulnerable to predation, especially from wolves. (500mm 4.5L)

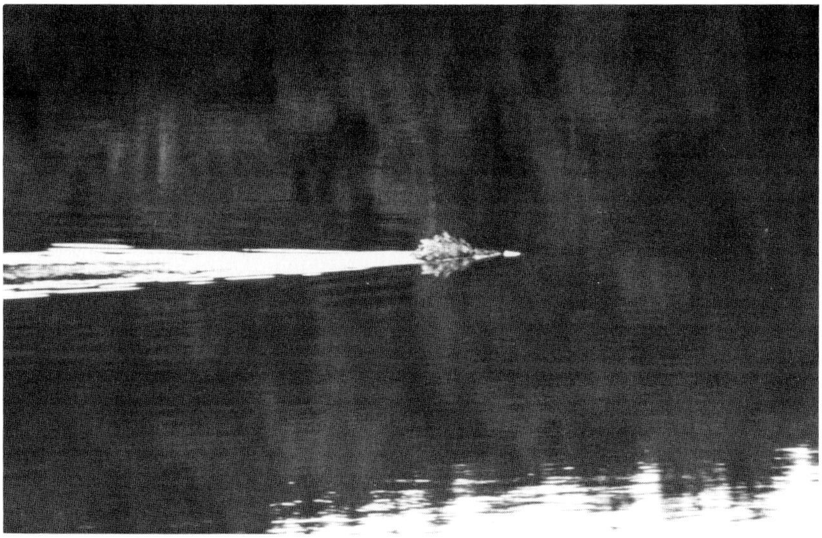

Beaver are tireless workers and as winter approaches will spend evening hours collecting cuttings which they will anchor in the mud at the entrance to their lodges so that when winter comes they do not have far to go to get food. (500mm 4.5L)

I find the Highway 60 corridor is the best place to get photos of these mammals. Although I have photographed them from a canoe many times, it is the highway that has provided me with my best shots. I suspect that is because the animals are used to cars and people and have a tendency to ignore them.

LAKES AND CLOUDS

For the slide show I wanted to do on Algonquin's ecosystem I wanted to combine the "60 corridor" images with ones taken of beaver lodges and dams on this trip. The Beaver Pond Trail at kilometre 45.2 is another excellent location to get habitat shots of beaver "workings" (dams, lodges etc.) too!

Soon the lake appears and our group finds ourselves in a new spacious environment. Scenic shots of lakes are usually taken under "blue sky" conditions. There's no doubt that they work well, but I prefer some cloud cover. Fluffy white cumulus clouds work well especially when taken with a standard (50mm) or wide-angle lens. I try to vary the angle I shoot at. The higher up I get, the more of the lake will appear in the picture. On the other hand, the lower my angle the greater the amount of sky. Both work.

Telephoto lenses, especially between 100mm and 300mm, can be effective too. They compact the image and create an illusion of tightness between foreground (the lake) and background (the forest) that can be quite nice. This works especially well in the fall.

Reflection shots on quiet days can be very worthwhile. At times, the park's lakes are so still that the reflection can almost be mirror-like. Sometimes a ripple will actually add to the surreal quality of this type of shot.

One of my favourite "lake" pictures was taken of Costello Lake. It shows a grey body of water broken in the centre by a splash of green. What I like about the shot is that the green is moving, shown by the "v" of trailing ripples. The green is a branch and it is being towed by an unseen beaver to its lodge. This shot combines the elements of forest, wildlife and lake to present an image that tells a story about the interrelationships found there.

OF MOOSE AND HIPPOS AND ENERGY SINKS

Which brings me back to a passage I read while researching material on hippopotamus for another project. The book was about the ecosystem of the African plains and the writer was making a point about the uniqueness of the hippo's role. Hippos, you see, are unique in Africa because of their lifestyle. During the day, they are visible as they invariably lie about in water, but most safarists don't realize that at night the hippo comes on land to graze alongside the wildebeest and zebra. Then it returns to the water where it escapes the sun's heat during the day.

The author's point is that this is very much a one-way street – the hippo derives nourishment from the land but returns little of it to the land. Instead, its energy-rich droppings fertilize the rivers and lakes it shelters in as does its body when it dies. (Few hippos die on land apparently.) Ecologists call this an "energy sink."

The author states that this is one of the few examples in the animal world where a mammal "makes a habit of regularly transgressing ecosystem boundaries." In other words, most mammals, whether whales or bears, usually stick to one environment and only rarely – sometimes never – move into another.

Here in Algonquin, however, we have two wonderful examples of this same "hippo principle" at work. The beaver (as nicely shown in the Costello Lake photograph) is one and the other put in an appearance as soon as we paddled from the lake into the river.

We had set up camp at the beginning of the river and our daughters had taken one of the canoes out for some fun. Suddenly they began shouting and pointing. From where they were on the opposite side of the river, they could see a moose. Cautioning them to be quiet and not scare the moose away, a couple of us slipped into a canoe and paddled over to see it.

I heard the animal before I saw it. Something was blowing bubbles and splashing in the water behind a screen of leatherleaf shrubs. We immediately slowed our paddling down and moved forward.

The moose was in water over its head and had to swim to keep its position. It reminded me of the hippos I'd seen in Africa except, of course, the moose was actually feeding in the water while hippos don't. Still, its large bulk and snorting brought back memories.

Moose, like hippos, are transgressors of ecosystems. They move freely from one environment to another, depending on the season and their feeding needs. Unlike hippos, though, they return their "borrowed" nutrients to their environments, both forest and river.

We will encounter moose again in this book along the Highway 60 corridor but for the sheer thrill of seeing them nothing beats "working" a moose from a canoe!

For one thing, you are eyeball to eyeball with them. For another, you can get very close for they seem not to bother with people too much. A word of caution here: never take an animal for granted. It is true that moose can be very tolerant of people but that does not mean that they are tame or approachable.

Animals have what is known as a "fight or flight" distance.

That is the point at which the individual animal either moves away or charges. There is no rule, no guide for this as every species and every unique being within that species will have its own level of tolerance. Even with a specific animal that distance will vary with season, environment and mood. It is not a very predictable thing but you can gauge it by watching for signs of agitation. Staring, raising its head, nervousness, snorting are all signs you should look for. Watch for the lowering of ears and the raising of hackles on moose especially.

Be careful not to corner any animal so that it feels it has no alternative but to charge you. A rule of thumb (yes, I know *another* one of those rules!) is to stop your advance as soon as you see the animal begin to move away. With moose this is not always possible when you are working from a canoe. On two separate occasions, gusts of wind have propelled me directly at one, catching me off guard while my paddle was down and my camera up. Fortunately, I had wisely left enough space that I was able to regain control before getting into serious trouble. In one instance, though, the moose did move off, depriving me of any more photographic opportunities.

Take time to "read" the moose and move up slowly on the animal. The quieter you are the better your chances will be. Pay close attention to your handling of paddles. Dropping them in a canoe, especially an aluminum one, can create a sound not unlike a cannon going off.

Waste a bit of film on the animal as you move up. It may not be the perfect picture but it may be the only one you get if the animal is the nervous type.

I use the zoom lens to put the moose in its environment and a long telephoto for those close-ups people like to see. Since moose are a member of the ungulate order, they spend a lot of time feeding. It takes awhile to consume fifty kilograms of feed a day!

In June and July they like to feed on the nutrient-rich lilies that grow in Algonquin's shallower waterways such as the edge of the river where I now found myself. I've never had this confirmed anywhere and I won't guarantee it's true but from my observations, a lake covered with the smaller reddish lilies is more attractive to moose than a lake or stream where the larger white water-lily and yellow pond-lily grow. I've never seen a moose eat these and I suspect it was the absence of the smaller lily on the earlier section of this stream that accounted for our not seeing any moose on that part of the journey.

In the two-kilometre stretch of the river where we found this bull, we encountered no fewer than a dozen different moose in two days of casual looking. The smaller lily is abundant on this stretch of waterway. I rest my case!

In any case, the moose come to the water for the variety of plants found here, all of which contain sodium – sometimes as much as 500 times more sodium than land plants – in order to replace nutrients lost over the winter. Sodium is necessary for their growing coats, bones and antlers. As we shall see in the next chapter, this same chemical draws them to the road in late winter and early spring.

The bull we were now watching paid little heed to our presence and kept right on feeding. After years of photographing moose in such a situation, I have learned that there are two basic images possible. The easiest is of the moose with his nose immersed in the river. Why?

Moose are ruminants, like domestic cows, and they consume food in large quantities, spending little time digesting it. Later on, they will find some safe secluded spot and regurgitate the food which has been fermenting in their first stomach or rumen. Here they will re-chew it (it's called a "cud") and then swallow it again, passing it through their remaining three stomachs.

The second shot is one with the moose with its head out of the water. This is a much rarer sight because being an ungulate, the moose does not have to spend much time chewing its food. It simply swallows it and then cow-like, regurgitates it later, safely bedded in the forest.

When I first started shooting moose from a canoe, I was surprised at how many of my shots were of the former type and how few the latter. I now force myself to wait for the moose to raise its head to briefly chew and swallow its food.

Although it was only early July, this particular bull had the most massive set of antlers I've seen on Algonquin moose. He exhibited a "double shovel" which is rare in this subspecies. There are three types of moose in North America: the huge Alaskan moose (about half again as large as our species), the Canadian moose (found across Canada) and the smaller Shiras moose. Typically, Alaskan bull moose have double shovels protruding over their noses while Canadian/Ontario moose have only tines. I estimated that the top of my head would come to the top of this bull's shoulder hump. A few weeks after this trip I photographed an Alaskan bull whose hump was another "head" taller than I.

This moose, though, was huge by local standards and I wondered what he would look like in the fall. That encounter would have to wait, and when he finally moved off into the woods, we moved on too.

We first saw the cow resting on the shore with her calf late in the day. The light was fading quickly but there was enough for me to use the 200 2.8. I took a few pictures before we left without disturbing her. I hoped that tomorrow they would still be nearby.

I do not approach a canoe trip the way most people do. For me it is not a case of "how far will I go" but rather one of "what will I see." "Seeing" imposes slowness. It takes time. When I go on a canoe trip, it is with "looking" in mind. Usually I will stay a day or two in one spot and explore that area.

This method is not for everyone. Many people go for the physical exertion and I say more power to them. True, they will see things that I won't see but my objective is to record and study. Even spending fifteen minutes watching a bull moose can be a strain for the gung-ho canoer. If you want to be a photographer, be prepared to invest the time. Fortunately, the friends with me on this canoe trip shared my philosophy.

We had the time the next day to go back and look for the cow and calf. We found them.

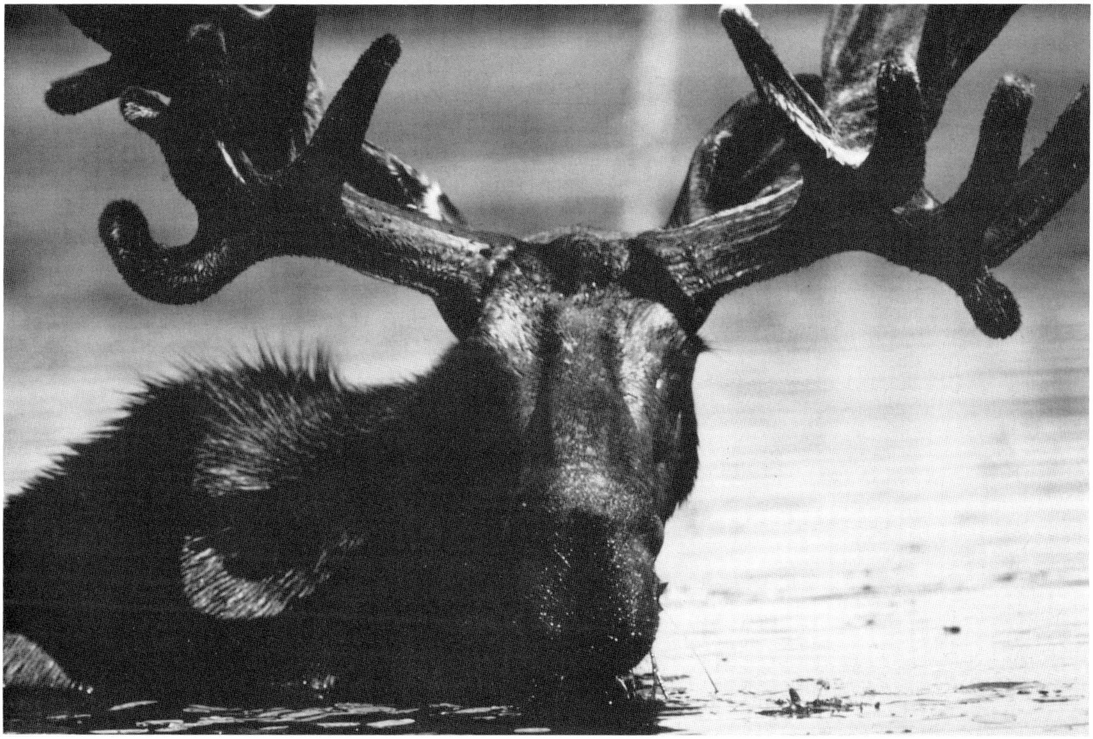

Being eye to eye with a bull moose can be one of the most memorable experiences of any canoe trip. I try to wait until the animal raises its head to swallow its food. This is a very large bull by Algonquin's standards. (300mm 4L auto-focus)

Time for another rule of thumb: ignore the common wisdom as to when animals are supposed to be out and about. In the case of moose, everyone will tell you that they are active early and late in the day. Hogwash. Anyone who tells you that has not spent time photographing Algonquin's moose. My files (and I have over 10,000 pictures of moose) are made up for the most part of shots of moose taken between ten and four.

Maybe somewhere there are moose that obey that "truism" of early and late, but if they do I suspect that they are hunted or pestered animals (by August Algonquin's roadside moose are a rare sight thanks, I believe, to all the summer traffic). My experience has been that moose may be found at any time of the day, especially in the spring and early summer. I've found this to be true in Alaska, Yellowstone and the Canadian Rockies. If there is a lull in their activities, it is around noon but then again that's when I eat and rest so maybe I'm just not out looking then.

The cow and calf were out and feeding at 11:30. She was unusually tolerant as our group were able to get fairly close. This time there was lots of light as the sun was shining in a clear blue sky.

If there is a drawback to shooting at "high noon," it is the intensity of the sun. Full frontal light can give a picture a flat appearance, and I try whenever possible to manoeuvre around a subject to get the light coming from the side. Under perfect conditions and with a little luck, you'll catch the sun glinting in the animal's eye while the neck is in dark shade. This makes the eye stand out and gives your subject life.

Always pay attention to the eyes. Auto-focus cameras focus on the first object in front of them, and in the case of a moose that can be a rather bulbous nose. The picture may look in focus, but unless you deliberately concentrate on the eyes your picture will be out of focus even though the nose is sharp. Why? People look at eyes and are naturally drawn to them. If they are sharp and in focus, then the rest of the picture is fine. If not, I toss the picture.

Some will tell you that moose take to the water in the summer to avoid the flies. I doubt that that is true and if it is, it doesn't work very well because moose are covered with flies, and when they swim or duck under the water hordes of them swarm above the moose waiting to land on it when it reappears.

The flies may be a nuisance but they do make for some interesting pictures. Wait until the moose moves and try to capture the mass of insects above it. Use a long telephoto and try for close-ups of the flies as they feed on the moose. Fortunately these flies do not feed on humans.

A WHO DONE IT, ALGONQUIN STYLE

Lurking in the ponds and marshes of the park is a deadly moose killer. You won't see it for it is small and hidden on the underside of the water plants.

The number of deer in the park directly influences the health and number of moose – the more numerous the whitetails, the fewer moose there are. Deer carry a parasite

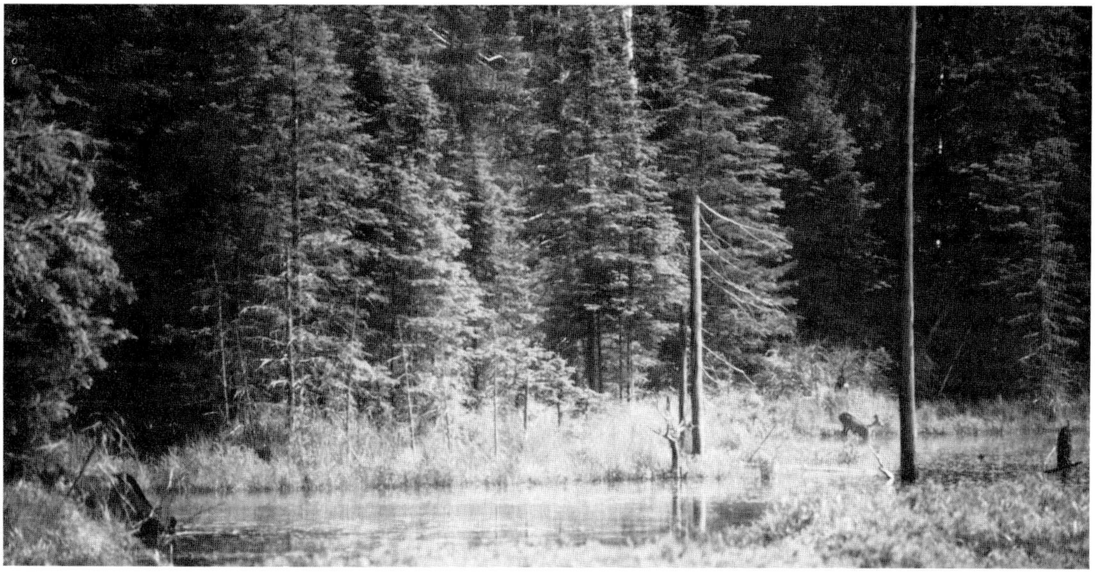

A cow moose and a deer both feed in the same pond; a deadly combination for the moose. Her life is in more danger from the presence of the deer than from any prowling wolf or bear. (500mm 4.5L)

known as brain worm that completes its life cycle by laying eggs which pass out of the deer into water. The parasite does not harm deer in the least as far as scientists know. Once in the water, the eggs hatch and the larva attaches itself to the underside of the leaves of water plants or to the stems and here they wait for a deer to feed on the greenery. The deer, in feeding, ingests the larva which then grows to maturity inside the deer, starting the cycle over again.

All well and good until a moose blunders into the picture. When it ingests the larva, the cycle breaks down. For some reason the brain worm is able to enter the spine of the moose where it works its way up to the base of the animal's brain. Here it grows until it is so large that it puts pressure on the host's brain, causing it to lose some of its muscular control. The moose becomes disoriented and off balance and either dies of starvation or, if it is lucky, attracts the attention of a wolf pack and is quickly dispatched.

I've wanted for some time to get a photograph that illustrates this part of the Algonquin ecosystem but until recently I had been unable to do so. Then one late spring day I got lucky. The picture shows a cow moose feeding in a boggy river and in the background is a whitetailed deer. It is not a great picture, but it allowed me to illustrate the complexity of life here in the park's waterways.

The picture of the two members of the deer family feeding together in the bog takes on a whole new meaning when you understand the deadly relationship the two have.

When I photograph Algonquin I am constantly looking for a variety of pictures. Some photographs, like the one described above, will be used to tell a story. Others will be portraits and others will concentrate on the environment. A final category will be those that hold some emotional appeal – a cute calf moose, a sunset or a pretty scene.

THE ANCIENT ONES

Before leaving Algonquin's waterways, I want to tell you about two other species I encounter regularly that share one common denominator – they are both incredibly ancient. The loon and the snapping turtle both can trace their ancestry back to the time when dinosaurs ruled the Earth.

It is rare to encounter a snapping turtle on a canoe trip in the summer. In twenty years, I've seen only one in July and

Snapping turtles are the Park's largest reptile. They are seldom seen except when they lay eggs in June or bask on logs on cool days. (400mm 4.5)

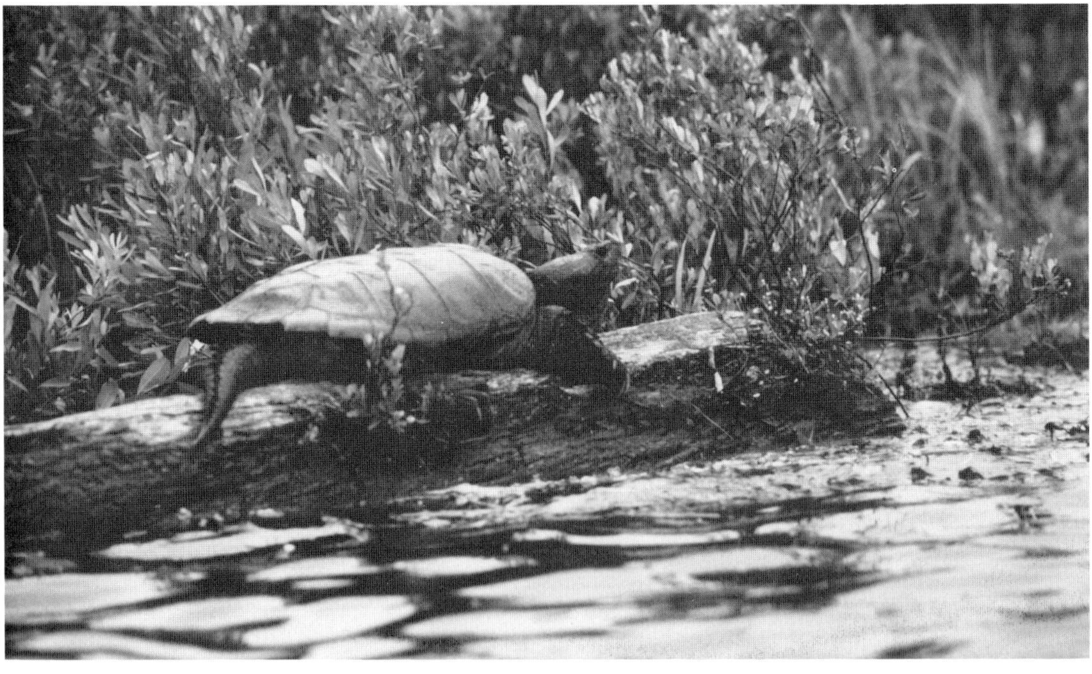

August. It was sunning itself on a floating log on a cool windy day. Like many campers, I have seen them when they come up to shore to steal a fish or two that I've left cooling in the water. My dad and one of his fishing buddies have caught one or two, as well, when the snapper took their bait.

The reason you don't tend to see them on canoe trips is that they want little to do with you. They are busily foraging or hunting below the water and seldom come up to sun. They are opportunists and will eat an amazing variety of foods. Animal matter, crayfish, fish and an occasional duckling make up their diet in the early spring when they emerge from hibernation. In summer, plant life tends to make up a large portion of their food but carrion is always attractive.

Even if you don't see them, they are there. Virtually every pond, river and lake has a resident adult snapper or two living in it.

As noted earlier, I enjoy hypothesizing about the life style of dinosaurs. The snapping turtle is a good example of why dinosaurs were more bird-like than reptile-like. One dinosaurologist makes the point that the one area where large cold-blooded predators, such as the snapping turtle, hold sway is the freshwater environment. There are, he states, few large warm-blooded carnivores that haunt rivers and lakes but there are many large reptiles found in these environments including crocodiles, alligators, anacondas, pythons and large turtles. His argument is that warm-blooded predators "ruled" the Earth because they were better able to cope with the extremes found there, while cold-blooded hunters found the more controlled environment of water to their liking. Since dinosaurs were found only on land, he argues, they must have been warm-blooded.

Snapping turtles are the largest water going predators found in the park. What about otters? Otters are common throughout the park. They are also predators and eat many of the same animals snapping turtles eat. An otter's average weight falls between five and thirteen kilograms. The average snapping turtle weighs between four and nine kilograms which would seem to argue against the warm-blooded/cold-blooded-theory.

However, the record weight for a snapping turtle in Canada is over twenty two kilograms. The world record snapping turtle weighed 143 kilograms! It was caught in Michigan in 1986. Although it may not be as evident here in the park, the theory does apply.

Surprisingly, many people think of the snapper as a vicious animal. It is not, but it will defend itself when handled.

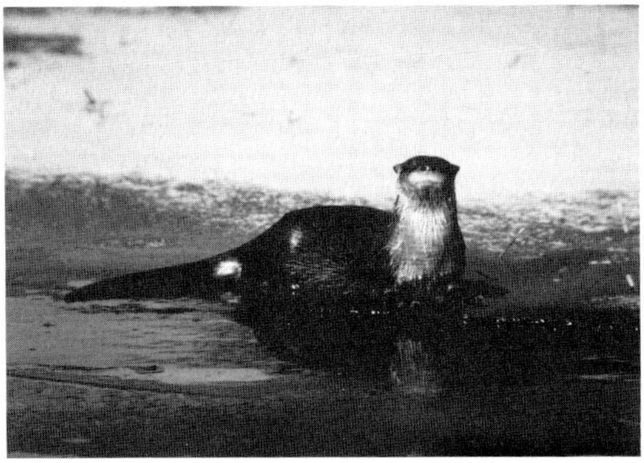

Otter are frequently encountered on canoe trips. Try imitating their cough ... They just might stay longer. (500mm 4.5L)

My best photographs of snapping turtles all come from encounters in early June. That is the time of year the females lumber back on land to lay their clutch of twenty to forty eggs. Here, deprived of the safety of water, the female has no option but to be aggressive if disturbed. (If you ever feel a need to handle a snapping turtle – to move it to safety, for example – grab it firmly by the tail. This is about the only safe place to hold onto one of these animals.)

You are more likely to encounter one in the morning as this is their preferred nesting time. I use the zoom lens to photograph them as it is possible to get quite close without unduly bothering the female. She will snap only if you touch her or she if feels you are going to touch her. Once she starts laying, she does little else no matter how close you get.

It takes awhile for her to deposit the eggs in the well-drained soil she has chosen and excavated, so use the time to compose your pictures. This is one of the few animals you will encounter in the park that allows you the luxury of having the time to do this. Try for a low-angle picture taken from the turtle's viewpoint. Another good picture is one of the eggs emerging. Since they are white, they show up very well against the dark moist soil.

Remember that over 50% of the eggs are eaten by mink, raccoons, skunks and foxes. Other eggs will perish if the weather is too wet or there are early freeze-ups. Do not disturb the nest. If the eggs you see are among the lucky ones that finally hatch, they will usually do so between early September and Thanksgiving (mid-October). Even then, most babies fall prey to herons and other predators.

Once finished laying, the turtle will head back to the water. She has nothing more to do with the eggs.

The loon, on the other hand, lays only two eggs but invests a lot of energy hatching them and then rearing the young. (There is now evidence to support the theory that some dinosaurs engaged in this type of pre- and post-natal behaviour too.)

I dearly wanted to include some nesting shots of a loon in this book but loon nests had eluded me, and I feared that despite my best efforts to provide new illustrations for this project, I would still have no luck finding a nesting loon .

But sometimes Algonquin can be a generous host and on this trip she was exceptional. I spotted something shiny on a small island of moss and grass; I thought it was the sunlight reflecting off the shell of a basking snapping turtle. Imagine my surprise and joy when I discovered it was the black back of a loon I was seeing!

Loons go on land only to mate and to nest and I knew the mating season was past. Algonquin had presented me with a loon on a nest! In my excitement, I moved too quickly and the loon dove into the water. Immediately I backed off. Wildlife photographers try to avoid disturbing nesting birds, and it is a practice I try to follow faithfully.

I anchored the canoe with the help of a friend on another small island and we crouched down hoping, she would return. It soon became apparent that we were still too close for her comfort, so we quietly paddled away.

An hour or so later, we returned and this time we handled our approach much better. Although she stretched out her neck low to the ground for a few minutes, she quickly relaxed and I was able to get the photos I wanted.

Loons are birds, of course, but very primitive ones. Fossil

evidence suggests that they have changed little since the time of the dinosaurs. The first true loons appear in the fossil record about 50 million years ago but birds very similar to loons in body structure had been around a long time before that. It is tempting to assume that primitive features, such as the loons' poorly developed legs, are somehow a mark of failure but that is not necessarily true. The fact that a species remains largely unchanged for millions of year can only mean that its adaptations have worked very well.

The Algonquin ecosystem has long been home to loons and snapping turtles, and a canoe trip through this watery world can be greatly enriched by encounters with these species.

I have always enjoyed the time I spent exploring the park's network of rivers, bogs and lakes for they offer a rich assortment of subjects for my camera. However, as wonderful as these environments are, they tell only half the story and like the moose I turned to the land itself for the other half.

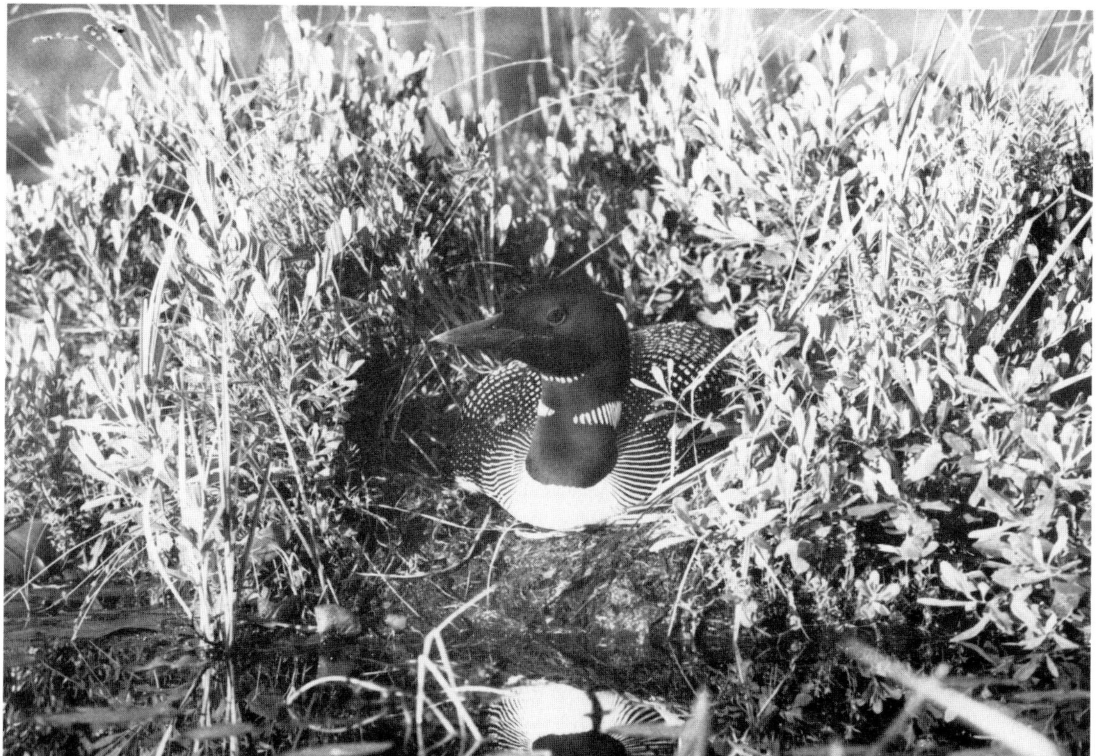

The Common loon nests on mats of vegetation close to the waters edge. Loons are ill suited for being on land because their legs and feet are well back on their body making it impossible for the birds to even waddle like a duck. (300mm 4L auto-focus)

Excursion 4

Friday, June 4–Saturday, June 5

After a long day of teaching, I was looking forward to this, our traditional early June weekend up in Algonquin Park. This was the weekend when my brother-in-law, Jim Markou, and I headed north to photograph the new crop of moose calves. Jim, like me, is both a teacher and a professional wildlife photographer and we have shared many trips to the wilds. We've photographed brown bears in Alaska, wolves in the Rockies and elephants in Kenya. He is the only professional I've worked with on a regular basis and that relationship (other than marrying my sister Nancy) has its roots in Algonquin.

It was Jim, in fact, who first "discovered" the tremendous opportunities for spring moose photography. He and Nancy happened to visit the park one June weekend in 1979 and they saw all kinds of moose. I had, until that time, confined my "moose" trips to the fall, but after hearing of Jim's trip, he and I made a spring excursion a regular part of our year's agenda. We try to visit the park at least a couple of times between April and June.

We discovered that the best shooting tends to be towards the end of May and the beginning of June. There is one major draw back to this season and that is the hordes of blackflies and mosquitoes that dine on you whenever you get out of the car.

At first I used to go to great lengths to avoid being bitten.

I'd wear long-sleeved shirts, long pants and a hat, all of which were sprayed with insect repellent. All of this worked, but if it weren't for a special fox I might still be doing it. A few years before this trip Jim and I were casually cruising along Highway 60 looking for moose when he suddenly stopped the car and pointed. "Fox." Trotting down the road towards us was a red fox carrying three chipmunks in its mouth. Naturally we were excited and began photographing it.

We followed it on foot until it disappeared up a sandy bank, at which point we lost it. As quietly as we could, we climbed up the bank hoping for another glimpse of the fox and maybe even her pups, which we felt had to be in a well hidden den nearby. Not seeing anything, we sat down and were amazed to see her a few seconds later trot out not twenty feet away and then, even more amazingly, she began to nurse her pups!

It was only when she disappeared that Jim and I became aware of the clouds of blackflies surrounding us. Despite the fact that we had neglected to put on fresh spray, we hadn't even given them a thought while we were busy "working" the fox. From that time on, I have seldom resorted to bug spray for I learned that the bugs were only "bad" when I paid undue attention to them. (This is not to imply that the bugs don't still bite me. They do, I just ignore them!)

We have often encountered cooperative foxes on these spring trips since then, although they have never been a sure thing. When Jim picked me up at 6:15 that evening for this latest spring excursion, we were both wondering what the trip held in store for us. As it turned out, it wasn't going to be red fox.

We were in the park by nine and the night sky was clear. As usual we slowed down our drive going through the park so as to avoid running into any moose. That is a real danger, especially since they would be still be visiting the roadside licks. We saw five moose that night as well as a deer and one black bear. Neither of us took any pictures.

By 10:15 we were at one of the motels in Whitney. We were asleep within the hour so we could rise early the next morn-

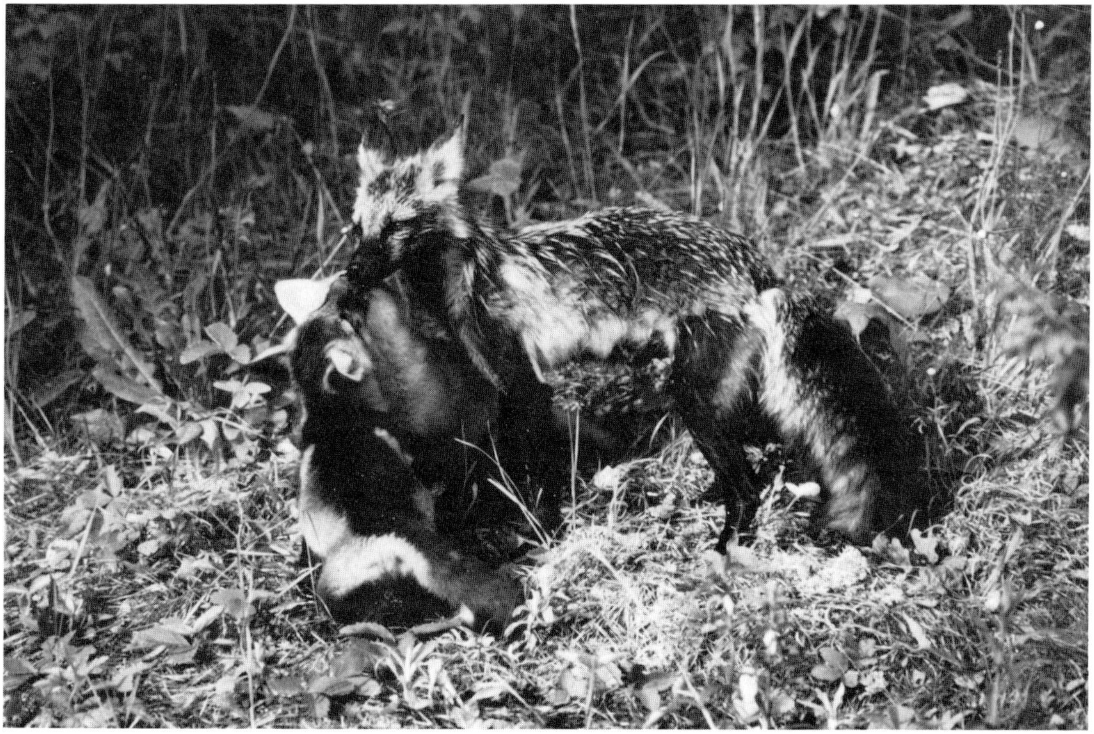

ing for what the weatherman promised would be a sunny day.

By 5:15 the next morning I was up and looking out at a clear early morning sky, full of anticipation. That was the last clear sky we saw. By six o'clock the clouds arrived and by two in the afternoon the rain had begun.

Moose, however, were everywhere. We saw thirty in less than twenty-four hours but not one was a young red-coated calf. Eleven were bulls, some with impressive racks, four were cows and the rest were yearlings. All the yearlings were on their own. It soon became apparent that we were one week too early, although it was the same weekend that had been so successful one year ago. The cows were still in the bush with their newborn calves. In fact, Jim would return the next weekend with his family and see several babies.

By nine that morning it became apparent we were not going to get the calves we had come for so we decided to check out one of the other roads within the park.

It is a remarkable event when a wild animal appears to trust people enough to bring out its young to be fed. I am at a loss to explain why red fox vixens will do this but I have had the experience three or four times in the park. Other photographers have noted this too but so far I have not read any theories to explain this behaviour. (500mm 4.5L)

The Basin Depot road is less than a two-hour drive east of Whitney and is quite a good road considering that it is not paved. In one of the guides to Algonquin Park we had read that there are several places for wildlife viewing and we were anxious to check out the potential for photography here.

Admittedly, it was late morning before we arrived on the road and the prime animal viewing hours were past, but we were singularly disappointed with this road's potential. From what we saw there I cannot recommend this drive to you for the purpose of wildlife viewing. I would be surprised to find that our experience was unusual, even during the more traditional wildlife viewing hours. There are several reasons to suggest you not bother with this drive.

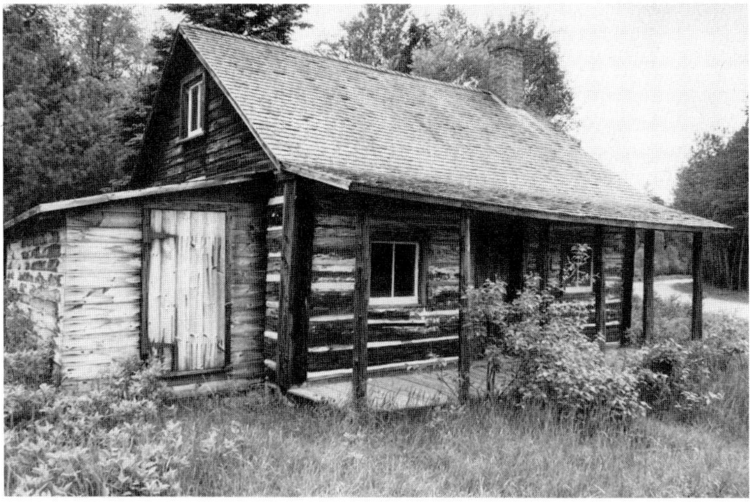

This cabin, at km 14.2 on the Basin Depot road is the oldest building in the park. It may date back to 1843 when the area was an important stop over for loggers. (200mm 2.8L zoom auto-focus)

First, the road is not salted so there is nothing to bring moose to it other than natural food sources. But these natural sources are everywhere in the park and presumably offer the moose and deer more seclusion and privacy. Why would they want to stay along the roadside?

Second, most of the road is lined with forest. There are few if any open spaces that either Jim or I identified as having much potential. We felt any wildlife we might see, early or late in the day, would vanish into the thick forest very quickly.

Finally, we saw no wildlife here at all but back on Highway 60 we saw thirty moose, one bear, one porcupine, two beavers, a few deer and a couple of loons. Comparing that abundance seen at all hours of the day to our dismal record on this road, I would not advise anyone wanting to photograph wildlife to make this journey.

However, the road is worth the drive for other reasons. Historically, the road offers the oldest standing building in the park at kilometre 14.2. This building was built in 1892 by the McLachlin Lumber Company during a time when both farming and logging occurred here. It is quite rustic looking and worthy of at least a few pictures.

Of more interest to us was the typical eastern pine forest that we encountered on the drive in. You simply do not see this forest type along the Highway 60 corridor and that alone makes the trip worthwhile.

If I ever return to this road, it will be to explore further the hydro line at the end of it. Here one finds a wide swathe cut through the forest; it runs as far as you can see. I'm certain bears could be found here during the berry season in July and early August.

None the less we, were not sorry to leave and by one o'clock we were back along the main corridor photographing moose again. We also made our first visit to the new Algonquin Visitor Centre at kilometre 43. It is wonderful.

The wildlife mounts are among the best I've ever seen and some of the background paintings blend almost seamlessly with the re-created habitats. The historical and cultural displays are also well done.

The new restaurant and bookstore add to the attractiveness of the building but it is its setting that makes it truly special. Built on a ridge overlooking Sunday Creek it offers a marvellous view of this habitat, which I suspect includes the occasional moose.

When we left the museum, it was just starting to rain and it did not soon let up. I remember photographing one bull moose feeding in a roadside pond while the rain splattered around him as I used my hat to keep the camera dry. It was about then that Jim and I decided to pack it in and head home.

It was the first time on a trip undertaken for this book the weather failed to cooperate. Even so, it was worth the drive.

CHAPTER 4

The Forests

I'm not certain but, I would guess that about half of Algonquin's area consists of lakes and waterways and the other half is (more or less) dry land. Photographing in the open spaces of the first half is relatively easy. Photographing the forest is far more challenging. To undertake a true study of this region takes time and skill. Like most photographers, I am not averse to using short cuts, especially when it comes to capturing images of the carnivores that live here.

Although this book stays true to my stated goal of having all the illustrations in it come from the park's ecosystem, it would be misleading to claim that when I illustrate slide talks or other books all my images of predators come from the wild. Like virtually all other professional photographers, I make use of animals in controlled conditions. That is, some pictures are from zoos and others come from game farms.

I used to believe that all those wonderful images of wolves and weasels, cougars and bears that grace wildlife and nature magazines were taken in the wild. As my experience as a wildlife photographer has grown my innocent notions have shrunk. I do believe (and increasingly so do other professionals) that it is only proper we acknowledge that photographers do use captive animals as a source of their images.

While my preference would be to photograph truly wild

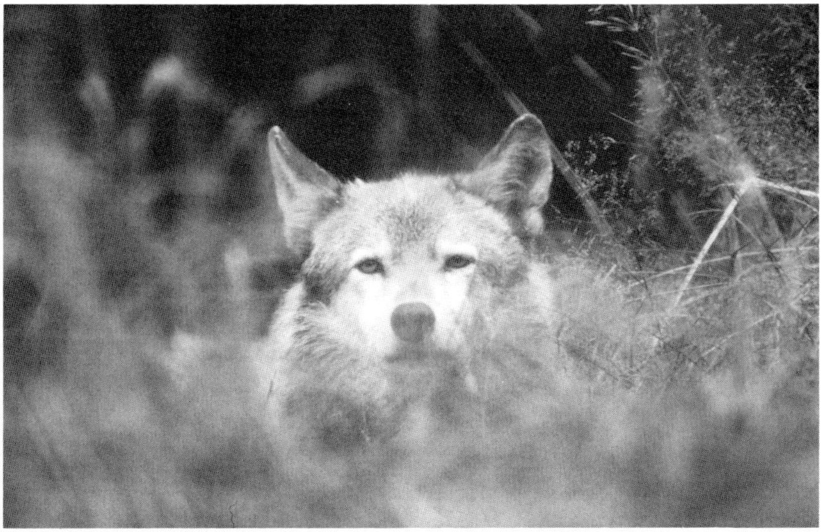

Boy, wouldn't I love to tell you this was a wild wolf. It isn't. It was taken under controlled conditions at a zoo. I used a long telephoto lens to get rid of the fence between us. (500mm 4.5L)

and free-roaming animals, I must admit that working with animals in these controlled situations is enjoyable. There is an art and a skill to it that make it more challenging than it at first appears to be. Certainly if your slide show on the park's ecosystem requires a photograph of a wolf, it is far easier to get the shot in a zoo than in Algonquin Park. One of the challenges of taking it in the zoo is to make it look like it was taken in the wild.

Although this book is about photographing in Algonquin, it would be unfair of me to mention the above without sharing at least one sure-fire technique to making photos of wolves shot in a zoo look at least a little wild. The telephoto lens when used at its widest aperture can almost magically make zoo bars disappear. The longer the lens the better, for this narrows the depth of field, blurring objects in the foreground and the background. If you use an automatic exposure camera, be certain to set the shutter speed as high as possible to insure a wide-open lens.

Although I elected not to use captive shots in this book or shots taken in other parks, I certainly would include such photographs in other books. I should also point out that my first intention when beginning to work on the illustrations was to enlist the help of Friends of Algonquin Park and the staff of the park. I chose not to go this route, although I'm certain I would have received their assistance in advising where and when to look for this or that. Such a request would have been fair under other circumstances, but I felt it did not fall within the spirit of this book. Please note that all sources of information called upon to enhance the success of my photography or the information contained within the chapters are available to amateur and professional alike.

THE FOREST-FOR-THE-TREES SYNDROME

The difficulty when photographing a forest ecosystem is that there are times you cannot see anything (the forest, for instance) for the trees. It is fairly easy to photograph lions hunting on the plains of Africa simply because there are few trees to interfere with your view. It is also relatively easy to work with grizzlies on the tundra for the same reason. A forested environment such as Algonquin's, however, requires luck, patience and knowledge.

Fortunately for photographers, Algonquin has several roads running through it that both create and lead to open spaces in which wildlife may be encountered.

An understanding of the park's ecology begins, on land at least, with the soil. How did it get there? Where did it come from?

With the final melting away of the glaciers, some ten thousand years ago the area that is now Algonquin Park was barren and unproductive. Hardly recognizable as the place we have come to explore.

This empty stage did not stay empty long. Soon plants began to arrive and with their arrival the slow build-up of soil began. These first plants were lichens. They are pioneering plants, which means that they are usually the first to colonize an area. As a family they are remarkably hardy, able to stand the sub-zero temperatures of the Arctic or the intense heat of hot springs.

Actually, lichens are made up of two different types of living things: fungi and algae. They form a living partnership

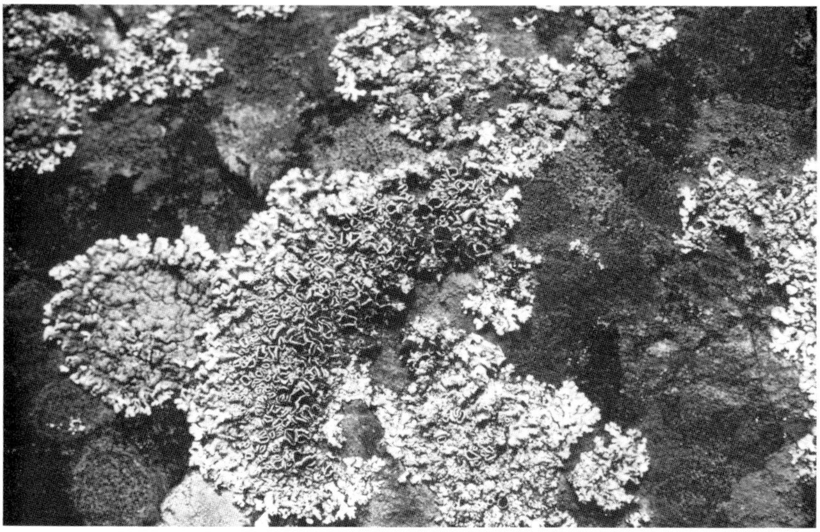

Lichen are among the oldest living things in the park. Some may well date back five thousand years before the present. They were the first living things to colonize the land after the glaciers departed. (200mm 2.8L)

which is mutually beneficial to both. This symbiotic relationship allows them to survive in the bleakest of environments. The fungal threads provide shelter, shade and a water absorbent anchor for the green algae. The algae is able to make direct use of the sun's energy (something no fungus can do) and through the process of photosynthesis produce food for both plants from rain and carbon dioxide.

Lichens also produce an acid that slowly breaks down the

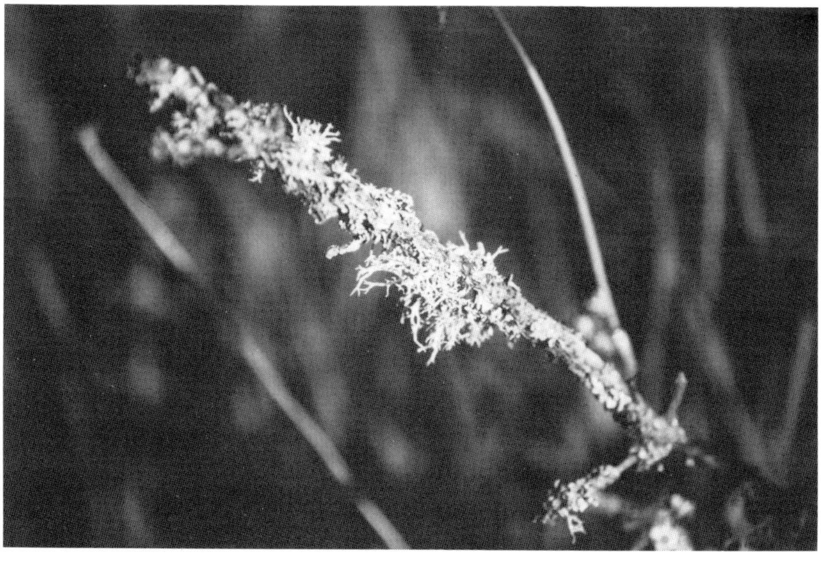

There are many kinds of lichen in the park. Some are found on the ground while others grow on trees. (300mm 2.8L auto-focus)

rock. As lichens die, their remains mix with the broken-down rock to form soil.

Photographing lichens requires close-up equipment although some patches are large enough that a standard lens may be used. Several groups of lichen can be found in the park and within each there are several species. One type spreads slowly across the rocks and may be encountered wherever you find undisturbed barren rocks. Rock Lake Road cuts through some good areas in which to find examples of this group. Another type grows just at the water line along the shore. A third is not flat but grows upward. One species, known as British Soldiers, sports red "helmets" and can be found growing on many roadside formations. My shots of this type come from the rocks near the Spruce Bog Hiking Trail at kilometre 42.7. Still another group grows from trees themselves. Some look like miniature reindeer antlers while others resemble an old man's beard.

Although it is easy to overlook these diminutive plants, they are the cornerstones of life here in the forest. They are doubly impressive when you know that some of these colonies have been living here for nearly five thousand years!

It could easily be a lifetime's work just to record and study this group alone. I contented myself with recording only a few types and then turned my attention to the forest floor.

DEATH AND THE "FUN GUY"

In any ecosystem, what lives there usually dies there. Why then isn't the forest floor littered with the remains of trees and animals that have fallen here over the past several thousand years? The critical role of converting this wasted energy back into more usable forms falls to the decomposers. Anyone who has ever practised backyard composting knows that living matter will break down into soil if the proper conditions exist.

Bacteria and other microorganisms are the final step in this progress, but it is very difficult to photograph them unless you have highly specialized equipment. Decaying leaves and rotting logs are the visible evidence of the existence of the decomposers so I set about to photograph them instead.

Once again I elected to use the wide-angle lens using many of the techniques discussed earlier regarding photographing the pitcher plant. Try and avoid shooting straight down on your subject as it will give it a flat appearance.

This is also a good time to remember the "rule of thirds." Imagine that your viewfinder is divided horizontally and vertically into three equal sections. Now frame a shot keeping the main subject in the middle third both horizontally and vertically. This will centre your subject. As a general rule, this is the most common and therefore overused place to put your main subject.

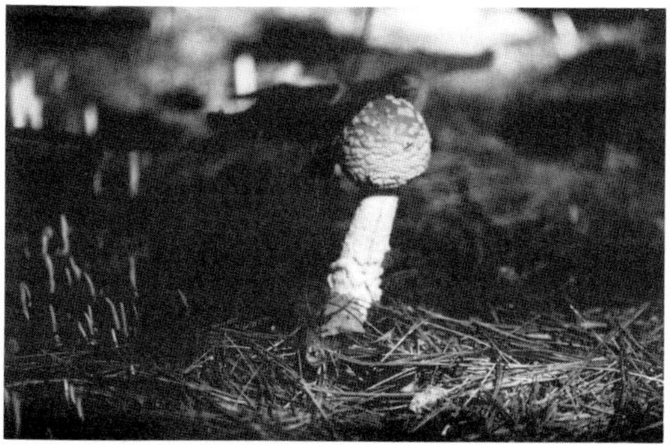

A single mushroom can produce over one billion spores, each capable of replicating its parent. (200mm 2.8L zoom auto-focus)

Try composing the shot changing the location of your main subject. Lower the camera so the subject appears in the top third. Now place it in the bottom third. One of these last two placements will likely be more pleasing than the one with the subject in the middle. Your own sense of creativity will determine which you select.

This rule is borrowed from the art world: great painters have known about it for sometime. With scenic shots, such as shots of the forest along the edge of a lake or bog where there is no specific centre of interest, keep the shoreline at the top or bottom third.

When your subject is isolated, such as a mushroom, flower or moose, apply the rule as well if the subject is fairly small in your viewfinder. With animals, especially large ones that fill your viewfinder, remember it is the eye that people will be drawn to so position it with this guideline in mind.

Be careful to leave your subject "breathing room." By that I mean you should leave space in the image for the subject to "move." A moose's nose pushed up to the very edge of the frame crowds the picture and will look awkward unless the animal's image virtually fills the viewfinder.

For most wildlife shooting, I find the centre-point auto-focus will generally produce pictures where the rule of thirds is followed automatically. For example, when you focus on the eye, the tip of the nose will usually fall in the right area. Of course, there is no guarantee that it will work for every shot so it is important that you, the camera operator learn how to focus and recompose your picture if need be.

Like all rules, this one should be ignored from time to time. Sometimes, as with fallen leaves, you will want to capture the pattern without having a centre of interest. At other times you will wish the subject to be dead centre because it works for the lay out you have in mind. Other images may look better if there is symmetry – that is, the right and left halves of the pictures are balanced. More and more, though, creative photographers are moving to asymmetrical images where the subject is off to one side.

For the shot of the rotting log I decided to have it run from the bottom third on an angle across to the top third. I delib-

Fungi decomposes about eighty percent of all matter that falls to the forest floor. Moss covered logs like this one are well on their way to being converted to forest soil again. (28mm 2.8L with flash)

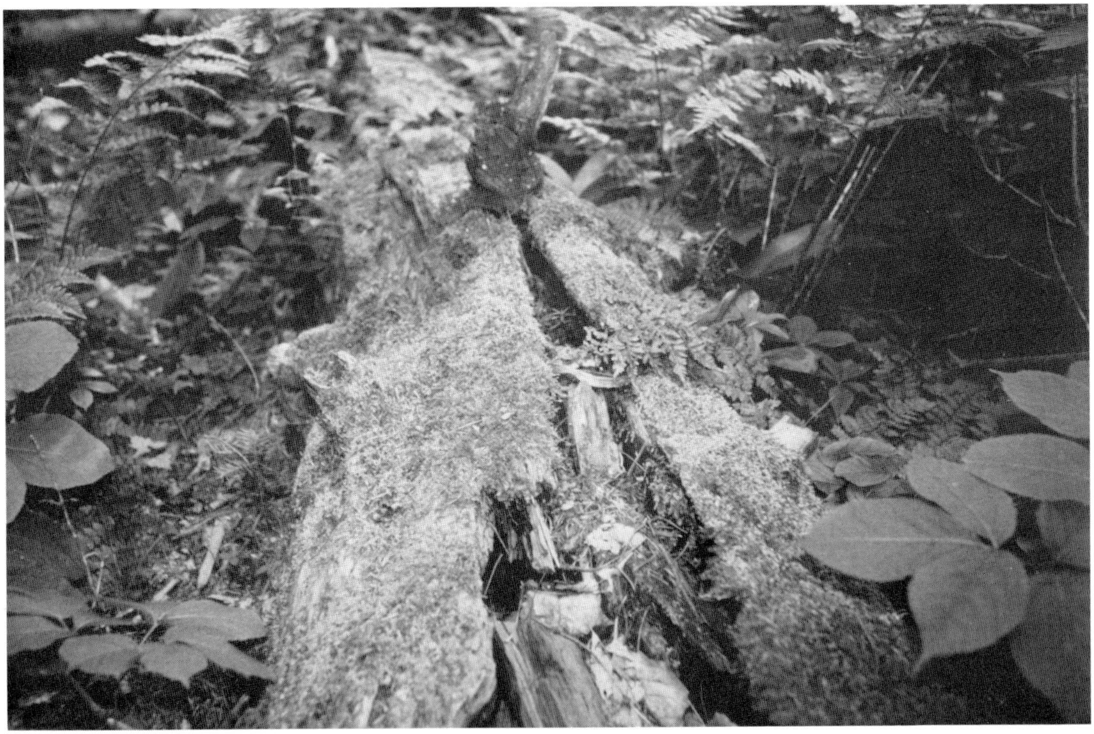

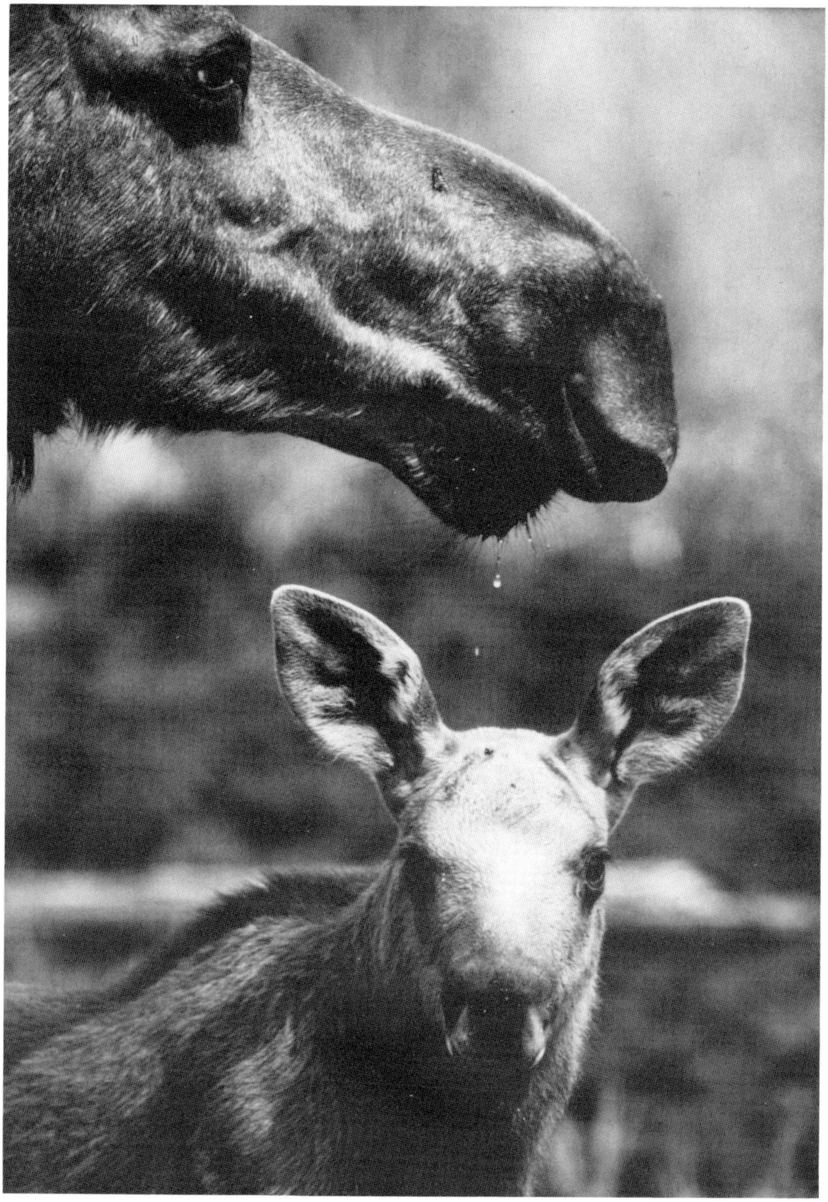

A cow moose is very protective of her young and should always be approached with caution. Notice the difference in the nose structure of the two. The calf moose will not have the prehensile nose of an adult until it is almost a year old. (300mm 4L auto-focus)

erately left space at the end of log where light could be seen so that the viewer's eye would flow along the log and out.

Remember that when you are composing your picture, to consider how it will be "seen" by the human eye. Avoid lines that lead out of the picture. For example, a picture taken of a moose with a telephone pole in the background should be recomposed to eliminate the pole. Otherwise the viewer's eye will be drawn away from your subject to the pole and out of the picture. It takes time and practice to learn how to avoid these distracting objects. It takes even more to learn how to compose a picture where the viewer is led to what you want him or her to see.

Since I was in the forest and the natural lighting was poor, I hedged my bet by taking a few shots of the log with the camera's built-in flash. Wasting film is a lot cheaper than having to travel all the way back to a spot a week or two later to re-shoot.

I also spent some time photographing some of the fungi that I found growing in the forest. Fungi are not true plants and have been given their own separate grouping. Plants are able to make direct use of the sun's energy thanks to the process known as photosynthesis. The members of the fungi family are unable to do this and must gain their nourishment from other sources.

What we think of as a mushroom or a bracket fungus is the fruiting body of the fungus – it's reproductive portion, if you like. The actual living organism consists of tiny hair-like filaments that grow through tree trunks or soil, removing nutrients and building up the portion of the organism we see. They are an important part of the forest ecosystem aiding in the breakdown of plant and animal matter and returning it to the soil.

Without fungi, the forest would be a vastly different place. Consider that over 80% of all vegetative matter on the forest floor is consumed not by bacteria or herbivores but by fungi. This is especially important in Algonquin's coniferous forests, where the acidity of the soil inhibits bacteria growth. Its possible that the largest living thing in the park could be a fungus. One species, found in Washington State, has a network of filaments covering nearly six square kilometres while a similar "mushroom" in Michigan has been estimated to weigh 100 tonnes, making these the largest living things on Earth. (Since I wrote this a researcher in the western United States reported that a grove of aspens is the largest and longest living organism in the world. To be classed as a living organism, all parts must be genetically the same and connected. The aspens and fungus both grow from underground root systems. The aspen grove is over one million years old!)

Fungi, decomposers and lichens may be fascinating, but for the vast majority of the park's visitors they are easily overlooked. Spend some time photographing them and let the rest of the world go bustling by looking for moose and scenery.

Algonquin's forests have changed in the last century due to the hand of man. We will explore the impact of humans on the ecosystem in the next chapter, where I will also discuss logging and reforestation. Let's treat the existing forest as we find it and worry about unnatural disturbances later.

IS THE FOREST STABLE?

Algonquin appears never to have had a truly stable forest for it lies in an area that because of variables in climate and altitude has been neither true northern boreal forest nor southern deciduous forest. It is a mixture of both, with one type dominating in certain locations or at a particular period.

In very general terms, the forest may be divided into two regions. The western two-thirds of the park is generally higher and contains soils based on glacial tills. Here hardwoods such as maple and beech dominate. The eastern third is, as we have seen, lower and covered with vast sandy outwash plains deposited by the ancient glacial rivers. Here pines (softwoods) are better suited to grow. Remember, though, that these are very general rules and other local factors such as ridges, bogs, fire and logging will create conditions that will vary this landscape.

Driving on Highway 60 you do get some impression of the applicability of this guideline but for the wrong reason. There is certainly a change in forest type from the big-maple dominated forests found west of the Pog Lake Campground to the birch-and pine-dominated forest east of there, but it is more a factor of human disturbance and fire than of past geological history.

I certainly am guilty of thinking that the east side of the park referred to any place east of Two Rivers on the park's highway. How wrong I was.

A look at the map will quickly show you that Highway 60 leaves the park at Whitney before it has travelled a distance equal to even a third of the true east-west width of the park. To truly explore the pine portion of the southeast, it is necessary to enter north of Petawawa. That's a good ninety-minute drive east of Whitney!

According to one of the park's guidebooks there are thirty-four kinds of trees found in the park not counting what it calls "shrubs," such as willows and ashes. It goes on to say that of these only twenty-six are commonly encountered. Some I have already discussed as they are found typically in bogs, but a lack of space prevents any detailed discussion of others. A list of guidebooks is provided in the bibliography so you can research various species in more detail.

As far as the ecology of the park goes I'll consider the trees not so much as individual species but rather as forest types. Should your interest lie in taking pictures for the purpose of identifying these various species, try to get pictures showing close-ups of the bark, leaf and needle patterns: fruit, nuts

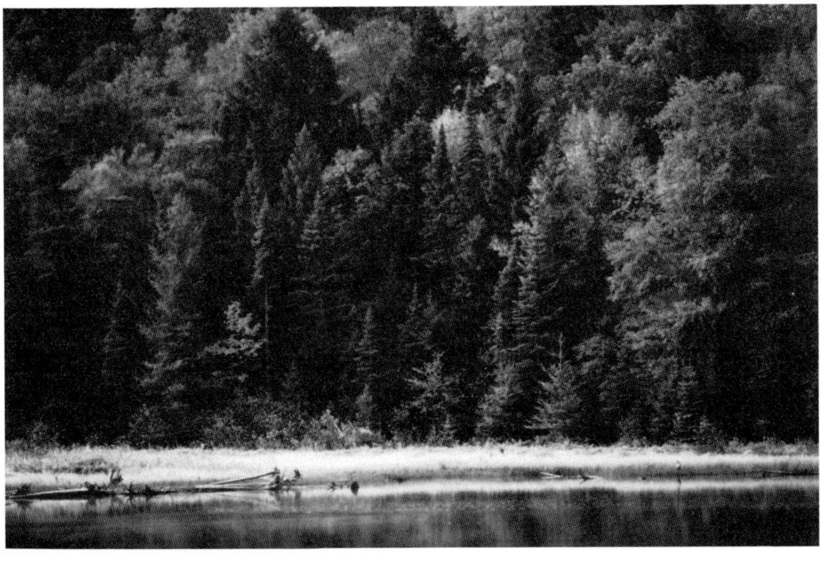

Algonquin's forests are a mixture of conifers and deciduous trees. Although the deciduous maples and oaks appear to hold sway along highway 60, most of the eastern half of the park consists of coniferous forests. (200mm 2.8L auto-focus)

and flowers; and summer, fall and winter shots of typical specimen trees. This is a project all in itself that could occupy you for years to come.

Instead of looking at the forest as individual trees and species, consider it as a living world in which all the trees are part of the whole. This way of studying the forest brings another way of understanding it as you explore it with your camera. Is this a climax forest or an evolving one? How do the trees interact with each other as well as other types of living things? Given what we know of the geology that creates a forest's basic environment, what other factors affect it?

Each question leads to a story, each story to a greater understanding of the whole.

ARE WE CLIMAXING?

There are few true climax forests visible in the park. A climax forest is one in which only a catastrophic change will alter it. Without such a disaster, it will remain unchanged for hundreds of years. In the past, white pines dominated the forest and such forests may be considered as examples of climax forests.

White pine are long-lived (up to 450 years) and huge, attaining a maximum height of seventy metres with a maximum width of 1.5 metres. They average an impressive thirty to thirty-five metres and sixty to one hundred centimetres across!

Once, these white pine forests covered large portions of the eastern side of the park, and so dense was the shade beneath them that only other white pines could survive and grow. In the western uplands, groves of white pines were common while individual trees towered throughout the forest. Today, thanks to logging and fire, there are few if any of these giants visible from Highway 60, although two stands do exist in the park, neither accessible by road.

An impressive stand of one hundred year-old white pine may be see behind the Achray campground on Grand Lake. As tall as these trees appear they have attained only a little over two-thirds of their full height.

White pines are a member of the conifer family. Other members include the jack pine, red pine, tamarack, black spruce, hemlock and white cedar. With the exception of the tamarack, they keep their needles year round. All of them produce seeds in cones, a method of reproduction that dates back over 300 million years before the advent of flowers and dinosaurs.

The needle-like leaves of the conifers serve them well in this environment. Being green, they are of course capable of photosynthesis, but it is their shape that provides the tree its true benefits. Most needles are long and narrow and are covered by a waxy coating. This combination prevents moisture from being lost allowing the trees to make do with less moisture than their broadleaf deciduous cousins who lose literally thousands of tonnes of moisture to the air each growing season.

It is, of course, for that reason that they grow so well in the porous, well-drained soils in the eastern part of the park. Pine trees do well wherever sandy soils are found, which is why they are a common sight along beaches as wide spread as those in Florida and Kenya, as well as parts of Georgia and other southern states. The notion that pine trees are at home only in the north just doesn't apply. The soil type rather than latitude is more important in determining this family's range.

However, the largest stands of conifers are found in the north. They are so well-adapted to the northern environment that during the crucial winter months they lose virtually no moisture to the cold winter winds. Their green tops provide shelter in winter for a variety of wildlife, especially owls, while other species such as red squirrels and crossbills have adapted their life styles using pine cones for food.

Where pine trees dominate, they affect their entire environment. Their needles alter the soil, making it suitable for pines alone. Indeed, these acidic needles take much longer to decompose than do the more basic leaves of maple. Therefore, it takes longer for soil to form in this mini-environment.

In a mature forest, their great height takes most branches far out of reach of browsers such as moose and deer. Black bear are much less common in the coniferous forest than they are in maple-beech forests where they find leaves, fruits and nuts more to their liking than pine cones.

Where pines are part of the mix, as they are in the western two-thirds, rather than the dominant species, they enrich the wildlife community by providing nesting cavities as well as year round shelter.

In the recent past, much of the park has been logged or burned. When a visitor drives or canoes through today's park what they are viewing is a disturbed forest, one that has grown up in the last fifty to one hundred years. The remains of the old forest are also there, if you look carefully. This is especially true of the area between and around Rock Lake Road and Opeongo Road. Here, if you take the time to look, you will soon see the stumps of giant trees long gone, many of them charred from past fires that swept the area after it was logged.

Here you will see large stands of white birch trees, which are quick to take advantage of disturbances in the forest. They sprout, grow quickly and then die off within a few decades as more shade-tolerant, slower-growing trees overtake them.

Eventually maple trees, which as saplings gain protection from the birch trees, will grow taller than their protectors and will kill them off by out-competing them for resources such as sunlight and water. Then the maples become the dominant species, as they are a long much of the western half of the highway. The maple is approaching a climax condition in this area. Six out of every ten trees here are sugar maples and their saplings tend to dominate the forest floor.

Each autumn over two tons of leaves fall in an acre of maple forest. They quickly decompose and help build up the soil but it is not the leaves on the ground you'll likely pay attention to. It is the colour of those leaves.

SHOWING THE TRUE COLOURS!

Every September to early October, thousands head north to view the fall colours along Highway 60. Reds, oranges, yellows and scores of shades decorate the road – and most of this show is dominated by the maples themselves.

To photograph all of this takes several visits spaced out over the seasons. Summer with its greens, early fall with its colours, late fall and winter with their stark barren look and spring with its halo of budding promises present different images. Along with these seasonal changes come other changes as different flowers bloom on the trees and the ground. Trilliums and spring beauties bloom in spring, columbines and hawkweed in summer and all enhance your photography possibilities.

A couple of tricks can help to bring out the colour of flowers and leaves. First you will need to be able to manually set your exposure by taking a light meter reading either off your hand or the plant.

The goal is to select a well-lit flower or leaf, then position it so that the background appears black in the exposed image. A simple way of doing this is to take along a large piece of black bristol board and line it up with the flower so that you get the required image. I've never resorted to that trick because it is usually possible to find some deep shade that serves as an appropriate background. Remember not to change your exposure once you've lined up the subject with the dark backdrop or the trick won't work and you'll get bland images.

Try shooting through flowers or leaves so that their out-of-focus colours frame your main subject. Short telephoto lenses work best for this style of shooting.

While the colours of leaves and flowers make for beautiful pictures, I wanted to include shots of the forest in winter and early spring as well. The winter forest is a pretty barren place for wildlife. Deep snow and dormant trees make getting even minimal amounts of nourishment difficult for the park's herbivores. To photograph this season I add another piece of equipment to my arsenal when I head out in winter – snowshoes. I've tried cross-country skis in order to get into the forest when the snow is deep but I find them awkward to manoeuvre in brush never mind trying to carry a tripod with lens mounted.

Early spring is another story. If winter is the season of death, then spring promises rebirth. It is the best season for photographing wildlife because the need for nourishment after a hard winter is so overpowering that many animals seek the roadway's margins to feed on new grass and buds.

A MONTHLY MOOSE GUIDE

Algonquin has one of the highest densities of moose in North America. A trip to the park from early April to late June comes with a virtual guarantee that you will see moose.

Here's what to look for and when you can expect to see it:

April

Expect to see moose along the road wherever meltwater has collected, and the muddier the better, for the mud holds on to the rock salt washed off the road which is what the animals seek. Look in depressions partially hidden from the road where moose can feed unseen by most motorists.

Don't expect to see moose with healthy looking coats. They are shedding their winter coats and many will have scratched off much of the long hairs in an effort to rid them-

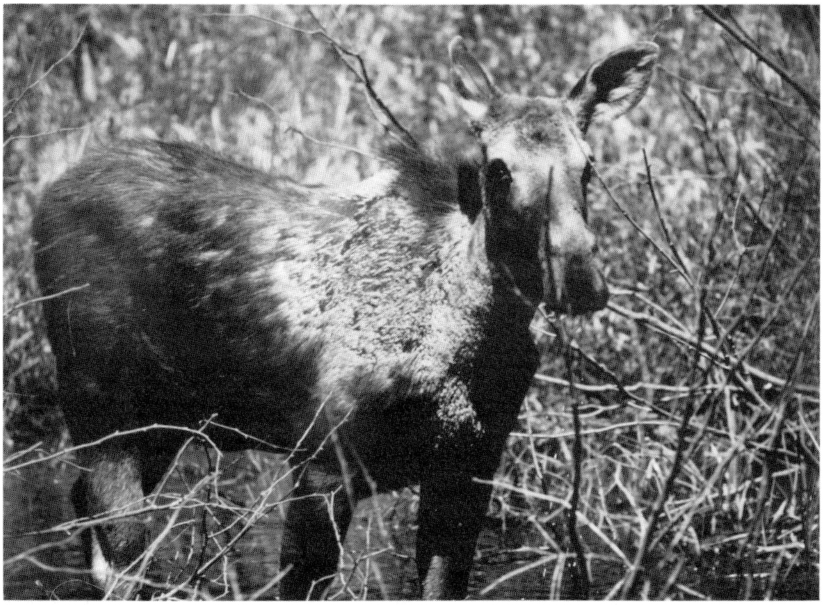

In late March and early April park visitors are likely to see "ghost" moose. These grey moose have scratched off their winter coats in an attempt to dislodge the many ticks that have grown large over the winter. If it turns cold, the loss of hair can contribute to the moose's death. (300mm 4.0L)

selves of ticks. Research has shown that a healthy moose will have up to five thousand quarter-sized ticks on its body. A badly infested one can host fifty thousand or more.

Pictures of these bald-looking "ghost" moose can illustrate once again the complexity of the ecology in the park. They have been the focus of much research recently. The understanding biologists now have about the relationship between the ticks and the moose was discovered here.

These ticks (*Dermacentor albipictus*) are parasites that rely on the moose for their survival. In the fall when the moose walks through the brush, the tiny ticks living there grab onto the moose's legs and then crawl up to its body. They bury their jaws in the animal's flesh and begin to gorge on its blood. The tick at this stage is about the size of a pin.

In spring the adult ticks drop off and lay their eggs under the mat of ground litter on the forest floor. After they hatch, the larvae go into a stage of dormancy through the summer. In fall they climb up onto vegetation and wait for a passing moose.

The ticks are not a major problem for moose during the worst of winter: but the warming days of March bring a real danger. The moose begins shedding and the ticks are at their maximum size now, they itch. In an effort to dislodge them, the moose rubs against trees or scratch itself with its hooves. The combination of loose winter hair and all the tick-induced scratching can be deadly!

Great amounts of winter coat are removed from the individual's body, making it appear an almost ghostly grey. In itself, this is not a threat for March can be fairly mild. A sudden temperature change, however, or a late winter-early spring storm may prove fatal as the moose, deprived of its insulating coat, freezes to death.

A healthy adult moose can sustain over five thousand of these parasites but calves and adults with huge numbers of ticks may be seriously weakened by the loss of blood. In their weakened state they are more vulnerable to disease and predators.

May

By May, the new growth of vegetation is well underway and I look for moose browsing along the forest edge as well as in the many mud holes. Bulls will be sprouting antlers by now , although in early May they are not very large. Cows and yearling calves are a common sight but a change is in the wind for the calves.

By late May, most cow moose are getting near the end of their pregnancy. It is time to chase off last year's young. This may be a gradual thing where the calf, like a wandering teenager, gradually distances itself from its mother, or it can be a nasty surprise as its mother kicks it and chases it off.

You may not see the event but you will encounter single or pairs of calves at this time. Sometimes an adult cow will be seen near them but not often.

June

Plan a trip for the first or second week in June to see the newborn calves. The calves are born in early June, usually on an isolated ridge or island safe from predators. When they are able to follow their mother, she leaves them as she seeks fresh food for herself. Normally, they are left hiding in the forest while she feeds on the pond lilies or the sodium-rich mud. However, along Highway 60 I have found the cows to be very tolerant of people and on several occasions found them leading their calves along the edge of the highway. The babies are at their cutest now, with short muzzles and reddish brown hair.

I have found the best places to look for them on the highway to be between the Rock Lake Road and Opeongo Road. I've also had good luck on the Beaver Pond Trail and the Mizzy Lake Trail.

Twins were the norm a few years ago when the moose population was expanding but now I am told single calves are more common. The moose population in the park may have reached or even exceeded the carrying capacity of the land.

As for the bulls, you can expect to see some major growth in antlers now and through the summer.

July and August

Summer brings crowds of people, and as a result the moose tend to move away from the highway. I've found them but not without a lot of looking.

It is in summer when the commonly held advice about looking for animals early and late in the day is most accurate. Summer is a time of abundance and heat, the combination of which means that the moose prefer to feed when it's cool and rest when it's hot. I also believe that the early-morning and late-evening sightings of moose at this time are due in no small measure to reduced car traffic, which encourages the animals to reclaim the roadway.

When I visit the park's highway for the purpose of photographing wildlife, I spend most of my day driving back and forth along the road. It can be tedious work doing this for eight or nine hours a day, but the rewards can make it worthwhile. I usually find a friend who can stand this type of photography (my wife can't) and off we go. Four eyes searching the forest are much better than two, especially when one of us is driving! We do between forty and sixty kilometre an hour and make frequent stops.

A frequent companion on these trips is Jim Markou. He is a nature photographer too. Although many photographers prefer to work alone I think there are a number of advantages to having someone else along. Jim and I learn from each other. We discuss how best to approach an animal. We pull and push each other to stay or to move on. Usually one of us is finished shooting a subject while the other wishes to go for one more shot. Sometimes staying is the right thing to do, sometimes moving on is.

Left to my own devices I do fine, but with a partner I believe I do better. I think I have a tendency to get into a rut no matter how much I try to vary the routine. Travelling with somebody changes my approach. I see another way of doing something, a new angle, a new slant.

My wife, Anne, who is not a photographer or naturalist, comes along on trips more than anyone. She enjoys the

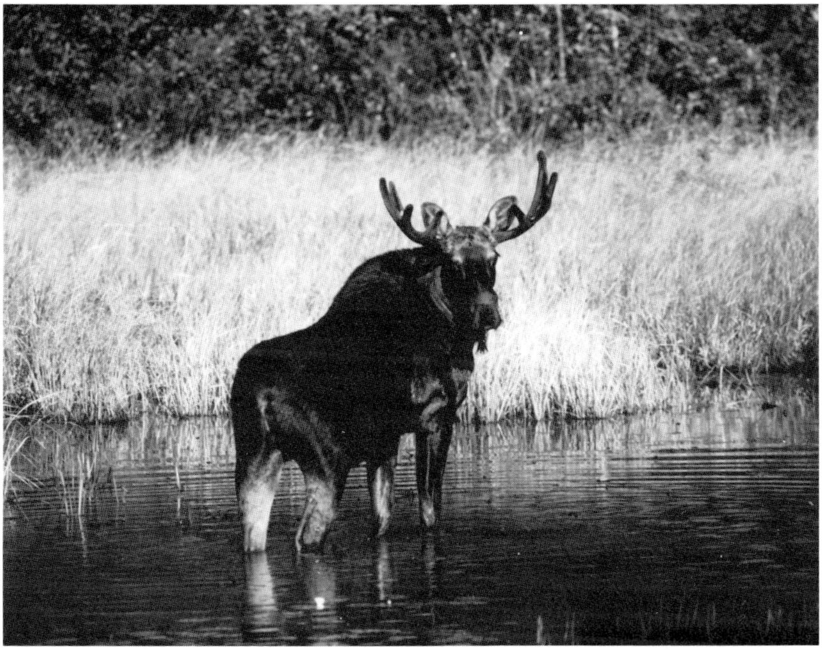

Moose can often be found near meadows and grassy waterways in fall. This bull has yet to shed its velvet. (500mm 4.5L)

travel and the experience. She usually simply waits and reads while I stalk this animal or that. When I return, she will often have seen something I missed and point it out to me. Perhaps it is a small bird or a flower. No matter, she has added to my experience and success. My daughters are becoming increasingly important in this capacity too.

You will also find that having a friend along can encourage you to take a risk: to move that little bit closer for that better shot. Knowing how much further you can or should push your luck is a matter of personal choice. It is nice to have the support of someone but it is equally important to have a person saying to you to let it go, back off.

I'm fortunate that the people I work with are blessed with common sense as well as creativity. If you can find a person who complements your skills, you will find it will pay dividends in your photography. Remember that this individual does not have to share your interests.

I find such a sharing is especially valuable in the summer when moose are rare. I need to be pointed in other directions while driving that road.

September and October

If there is a perfect time to be in Algonquin Park, it is during these two months. The air is cool and crisp, the fall colours are at their peak and the bugs are gone.

Moose are harder to find than in the spring but somewhat easier than they were in the height of the summer tourist season. My days start early now, sometimes before dawn as I listen for the sound of a cow moose calling for a mate. It is the season of the rut, when moose seek each other out in order to breed. I've camped out here and been kept awake all night by the "maaaaing" of a love-sick cow. Why are they so noisy?

Moose are a product of the northern forest in which they live. They have had to adapt to this environment and have done so to near perfection. Long legs carry them through the muskeg. Their huge bulk stores enough energy to see them through the winter. They are loners for the most part so that they can seek out the limited supply of food and not have to compete for it.

When it comes to sex and reproduction, they have solved that problem in a grand matter. When you are single and living in a forest, it is difficult to see let alone find another moose to mate with. Compounding this problem is the fact that a cow moose is receptive for only a day or so a month. The odds of a bull finding her at the right time would seem long indeed.

The solution moose have evolved is to become very noisy. Cows start bawling a few days before they reach their peak of fertility. Their huge lungs and nasal passages produce a sound that will travel through the forest for a kilometre or two. They swing their heads as well to help broadcast their call as they wander about.

They also make a performance of urinating, preferring to do it in the water so that it is noisy as well as scenting the air. They also do it more frequently, leaving on land a telltale trail of their readiness that any bull can sniff out.

As a photographer, I make use of these same tricks to call a bull out. Any good hunting store will stock a record that will teach you how to imitate the cow's call. As well they usually stock a variety of commercially made artificial calls to enhance your natural abilities.

Calls work best in early morning and late evening when the moose are most active. These are times when the light for photography is at its poorest, so you may want to have a fast film in your camera. Scooping water up and letting it dribble back into the lake imitates the sound of the cow urinating, which increases the effectiveness of the artificial call.

I've had some luck with calling moose out but I've had much better luck with my vocal imitations once I've found the moose. I find that a cow call will usually stop a bull long enough for me to get off a couple or more shots. I've never been sexy enough as a moose caller to get him to seek me out as a mate (thank goodness!).

If a cow is present, I've found mimicking a calf's call very effective. She calms down and will sometimes approach quite closely to check me out. I had one come to within a metre once, which, let me assure you, was more than enough!

Should you ever feel truly threatened by a large mammal, my advice is to make yourself look big and aggressive. Over the years I have had elk, bison, moose and black bear all approach me in a manner which I did not like. Backing away is one option, and it is the one I prefer but sometimes you get yourself, foolishly, into a situation where you have no option.

When that happens, I grab my tripod or cameras, stand up and lift my arms high and wide and yell. It works well... once. I've never seen it work twice on the same animal so after one use of this trick, I back off. No picture is worth getting seriously hurt over nor is it worth endangering the life of an animal.

If you can keep the cow moose calm, the bull will stay. They are addle-brained with their desire to mate and will not leave the cow.

If a bull decides you are a threat to his mate, he will usually signal you by twisting his head and rocking his antlers back and forth before charging. If you see this back away, immediately. I had a small bull do this to me once when I got too close to his cow. It was a very scary experience!

By early September, the bull's antlers have completed their growth. Since early spring, blood vessels have been depositing calcium beneath a layer of skin known as velvet. In August this layer of skin begins to dry and turn white as the antlers harden. The bulls have feeling in the antlers as they are growing and take care not to bruise them. When bruises do happen, the result of these injuries can be odd-looking points growing from the antlers. By late summer, the antlers begin to itch and so the bulls rub them against trees and bushes, scraping off the layer of dead velvet.

At the same time, their testicles drop and begin releasing testosterone, causing the bull's neck to swell and his attitude to become aggressive. These changes are directly related to the angle of sunlight. This is a process called photoperiodism and scientists are only now beginning to realize the extent of its importance in timing nature's cycles.

Photoperiodism turns off and on the moose's reproductive systems. The desire to mate is not just an isolated event that happens in the fall as the light wanes. In the spring, the rising angle of the sun stimulates the bull's hormones, causing its antlers to begin growing. Deer respond to it as well.

Photoperiodism plays a role in plant cycles too. The fall colour in leaves is a result, not of cold temperatures, but of decreased sunlight altering the chemical balance in the leaf, thus turning off the process of photosynthesis and causing the green chlorophyll to die off. This in turn reveals other colours in the leaves, colours that were always there but were overwhelmed by the green chlorophyll cells.

Even meadow voles and other small mammals living beneath the winter snow cover are affected. A recent study suggests that even snow-filtered sunlight will cause their reproductive systems to turn off and on.

For bull moose, the arrival of the rut begins with the first scraping of velvet from the antlers. This occurs a few weeks before the cows come into heat and it may be that the bull's increased interest stimulates the cows to cycle. In any case the bulls start to seek out the cows.

A bull's antlers are his way of advertising stature as a potential mate. Big antlers inform a cow that the owner was successful in finding the best feeding spots. They also tell her that the bull is into its prime, usually reached by age seven and lasting until the animal is ten. After ten, a bull starts to produce somewhat smaller headgear than when in its prime.

The antlers are easily seen and they help cows spot a potential mate. The large palms of the antlers bleach in the sun and reflect light like a mirror when a bull emerges from the forest.

Antler size also prevents wasted energy for another bull will judge a competitor by the size of his armament. If you're a moose you challenge a rival only if he is equal in size.

All of this action can make for some exciting photography. Along Highway 60 I find the meadows along Opeongo Road are often excellent spots to look for rutting bulls. Moose can and will be found everywhere in this season as they seek each other's favours, so be prepared. I carry my 80-200 lens beside me and keep a long telephoto mounted on a camera in the back seat. If you see a lone bull in a roadside bog, he will likely be just moving on so you better be ready to shoot.

The day I regard as my best in the spring I saw thirty moose. My best day in the rutting season to date has produced five, my best winter day only two. Do not go expecting moose in the fall to be as visible as in the spring. They have other things on their minds beside road salt!

Are September and October the only times to see the moose rut? Yes – fall is the only rutting season moose have and in Algonquin it is winding down by mid-October. At least it is for the cows, for by then most have been bred. A few are not and will continue to seek mates sometimes up to December but your chances of encountering them are scarce. I've found that the bulls' ardour has decreased as well. I suspect that they are just plain tired. However, from November through to the end of January it's still worth a "moose" trip because some moose will retain their antlers well into the winter, although the biggest bulls usually drop theirs by December.

An added bonus of a late-fall or early-winter trip is that the bulls begin to associate with each other again, and this provides an opportunity to photograph some sparring. These fights lack the aggression of the early rut battles but are still impressive.

The transitional nature of Algonquin's forest supports a wider variety of wildlife not found north or south of here. For example, there are really very few places in North America where you will find whitetailed deer and moose living together except where these mixed forest types meet.

THE NOT SO BAD WOLF

These days deer are scarce in the park and I see them only rarely along the roads. In the fifties, they were everywhere and when I first came to the park in the mid-sixties, they were still a common sight. By the seventies, they were all but gone. What happened?

The popular belief was that Algonquin's three hundred wolves killed them off but biologists disproved this. Deer were not found in the park until logging cleared away the old growth forest in the mid- to late 1800s. Deprived of their food and infected by the deer-carried brain worm, moose all but vanished and the deer herds took over.

By the late fifties the park's forest was growing older and was less nutritious for the deer. Their numbers declined, and then severe winters in the late sixties and early seventies all but eliminated them. These bad winters were no problem for the moose and their numbers rebounded at an unprecedented rate. By the 1980s it was possible to see moose in numbers that rivalled deer sightings in the fifties!

Now deer, thanks to mild winters in the mid- to late 1980s, are once again re-invading the park and are quite numerous in the eastern portions and west of the park gate. Excursion 1 suggests a place just south of Dwight where you can easily see whitetails in their deer yard. This is the best place to see deer in the park's ecosystem that I know of although they may be seen in smaller numbers almost anywhere along the park road.

Like moose, whitetail deer also have a rutting season. Theirs peaks in November but I've never found it worthwhile to travel to the park to view it as the deer numbers are so low there is little opportunity to photograph the "action."

Photographing the park's predators is also not very easy. Otter, which are a member of the weasel family, have of late been very common in the lakes and rivers along the highway but wolves and bears have proved elusive.

Algonquin's wolves are easier to hear than they are to see. In all my years of visiting the park, I've seen six and these few occasions stand out in my memory. My mind's eye is the only place I can view them, for with the exception of three shots taken at the Beaver Pond Trail none of my Algonquin wolf pictures were worth keeping. Even these three are not all that great, for that matter.

Wolves are not a common sight despite the presence of some 300 of these predators in the park. Recently some appear to have become more tolerant of the traffic on highway 60 and more sightings are being made. So far though I've only succeeded in getting distant shots. (500mm 4.5L)

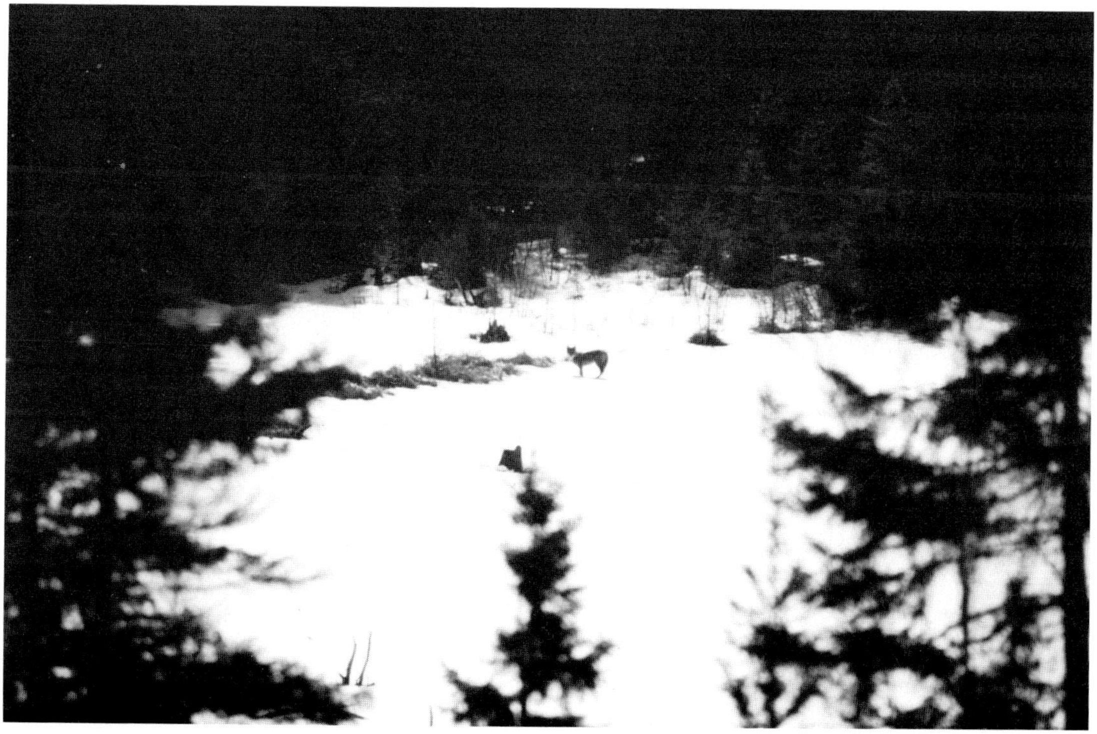

Some people have been luckier than I due simply to having spent more time in the park than I did. If your goal is to photograph wild wolves in the park, you will need to spend time looking and listening. Ask park officials and naturalists where wolves have been seen and then frequent these areas. Apparently the eastern third of the park is the best, but to be honest, your chances anywhere will be slim to nil.

BEARING IT ALL

Bears, on the other hand, are easier to see, and in the past few years I've seen five and photographed three of them at least well enough that I kept the pictures. In the sixties I used to go behind the old dump along Highway 60 with my dad's Brownie movie camera and film the bears. Back in those days, twenty bears was a poor night.

Wild bear photography is chancy, but until recently, dumps bordering the park provided me with opportunities. Bears are drawn to dumps because, like you and me, they are omnivorous. Also, like humans, they have very poor digestive systems and need very rich food. Cooked and processed food that we throw out is more than acceptable to bears.

Today, every dump that I used is closed down or securely fenced. While much more personally satisfying than my dump encounters, my recent meetings with bears in the park have not been the stuff from which great pictures are made. As with wolves, it appears that future bear photography here will be a hit-and-miss proposition (or accomplished elsewhere).

Algonquin imposes few rules on its visitors. In some places, calling of animals is forbidden but in this park you can try to call moose or wolves. You can get out and approach animals, too, but one rule virtually every park in North America enforces is that feeding of wildlife, especially bears, is not allowed.

It may be tempting to try to attract a bear by baiting it, but to do so is against park rules and very foolhardy. Remember that more people have been killed *and* eaten by black bears in this park than in any other park on the continent. I say

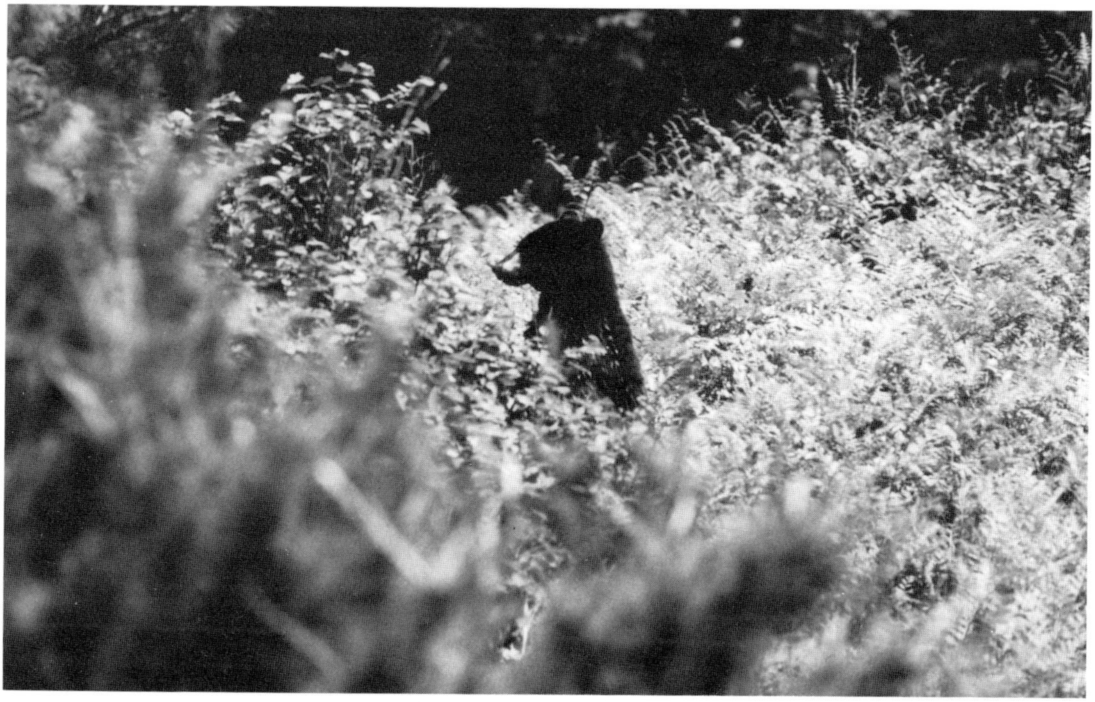

that not to scare you, but to bring home the point that bears can be dangerous animals.

To date there have been only five such incidents and I certainly wouldn't worry about the danger from bears unless I were doing something to attract them to my campsite. Bears are generally very tolerant of people, and if you see one ambling along you will be quite safe photographing it from a reasonable distance.

"Killer" bears appear not to have had much experience with people. They tend to be true wilderness bears and are encountered in remote areas. They are not the ones you see wandering Highway 60 or the more travelled canoe routes. Still, bears do wander and one of these bears could appear anywhere, so be alert. This type of bear will treat you as it would any prey. It will lock on to you and stalk you. Playing dead, running or being aggressive will do little to deter it. It wants to eat you, not remove you as a threat.

I work with bears a lot and I always watch for this type of abnormal behaviour. So far (knock on wood) I've never seen it.

Black bear are a rare sight in the park but they can be seen just about anywhere. The majority of nuisance bear reports come from back country users where park officials are less able to deal with the culprits. (500mm 4.5L)

If I do I will get to some safe place, such as a car, a boat or deep water and I'll do it fast. Otherwise, I'll use common sense when I encounter a bear putting my, and its, safety first.

THE REMARKABLE CATLIKE DOG

There is one road side predator that I have had great luck with – the red fox. If you drive the road often enough you will meet this engaging little dog. Some in the park are quite tame and on more than one occasion I've had them actually bring their kits out to feed in front of me. I have no idea why they do this, but I do know that I am not the only photographer to have had this experience.

Red foxes are small catlike hunters that prey on the park's smaller animals. They will eat birds, turtle eggs, chipmunks, mice and voles, groundhogs and even insects. I've found that by sitting still and sucking on my knuckle to make a squeaking sound, they will come to investigate. I've also found them

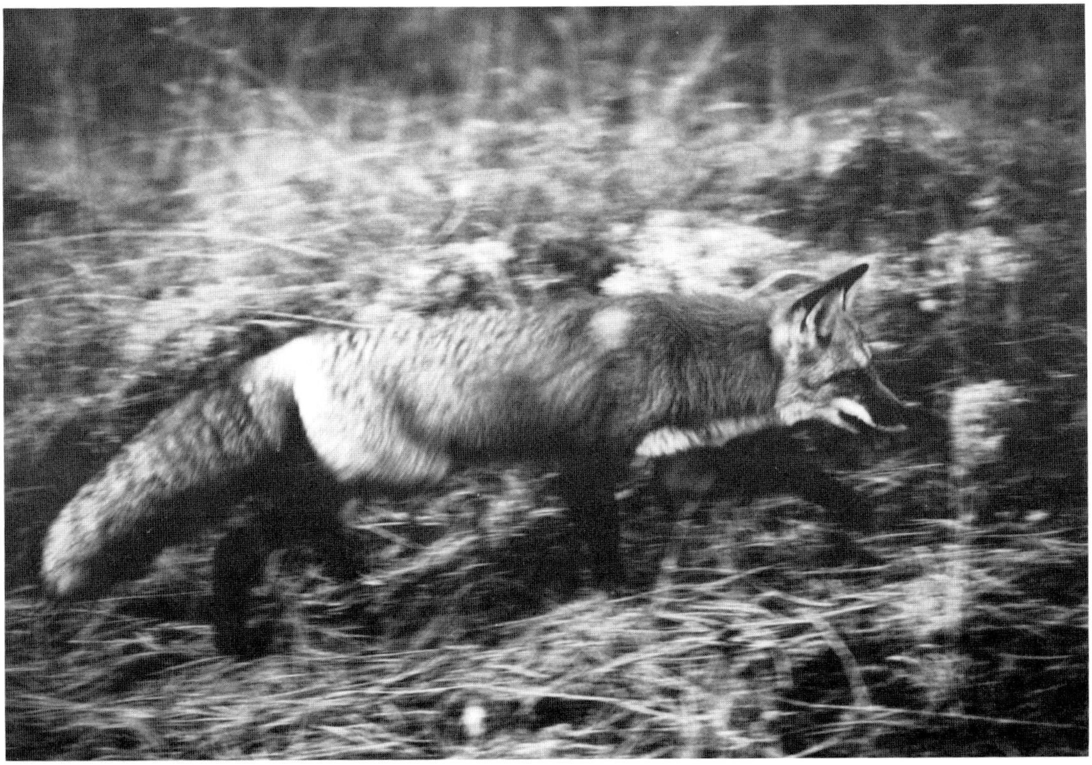

Red fox are the most cat-like of all the dogs. There is only one species of fox in the park but it comes in several shades, the black phase, sometimes called the silver fox, and the red, shown here. (300mm 2.8L auto-focus)

to be so tame that they approach me without any inducement at all. I suspect that some of these foxes have been fed by visitors, but I do not feed them and suggest that you should not either.

Rabies is a concern, of course, and if I saw a fox approaching me like this at home in Mississauga I'd be calling the humane society. Up here, though, I've encountered enough tame foxes during the day to accept that these animals live by different rules. They are more used to friendly curious people, I guess, but to be on the safe side I do not let them get too close.

A bite from any park animal should be treated as serious. That goes for chipmunks as well as foxes or bears. See a doctor if blood is drawn.

THE FOREST IN WINTER

In winter I often visit the Mew Lake Campground, where I can usually find a variety of birds making do with scraps left by the winter campers. Red breasted nuthatches, chickadees and blue jays are fairly accommodating here.

Both gates usually have bird feeders up and so does the museum. Downy woodpeckers are frequent visitors. The Minnesing Cross Country Ski Trail at kilometre 23 also has a feeder that is quite active.

As a general rule, there is a feeding order that will become obvious to you after a while spent photographing birds at a feeder. Smaller birds will appear soon after you set up your camera. Chickadees are usually the boldest. Then other small birds feed while the larger blue jays wait in the background. The reason for this apparent order has to do with the food requirements each species needs. The smaller the bird is, the more rapidly it uses up its energy supplies, because the ratio of heat-losing skin surface to body weight is greater in small animals than it is in big ones.

Standing at a bird feeder you will come to know the truth of this law of nature. Your small parts fingers, nose, toes and ears will chill much more rapidly than your big parts (legs, chest and upper arms). The apparent tameness of chickadees is not the result of trust but of desperation. If they wait until you depart, they may well hinder their chances of survival!

Blue jays, with their bigger size, can afford to wait. I've tested this rule at feeders in southern Ontario, my own backyard and out west, and it applies in all situations I've encountered if conditions are similar.

Leave it to Algonquin to have a classic example of a bird whose behaviour flies in the face of this logic. One of my favourite birds at these feeders is the Canada (grey) jay. You won't see these birds very much in summer but come fall and winter they will find you, especially if you have food about. These birds have adapted well to Algonquin's winter by collecting and storing their food supplies in the summer. During that season, there is so much bounty that the birds have little need for human charity. With the onset of fall and winter, the bird's natural food supplies dwindle and it turns to people to augment their larders.

Canada jays or whisky jacks, as they are also known, are well known for their abilities as camp robbers. They are bold and will hop right up onto your picnic tables in order to get their bounty. As I said earlier, I do not, as a rule, hold with feeding wild animals, but for this engaging bird I break my rule.

A piece of bread or bacon held out will usually tempt the bird to land on your hand. Take a picture of this with a wide-angle lens for a different view of these birds.

Why do they tame so quickly? The whisky jack is one of the very few birds to nest in the park during the winter. By the third week of March, they are sitting on eggs and by the end of March or early April, the young have hatched. The energy required to do all this (mating, nest building, laying and feeding) has to come from the food stored throughout the forest. There is no other source at this time of year.

While it would seem impossible for such a small animal to remember where it has hidden thousands of bits of food, the fact remains that they somehow accomplish this feat. Even the food they take from my hand gets deposited somewhere out of sight.

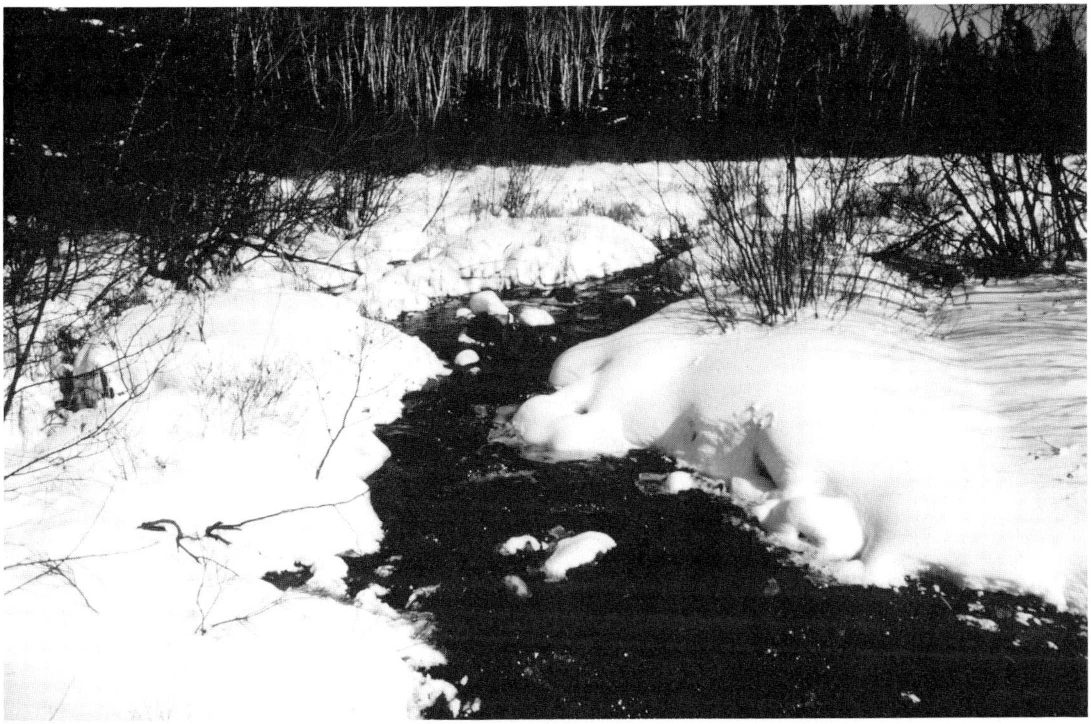

The first melting of snow in March brings the promise of spring to a land that has been frozen for four or five months. Underneath the snow, protected by its insulating blanket, voles are giving birth and plants are already growing. (28mm 2.8 auto-focus)

Come winter, any food offered will be gratefully accepted in order to boost their chances of survival. This is the reason for their apparent flouting of the feeding order. Unlike their cousins the blue jay, who nest in the spring when insects and seeds are available, the Canada jays have young to feed in winter as well as themselves.

When I work a bird feeder, I usually have my longest telephoto lens mounted on a tripod so that I can catch the more distant larger birds and get extreme close-ups of the smaller ones. I keep a shorter telephoto lens, normally a 300mm, hung about my neck for snapshots or for shots that require some movement on my part to get the right angle.

I typically use two or three camera bodies whenever I shoot. The freedom to select from more than one focal length is invaluable for the time it saves.

Birds at a feeder are one thing – they are in effect baited and come to me – but what about animals encountered in the "wild"?

Photographing from a blind is a popular image of wildlife photographers. In many places, it is the method of choice. It is ideal for shooting waterfowl on ponds or nesting birds but to be honest, I've never used one in Algonquin. In fact, I've never heard of or seen anyone use a blind in Algonquin Park.

Traditional blinds are of little use here unless one is working with a nesting grey jay or other bird. Visit the park often enough and you will find that most of the species found here are fairly accommodating (if you can find them). Moose seldom snort and run away even in the fall when they are harder to find.

Photography of predators, such as fox or wolf, might be better from a blind, but in photographing wolves, it would be useful only if you somehow found a den, while for foxes my experience in the park suggests it is unnecessary.

The truth is that your automobile is a superb blind. As in Africa, the presence of cars is not directly associated with the

Red breasted nuthatches are often found at park bird feeders in the winter. They also frequent the winter campsites at Mew Lake and will come readily to you if offered food. (300mm 2.8 auto-focus with 2x tele)

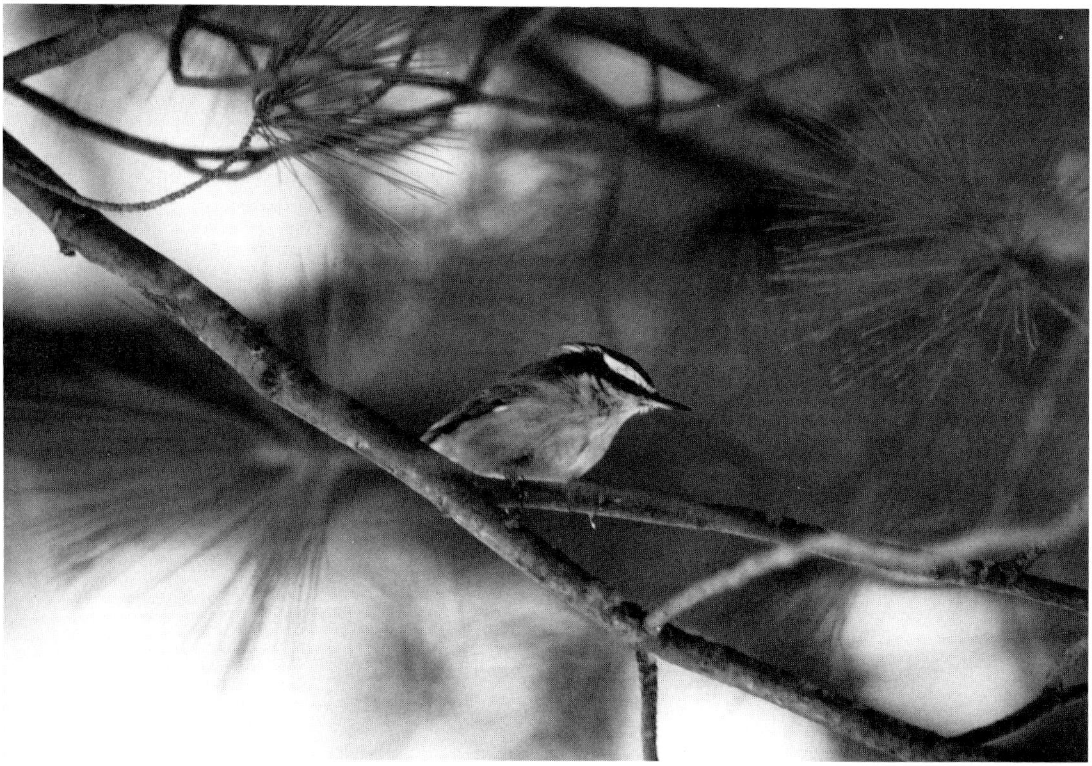

danger of human beings. When my photography companions and I spot a subject, we've learned from bitter experience how to use the vehicle to advantage. Slamming on the brakes as soon as you've seen an animal does not work!

Instead we mark the location using a distinctive tree or rock and then drive up the road a distance (five hundred metres), turn around, come back past the animal, and if it is on the opposite side of the road, repeat this procedure, coming back to the location slowly until we stop in position.

Always bear in mind that there may be traffic coming so signal your turns and make them safely.

Once in position, the person on the side closest to the animal begins shooting, with the camera lens supported by the edge of the open window. Turn the motor off to avoid vibrations.

If the animal is skittish, it is usually possible for the other photographer to shoot over the shoulder of the first. If the animal appears calm, the person on the far side of the car quietly gets out, taking the keys out of the ignition so the car doesn't "beep." Do not slam doors. I find it best to start shooting while partially hidden by the car, using the roof or hood as support.

Once outside the vehicle, move closer and take up a position that does not make the animal nervous. Now it is time for the first photographer (the one closest to the animal) to open the door and emerge as quietly as possible.

If the animal is still there, you should be able to work it at leisure. At least you will until someone comes along, slams on the brakes and leaps out yelling, "Look, Henry! A moose!"

Photographing along the park's roads can be a harrowing experience thanks to *Homo tourista.* Try not to let them bother you. By far the majority of the park's visitors behave themselves well around animals and respect them, but a few will attempt to pet a bull moose – the bull usually dispels that notion quickly.

I try to remember that the same animals I marvel at are also a rich part of other people's visit to the park, so I avoid bothering the animal to the extent that it moves off the road and out of sight. This code of ethics is enforced in some parks where photographers are restricted by the park officials. That you and I have a great deal of freedom in Algonquin is something I take care not to jeopardize.

Besides, if you spend a lot of time watching animals, you will soon see that you are a rarity among the park's human visitors. Many times we've had a moose or fox all to ourselves as people stop, watch for a few minutes and then drift on. My success, whether in Algonquin, Africa or Alaska is due largely to building in time to sit and watch. I used to rush about fearing I'd miss something but I'm not like that any more (except sometimes).

Cars do make excellent blinds, but for a true feeling of working the "wild" Algonquin it is necessary to get out of the car and work away from the road. Algonquin's trails offer much to the hiker but wildlife sightings are never guaranteed. I've already mentioned some of the better ones such as Mizzy Lake, Spruce Bog and the Beaver Pond Trails. Hiking logging roads can pay off, as well, as they are seldom used by large numbers of people; however, do keep an ear cocked for an approaching logging truck for safety's sake. There are three or four such roads that I know of along the Highway 60 corridor, all marked by chains and signs prohibiting public vehicles but not hiking. Walking any of these will lead you into the forest, and while animal sightings may be few, tracks of moose, wolves and even bear may be encountered in the earth along these routes.

If you wish to photograph these tracks, try it when the light is at an angle for best results. Don't overlook droppings, either, as a fit subject for your camera.

Berries in season are a favourite food of bears. Most berries have seeds coated with a resin that protects them from the gastric juices of the animal's stomach and gives the bear a tummy ache. These seeds pass through the animal with its droppings. One scientist who counted these seeds found that they averaged about 1,500 per steaming pile. There were several such piles within a few metres radius!

READING SIGN

Wolf droppings often contain moose, deer or beaver hair and it is fun to study them and guess what the canine's last meal was.

Moose droppings look like those little baked potatoes you are sometimes served – sort of like half-baked brown marshmallows. In winter, they are dry and hard because the animal conserves its water by producing dry stools and minimizing its loss of moisture. In spring, they look like small wet chocolate-covered raisins, because the animal is now feeding on moist vegetation.

As for their relevance to the ecosystem, droppings represent one way in which animals return energy to the system. The droppings are made up of food which the animal, for whatever reason, was unable to digest. They still have energy stored in them and are sought by all kinds of other organisms from bacteria and fungi even to (at times) the animal that produced them. Rabbits and hares are known to eat their own stools to get that extra energy left in them.

A principal of ecology at work here is that no organism ever gets 100% of the energy available. Some is always wasted, and droppings are one example of this waste. Body heat is another.

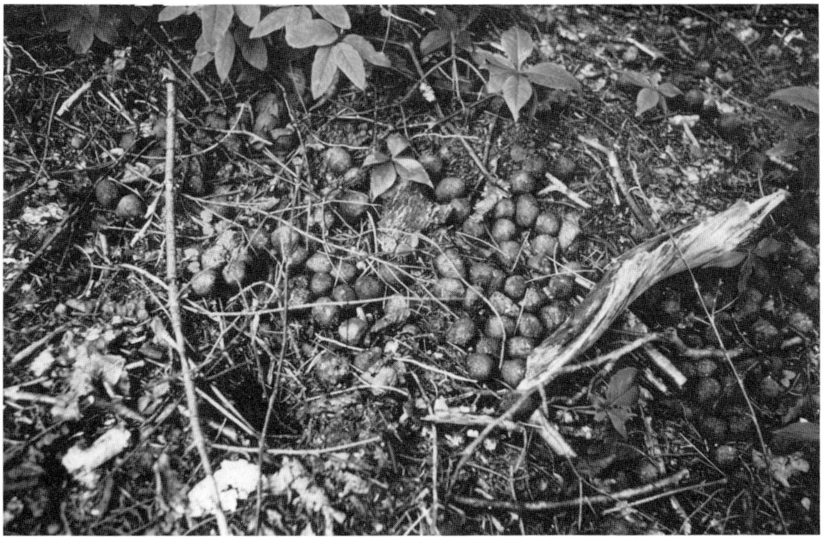

Moose droppings can tell you a lot about the animal that left them. This set is from a winter feed. They are dry and made up of woody vegetation. (200mm 2.8L zoom auto-focus)

THE STALK

Sometimes if you are lucky, you will find an animal that requires some stalking. I never feel more alive than when I am moving quietly through the underbrush stalking a large mammal be it bear or moose in Algonquin, hippo or elephant in Kenya. Every sense is working. Sounds, smells and movement are analyzed and filed away.

I first became interested in animals from the point of view of a hunter. I've long since laid my shotguns and rifles aside in favour of my cameras, but the thrill of the hunt and the stalk is still there.

Stalk into the wind. Be careful with each footfall. Avoid snags. Move with care. Don't get cocky. Move slowly, very slowly. What you could cover in a few minutes of normal walking will often take ten, fifteen or twenty minutes of careful stalking.

Chances are in Algonquin the animal will know you are coming long before you are within decent camera range. Don't let that fact deter you. Many times the animal will stay as long as you don't do something foolish, like falling down or yelling.

Each animal and the ensuing stalk must be judged by its surroundings, sex and season. As we've seen, moose vary in their approachability with the season. Spring is best. Winter is the worst.

If the animal you are after is a "park" animal, your stalk should be aimed straight at it as that is what it is used to. "Park" animals are those that are commonly found along the roads and canoe routes where people are frequently encountered. This applies as much in Algonquin as it does in Yellowstone. These animals are used to people looking at them and moving straight towards them. This is the norm, and they more or less accept our behaviour. Your stalking method will be much different with them than with "wild" animals.

We will define wild animals as those that are not used to encountering our species. Most deer in the park, along with all bears and wolves should be placed in this category in my view. Highway moose are usually in the former group as are some individual foxes and grouse.

This second grouping requires a more traditional stalk. Don't look at the animal except when you take a quick photo or two. Don't walk at it but zig-zag back and forth, moving a little closer with each pass. Stop frequently and move when the animal is not looking at you. Freeze if it stares at you or become very interested in something else – a blade of grass or a twig. With practice and luck, you'll succeed.

I do not normally carry a tripod or really long lens for this type of shooting. Instead, support the camera with a monopod or against a log or tree trunk. Begin shooting when you begin your stalk. Sometimes, if the stalk is successful, those first pictures are thrown out because they are too far away and the subject too small. Sometimes, unfortunately, they are the only shots you will get.

Algonquin can be an excellent place to photograph wildlife, but as noted in the introduction to this book, it can also be a very frustrating park to "work." A visit to the park's museum or the various outfitting stores may provide you with current information. On one occasion, a visitor centre stop led directly to some of the best moose photography I've ever had. A truck driver had just seen two big bulls along the road and had stopped to inform the centre's staff. My companion on that trip, Don McClement, and I headed straight for the spot.

We found tracks but no moose, so we followed the tracks, which were in about sixty centimetres of snow. We soon discovered that moose were not as easy to track as I believed them to be and we became mired in a host of tracks that crisscrossed and meandered through the forest. We had no idea which were the freshest so we went back to the road to see if we could conjure up some clues to the moose's current whereabouts.

We heard from someone busily cutting small trees down along the roadway that a pair of bulls had crossed a few hundred metres down the road just minutes ago. We soon had fresh tracks to follow and within minutes we saw the moose rush away, crashing through the forest.

We nearly gave up then but a slow drive along the road soon located fresh tracks where the spooked moose had crossed. To our amazement, they were standing about fifty metres inside the forest. We stalked them using the technique described earlier for park moose and it worked. For over an hour, we filmed these two bulls as they rested, sparred and fed.

Such luck resulting from inquiries is sadly rare. Most of the time, such stops result only in general impressions based on what visitors report to the park staff. It helps to know moose are being seen frequently but it does not guarantee you will see them. Indeed, with a slow purposeful drive through the park you will likely see far more than by asking around.

CHASING GHOSTS

While driving the park highway, I always watch other drivers. A parked car merits an inspection, and several cars stopped at the same place usually means an animal is present.

Sometimes I'm lucky enough to run into Ron Tozer, the Park's resident naturalist. If anyone knows birds, its Ron. If you're lucky enough to spot him "birding," a few minutes' conversation with him will likely lead you to some interesting species you would otherwise have missed. That's how I saw my first bald eagle in the park.

I try to avoid chasing "ghosts" as much as possible. The temptation to do so is very real, especially when somebody tells you that he or she has just seen an animal "down the road a piece." This phrase can mean anything from half a kilometre to several kilometres and should be taken with a grain of salt. Also I try not to rely on directions based on distinctive trees. Experience has shown that whatever was there has gone before I get there or perhaps it never existed – a "ghost" sighting. And that's assuming I can find the unusual tree in which the bird was first sighted.

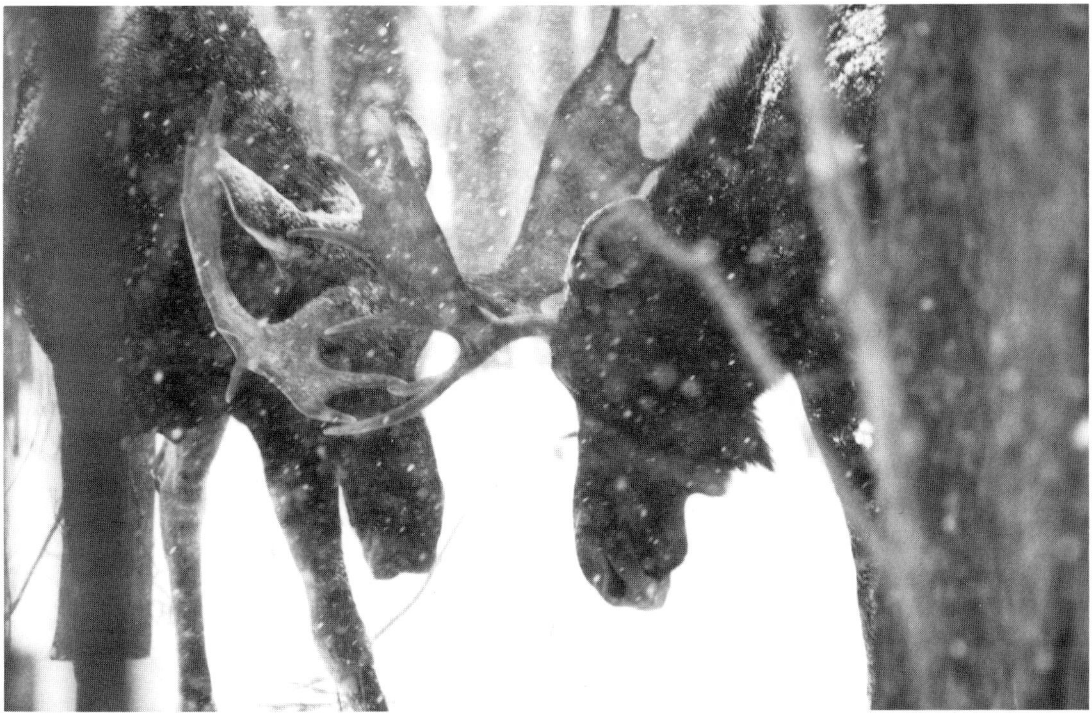

Remember, "a bird in the hand is worth two in the bush." Many times I've left a subject such as moose or bird, figuring that I could find another or come back to this one, only to discover that by leaving I've lost an opportunity. When you leave, a subject be confident you are finished with it. Rushing around seldom pays off.

Finally I word about being in "sync." What follows will sound as if it is out of Star Wars but in my years of wildlife photography, I've found too many examples of this to reject it out of hand. Simply, what I and other wildlife photographers have found is that if you get into the rhythm of the day, your shooting will be good. Whether you call this phenomenon "luck", "the force being with you" or just "being in sync," it is something that happens.

You will know it when it happens because an ordinary day will turn into an extraordinary one. A fox will catch a chipmunk in front of you. You will see twenty-five moose in a day or find a nesting loon.

Besides the incredible good luck, the thing I remember most about these two sparring bull moose was the sound of their antlers hitting together. The fight was not serious and they kept at it off and on for an hour while Don McClement and I followed them. (300mm 4.0L)

(Facing page) Fall colours in Algonquin generally peak between the last week in September and Canada's Thanksgiving weekend in October. Weather, both in the summer and the early fall, is a factor in determining when the colours will be at their best. (300mm 4.0L)

You will know it when it is not happening, too. You'll see nothing or – worse – you will see something but not be able to photograph it. When I have a bad day, I usually pack it in early and head home or I change my routine and do something I hadn't planned on doing, such as having a nap or going into Whitney for lunch. Sometimes it works.

Being in sync with the day is much more than simply being in the right place at the right time. It is also pacing yourself so that the day or the trip becomes that much more enjoyable. My wife is not smitten with wildlife to the same extent that I am, and we've had a constant give and take when she accompanies me on trips. During the first years of our marriage, I usually won out and we'd rush around spending hours looking for the perfect shot.

Now it is a much more balanced experience for us. I still get out and do my photography but a typical day includes "family time" too, whether it's a picnic, a quiet spell by a river or sightseeing. These breaks help relax me and re-focus the day and they do make for a more enjoyable experience for all of us. Most of the time these "delays" tend to put me into sync and I find my photographic opportunities improve.

When the four of us, my wife and two daughters, were in Alaska recently I trusted my luck to the rhythm of my family's pace. I don't know what it would have been otherwise but I do know that I was very pleased with what we saw. On the other hand, I did give up a morning whale watch a few weeks later and missed the only time anyone saw humpbacks breeching. So my system isn't perfect but I'd bet on average, I benefit more often than not.

Now I know this idea of rhythm and sync seems a tad hard to believe, but I have not yet met a professional wildlife photographer who doesn't nurture a similar belief. One thing is for certain, whether you subscribe to this theory or not, and that is that you will have no luck unless you get out into the field and look.

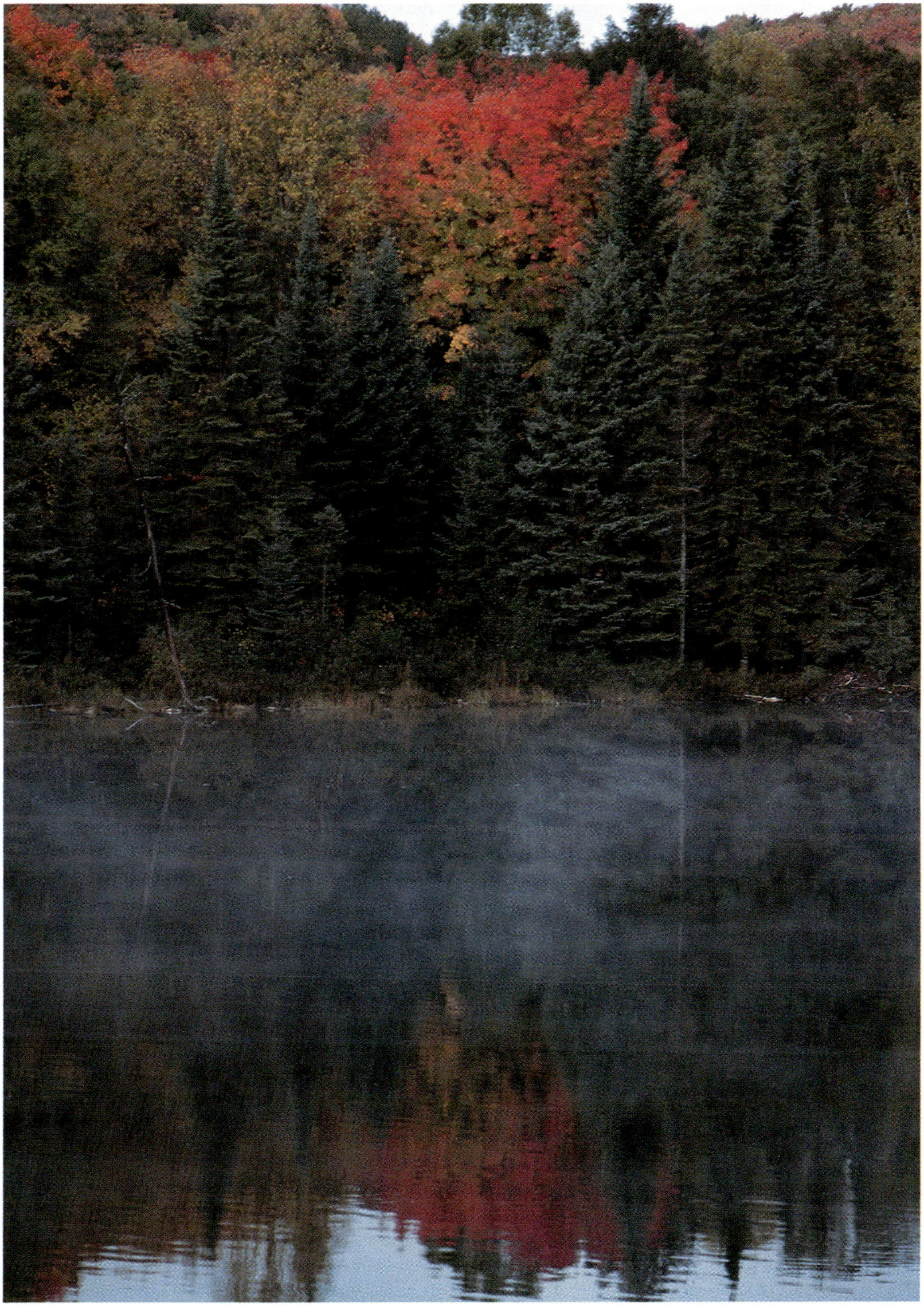

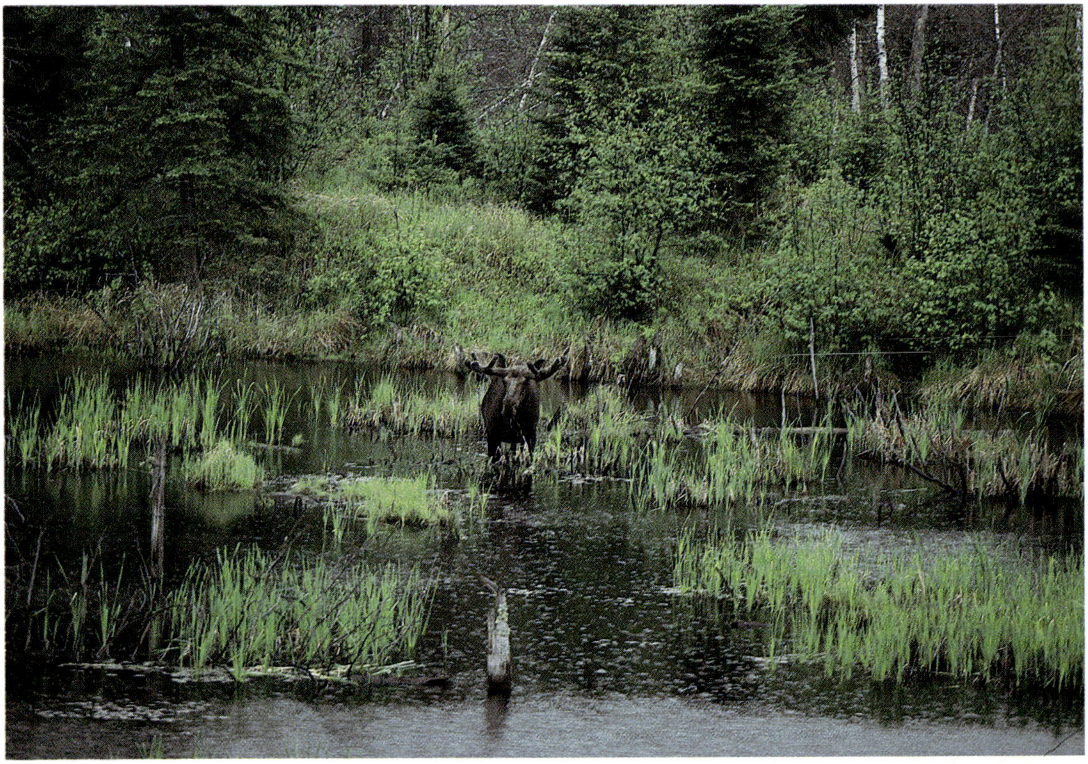

There is a good reason why the forest here has earned the name the Algonquin Rain Forest. Still, the animals don't stop their activities for the rain. Why should you? (200mm 2.8L auto-focus)

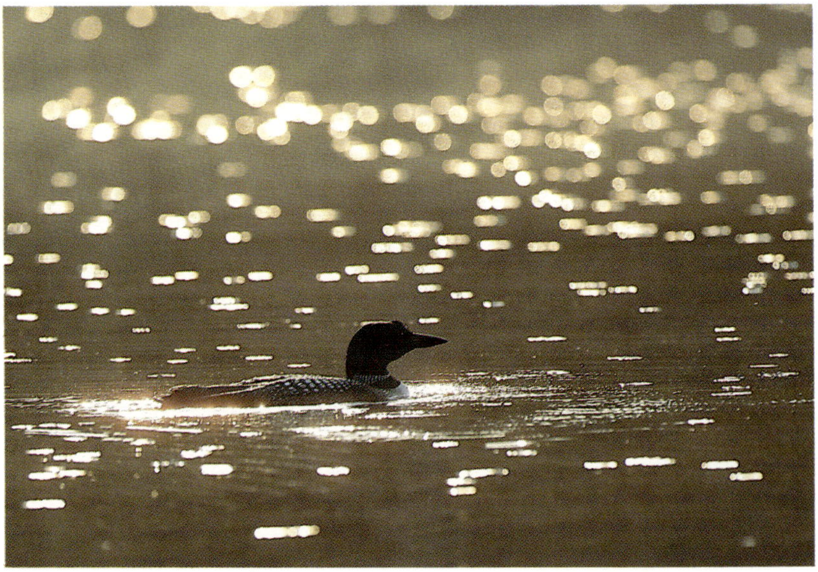

There is no other sound that personifies the park more than the haunting call of the common loon. Their yodels, calls and laughter are a special part of any summer trip. (500mm 4.5L)

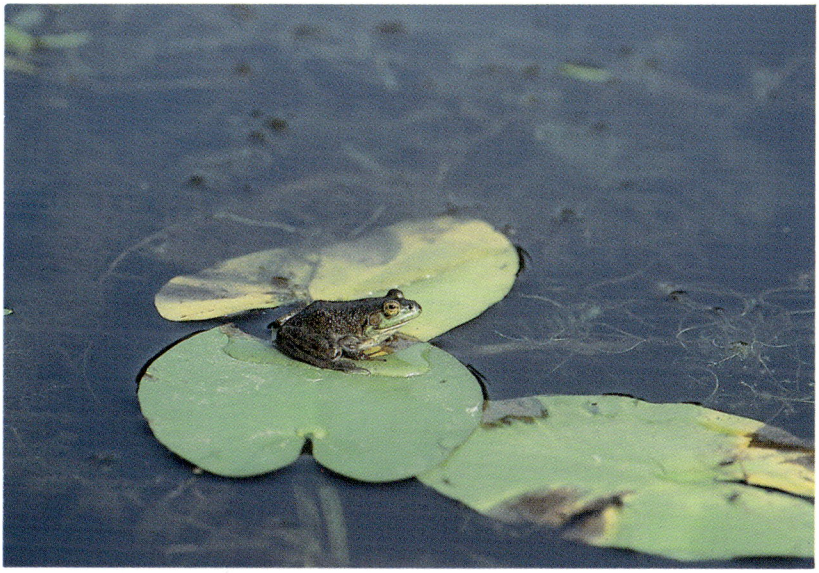

Frog numbers are down throughout the southern portion of Ontario due in part to increased levels of acid rain. Even in the park it appears that their populations may be decreasing. (300mm 4L)

The female common merganser (below) is often encountered by canoeists in the summer. Usually her brood of ducklings is close by, hidden along the shore. They will join her if there is danger and may even hitch a ride on her back. (300mm 4L auto-focus)

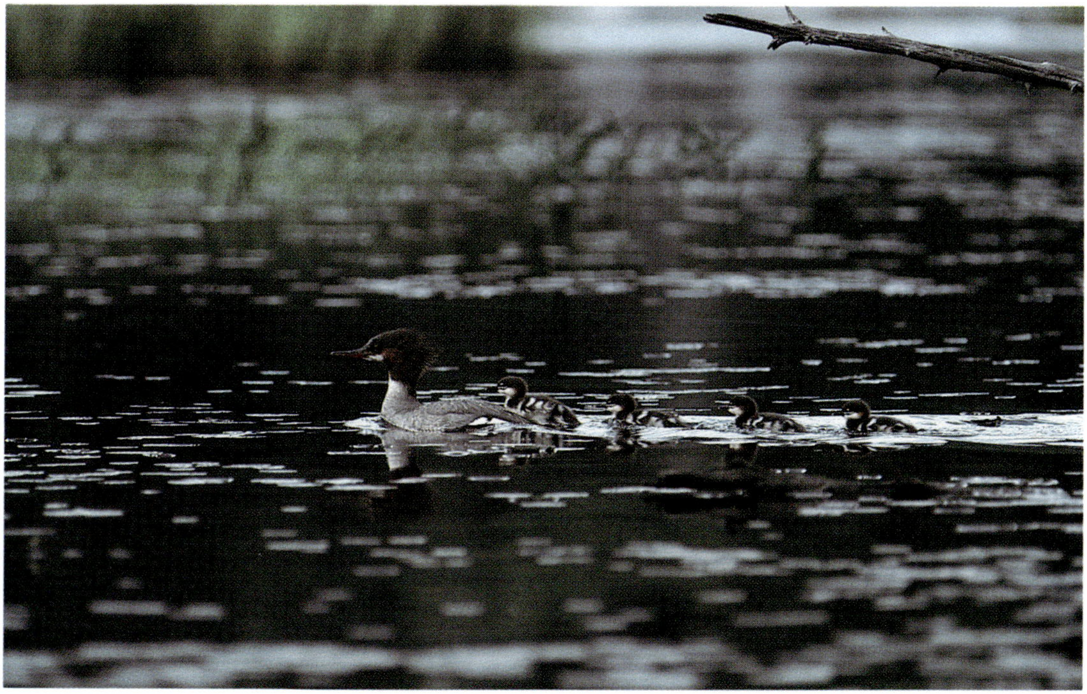

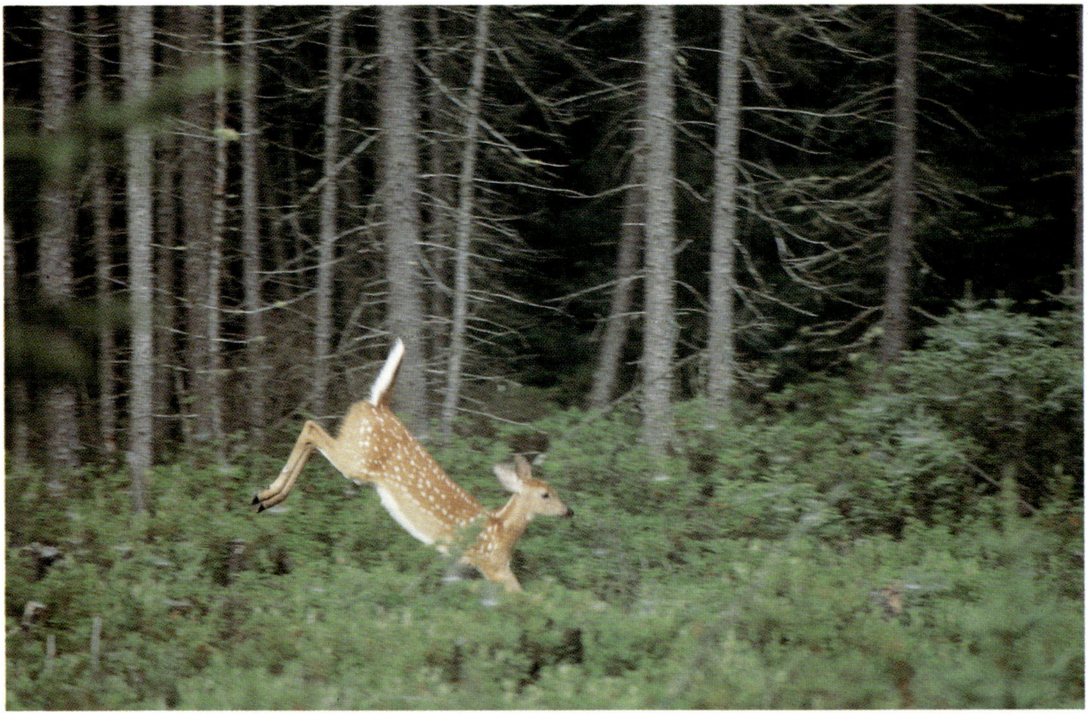

The whitetail deer holds its tail high when alarmed. This probably serves as a warning to other nearby deer and may also confuse a predator if there are several deer leaping at once. (500mm 4.5L)

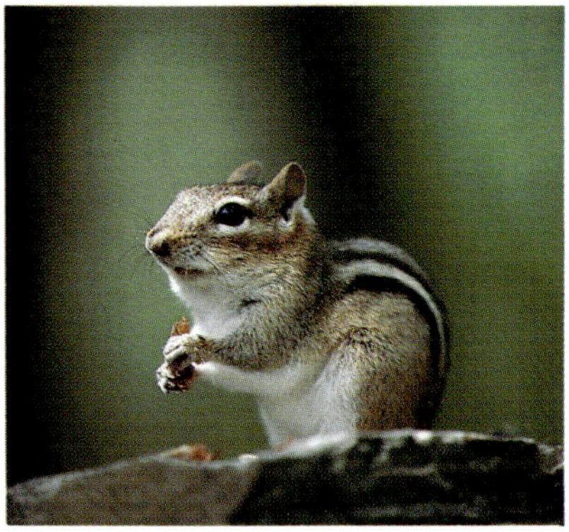

It is tempting to feed chipmunks but they do carry fleas and ticks that can cause diseases and should not be encouraged to come too close to people. (200mm 2.8L auto-focus)

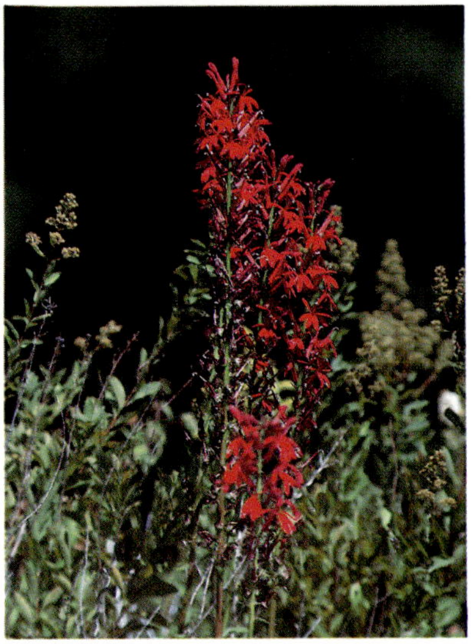

There are cardinal flowers growing below the visitor centre. I try to photograph them with the flowers in sunlight and the forest background dark. (200mm 2.8L auto-focus zoom)

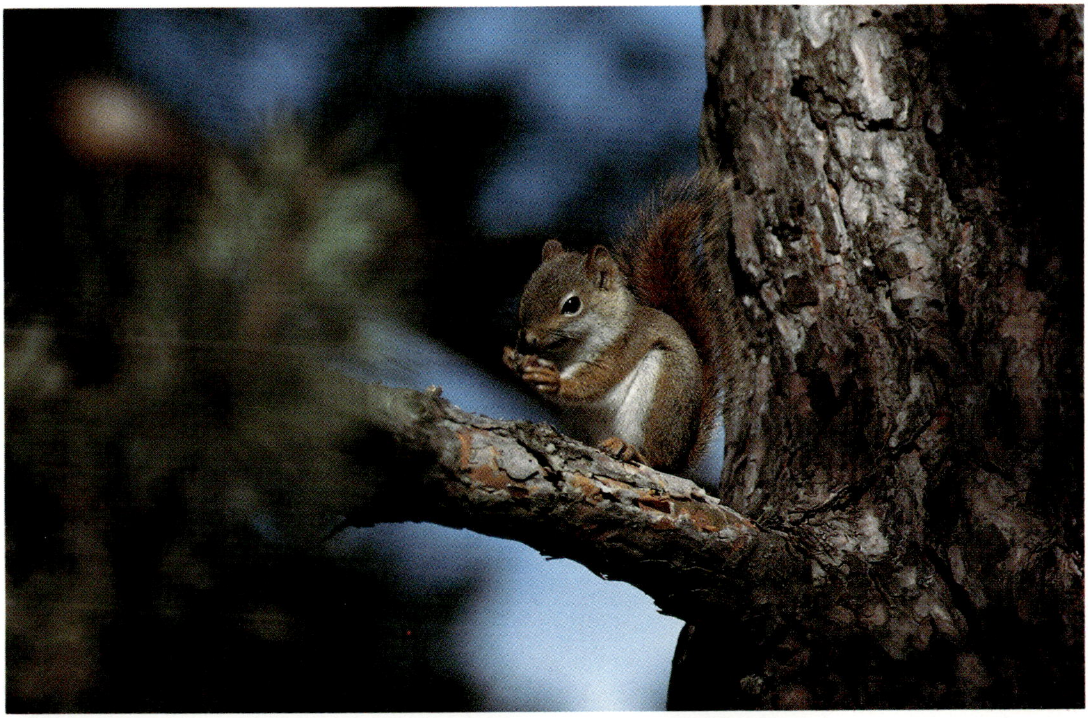

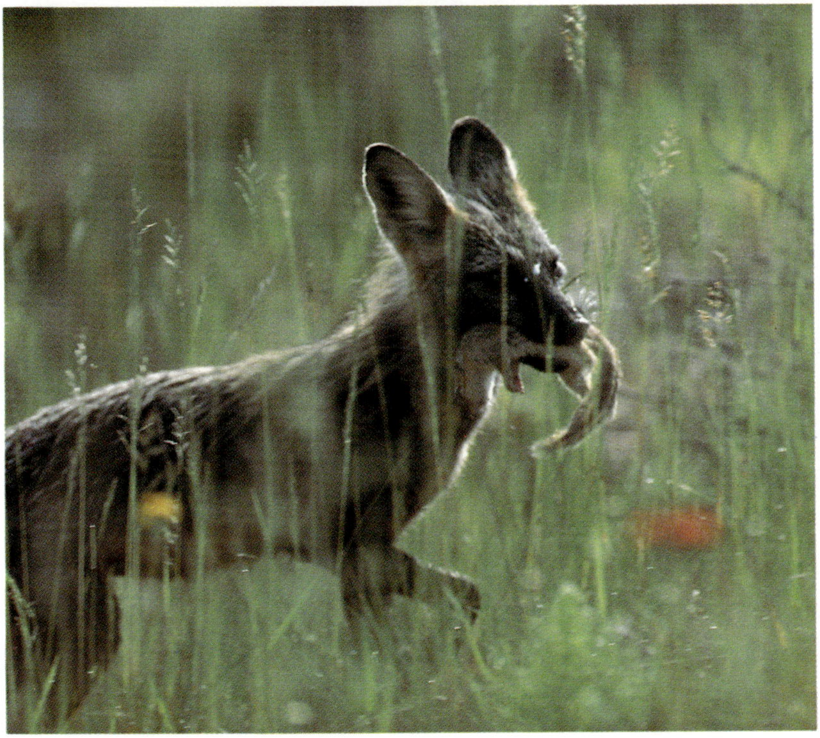

(Above) The red squirrel is the common squirrel in the park. I've only seen two black ones there. Red squirrels eat pine cones, which helps explain their relative abundance. (300mm 4L)

(Left) Predation is rarely witnessed in the park. I've never heard of a photographer who has actually seen a wolf hunting. Red fox are more common than wolves, but even so I've only witnessed them hunting chipmunks twice. (500mm 4.5L)

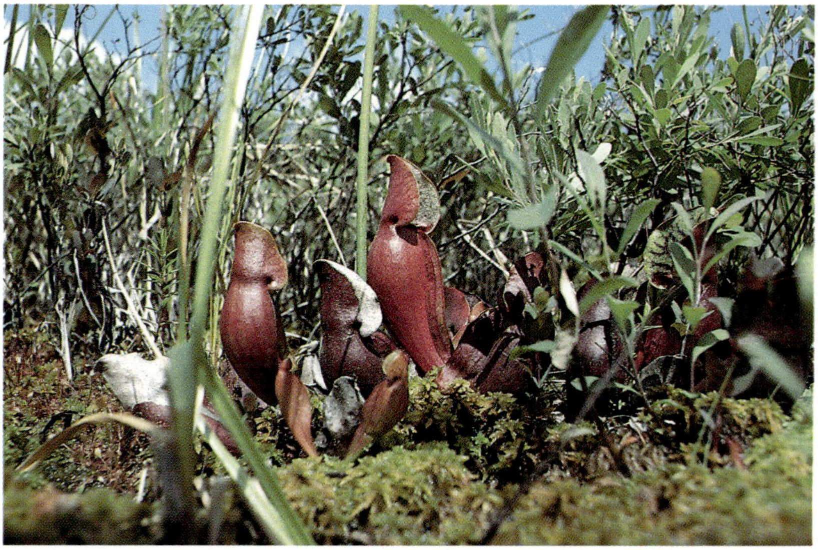

Pitcher plants are one of the most interesting bog plants. It was once believed that they ate insects, and at some point in their evolution they apparently did. Recent findings show that they develop a partnership with the insects they trap, with both plant and "bug" benefiting. (28mm 2.8 auto-focus)

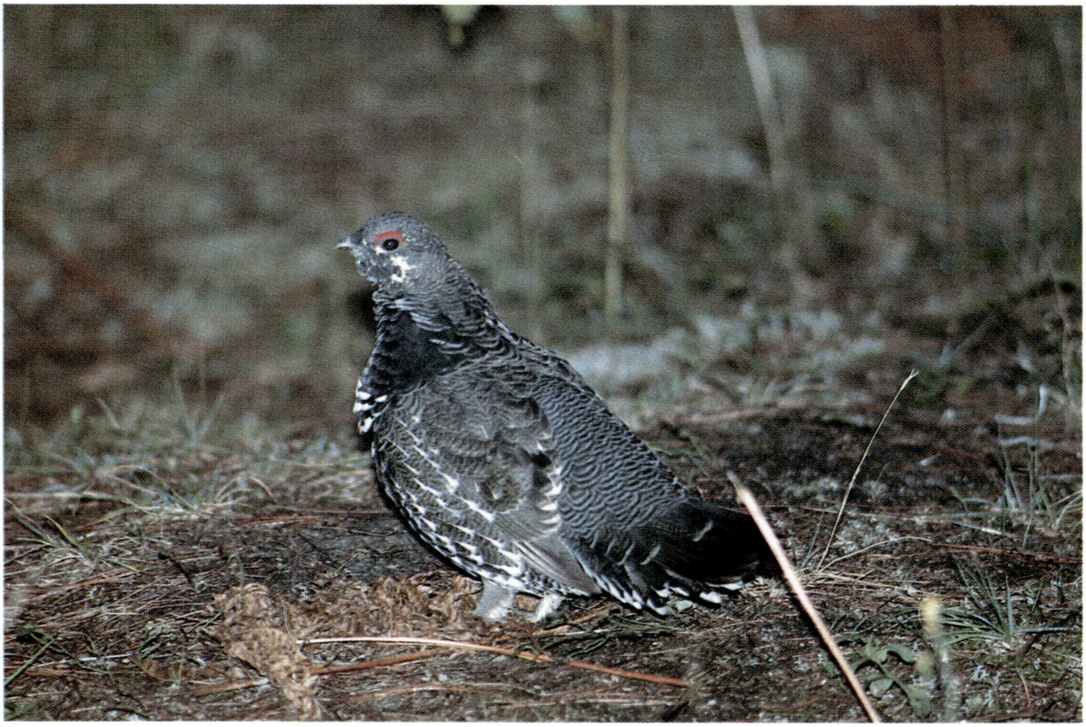

Two species of grouse make Algonquin Park their home. The spruce grouse is a northern species that prefers cool damp spruce bogs to drier woodland areas. The Spruce Bog Trail is often a good place to see them. (300mm 4L with flash)

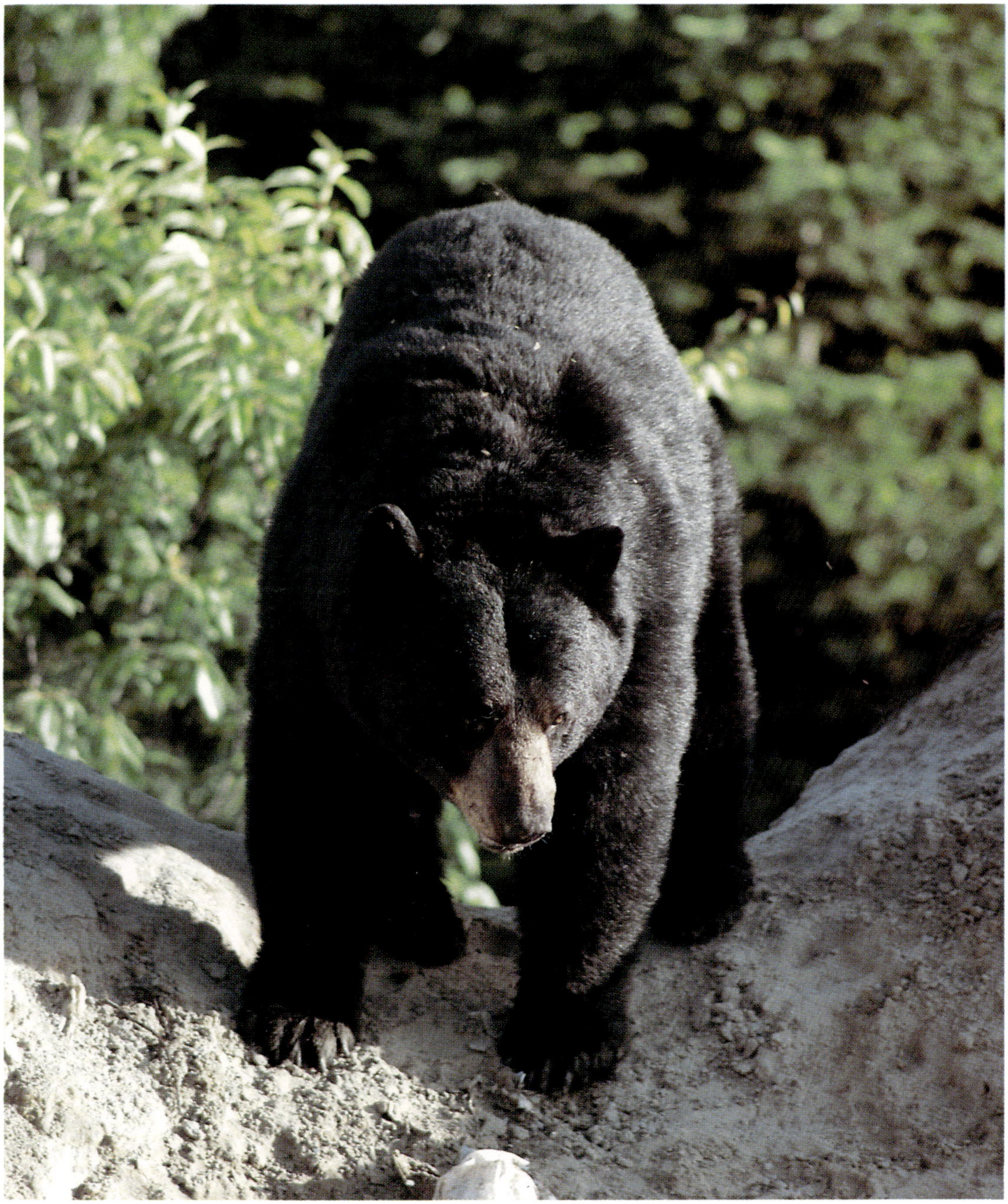

Black bears are common throughout the park and you are never far from one no matter where you are. They are generally shy and retiring and prefer to vanish into the forest rather than confront people. (500mm 4.5L)

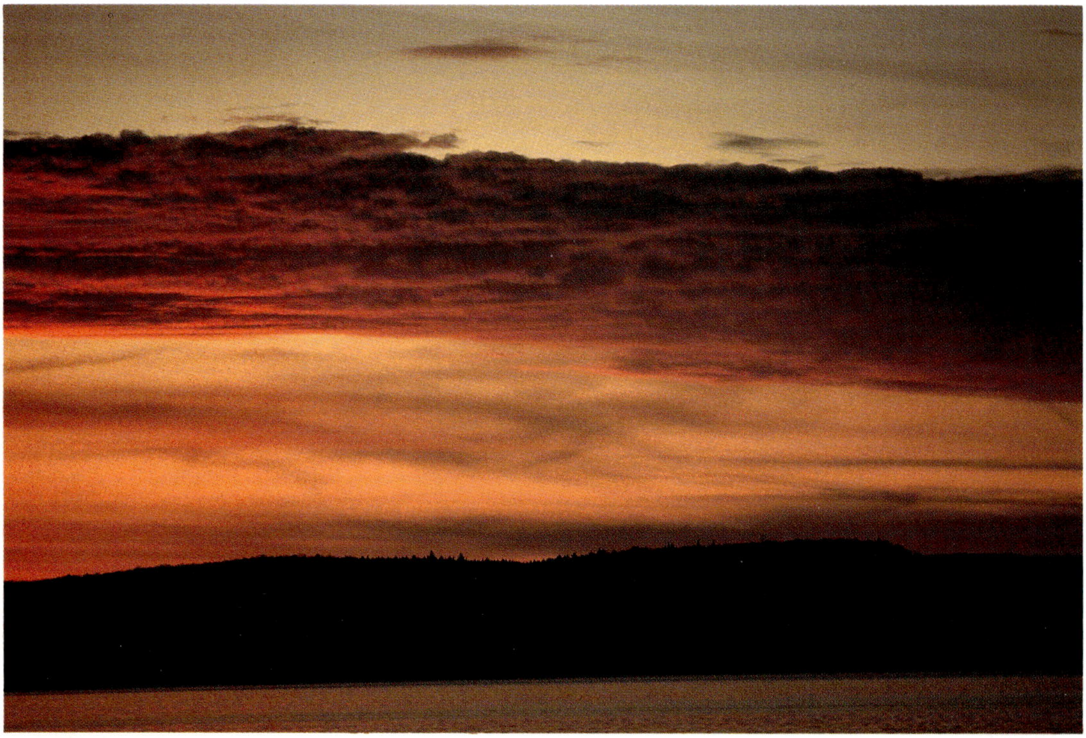

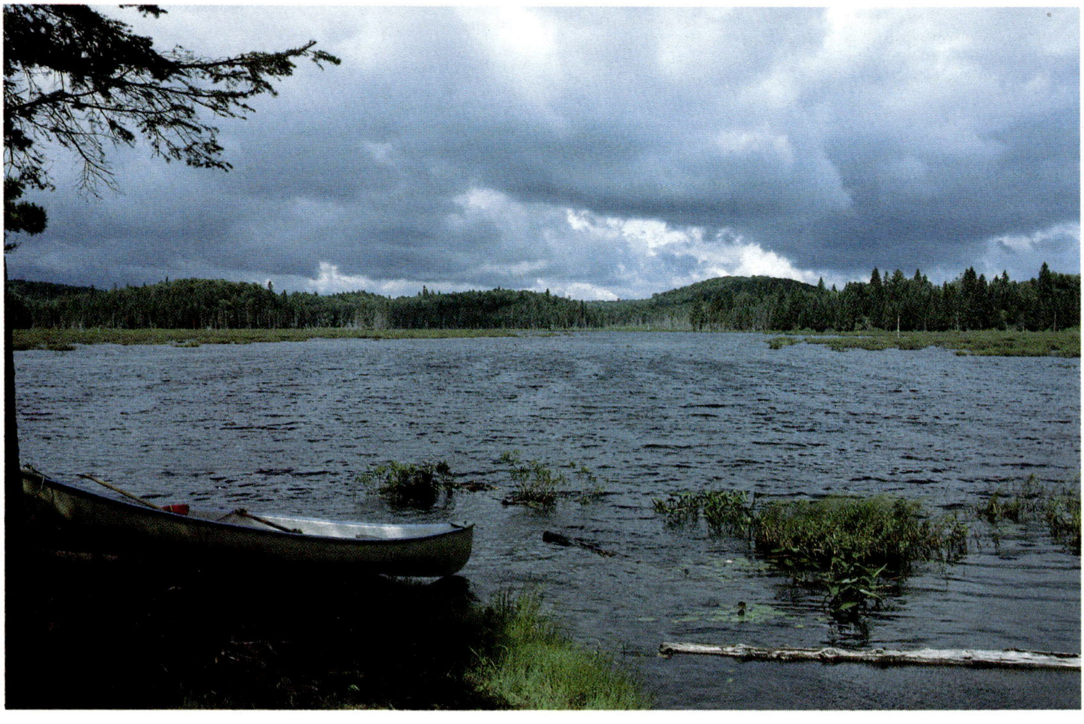

Excursion 5

Tuesday, August 17–Wednesday, August 18

Don McClement once again joined me for this late summer trip north to the park. I'd been back to the park only once since June 5 and that was for a three-day canoe trip, which is describe in the chapter on photographing the park's waterways. For most of the intervening weeks, my family and I were in Alaska where I had to do some work with grizzly bears and sea mammals.

Alaska had been wonderful but I was anxious to visit Algonquin again. When I asked Don if he'd like to join me, he quickly agreed and off we went.

He was unable to leave home until 1:00 p.m. so it was quite late in the afternoon when we arrived in the park. Our first and only stop that day was a visit to the museum. Don was anxious to see it and I was more than happy to go back. By coincidence I ran into another friend, Sonny Allinson and his wife Pat, who happened to be camping in the park with their daughters.

Sonny and I had met in the park in the mid 1960s when our families camped at the South Tea Lake extension. This campground is closed now and is being allowed to return to a natural state. It was, in our view at least, the best campsite in the park.

I was with Sonny when I saw my first wild moose in the park. That was a big deal then because moose were not very common in the sixties thanks to the brain worms carried by

(Facing page, top) Algonquin's sunsets are pretty but not spectacular unless there is a lot of dust and pollution in the air. The sun itself is the source of energy for all of the park's life forms. (300mm 2.8L auto-focus with 1.4 tele)

(Bottom) Clouds, water, forest and land are the elements that combine to make Algonquin such a wonderful place. A canoe remains my favourite way of experiencing this wild park and Tim Lake is one of my favourite places. (28mm 2.8 auto-focus)

deer. Looking back, I often wonder if that first moose was the vanguard of change that was to sweep the park and see moose replace deer as the most common large mammal seen here. (We saw it at Wolf Howl Lake which is still one of the best places to see them.)

Seeing Sonny brought back memories of bears too. Back in the sixties he was one of the friends that often accompanied me to the park dump to see the bears. In those days the dump was a popular tourist attraction and on some nights you could see up to twenty bears there. Of course there might well be three or four hundred people watching them, but it was the bears that counted.

Most of those bears wound up being shot because they were becoming habituated to people. In those days I used to keep track of such things and I was aware of at least a few hundred being killed over the years ending in the early seventies when the dump was closed.

One night, back in those heydays of bear watching, I even went on a park raid but unfortunately (or fortunately) there were no bears present that evening so there was no "action" to see.

Today, thanks to a better understanding of bear ecology the dumps along Highway 60 are a thing of the past, and the bears are back to feeding on wild foods again. This is no doubt safer for bears and people, but for a photographer it can be frustrat-

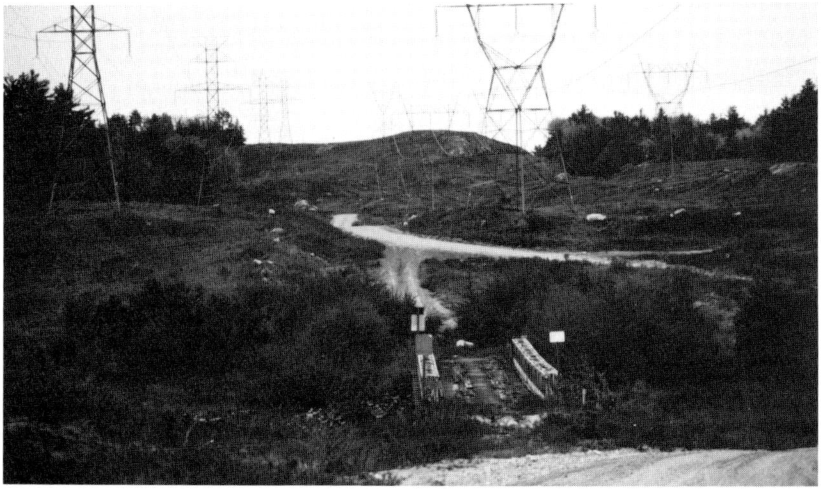

The hydro line at the end of the Basin Depot road might be a good place to see bears as they feed on summer berries. One day I'll go back and try it. (200mm 2.8L zoom auto-focus)

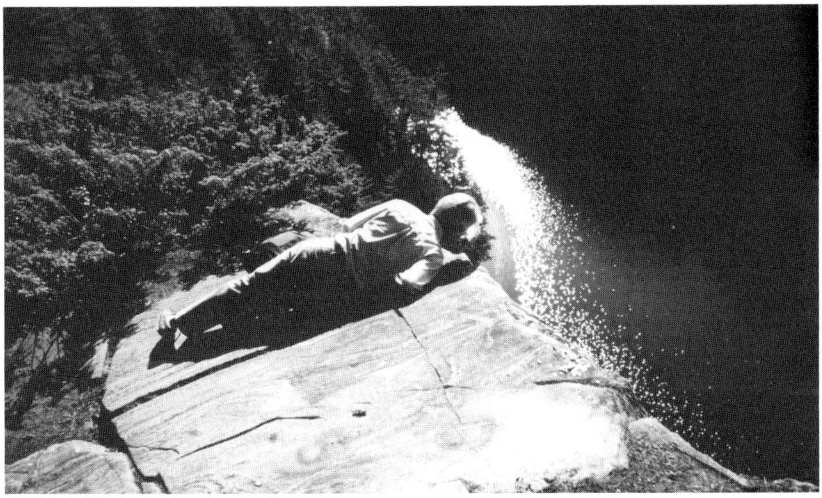

The Barron Canyon is not for the faint of heart. There are no fences here or barriers so Don McClement opts for a safer approach. It is a long way down! (28mm 3.5 auto-focus)

ing. (Since the dumps were closed and the bears have returned to more natural foods, few bears have been shot and the number of bear "incidents" greatly reduced.) The few bears I've seen in the park since the dumps closed have seldom stayed long enough for any serious photography.

It is a pity in a way that those days are gone. Some of those dumps provided ideal shooting conditions where, with a bit of luck, you could get pictures that made it seem as if the bears were in the wilds of Algonquin. Most of the bear pictures in this book are from those dumps.

When Don and I left Sonny, our goal was to see bears at what I was led to believe was an active dump site still in the park. It was a two-and-a-half hour drive away on the road into Achray. This road enters from Highway 17, north of Pembroke. Due to our late departure, we decided to spend the night in a Pembroke motel and head in early the next morning.

The road to Achray has three things to recommend it, we found out the next day. First, there is the Space Camp (the Institute for Space and Terrestrial Ecology) at kilometre 71.5 although we did not see it. The second is the "town" of Achray, which is still a whistle stop on the railroad. It was here we photographed some impressive one hundred-year-old white pines, the oldest pines in the park that you can reach by road.

The third is the Barron Canyon which is reached by an

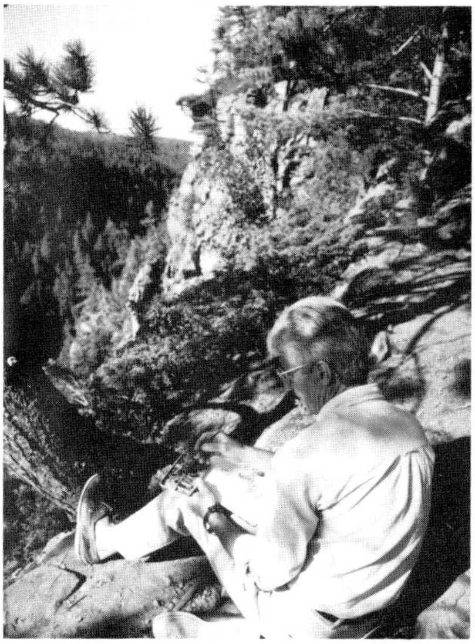

Don McClement produced a small jar of water, some watercolour paints and a sketch pad from his backpack and was soon busy sketching the Barron Canyon. Cameras are not the only tools for exploring the park! (Image 16 & 17; 28mm f 2.8L)

easy hike along a good trail at kilometre 28.9. Be warned that there is no railing or barrier at the edge of this one hundred metre high cut through the park. The view is well worth the hike, and Don couldn't resist taking the time to do a watercolour of the scenery. I, of course, couldn't resist photographing him doing the painting.

Now you will note that none of these three things bears any resemblance, even remotely, to a dump. Oh, we found the dump that we had read about in one of the park guides: it was closed! No garbage ... no bears.

The road itself is more scenic than the Basin Depot road discussed in Excursion 4 but its attraction for wildlife photographers is not much greater. The same comments about wildlife viewing made concerning the Basin Depot road apply here. We did see a moose on this trip; it ran down the road ahead of us only to veer off and disappear into the forest.

By one o'clock Don and I were back in the Highway 60 portion of the park. We were glad we made the trek to the Barron Canyon, but we both agreed it was a long drive from Toronto and not one we'd do in a hurry again.

As I needed photographic material for the chapter on mankind's impact on the forest we stopped at the new Logging Museum in the park. For me it was another trip down memory lane as I had worked one summer as a park naturalist here in the old logging museum back in the sixties. The museum has come a long way since then, and I like the new displays better. I was a little saddened, however, to see that much of the exterior wood of the alligator boat had been replaced since the days I guided tourists around through it. Somehow the old rustic look suited it better, at least I thought so.

After that it was a leisurely drive through the park and then a stop in Port Carling at the Muskoka Lakes Museum where I presented for the first time the slide show I developed while writing this book.

CHAPTER 5

The Human Factor

The ecology of Algonquin Provincial Park relies on many factors, both abiotic and biotic. So far we've looked at the ecosystem here as if it is a natural thing free from the influences of humans. This, of course, is nonsense. Humankind has made its presence felt here and continues to do so.

One might argue that the remote Arctic or the peaks of some mountains are far removed from our influence, but scientists have found traces of pollution from factories even in these spots. Safarists journeying across the African plains

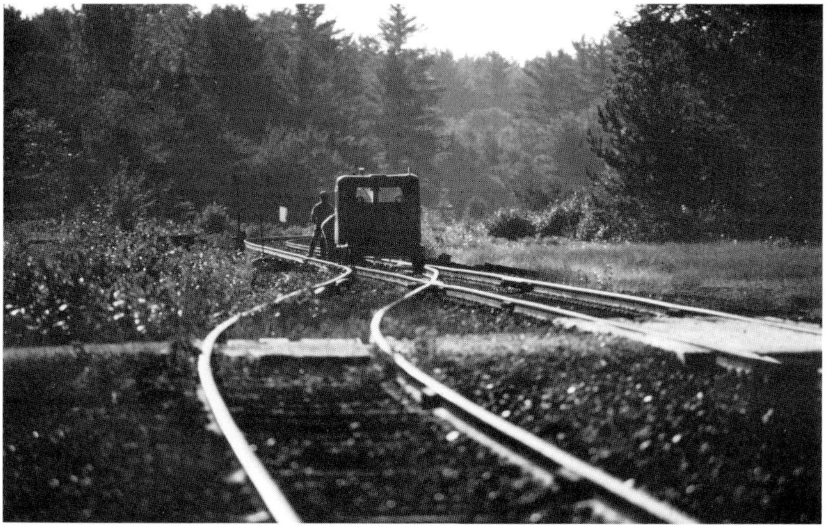

Achray is still a whistle stop for trains. There is a small campground here too. (200mm 2.8L zoom auto-focus)

might feel they are viewing a Pleistocene world but they are not. We cannot escape the influence of our species no matter where we journey.

Indeed, the very fact that Algonquin is a "park" is a direct consequence of our fiddling with nature. Man-made boundaries do not define ecosystems or natural places. A black bear visiting a dump or cottage outside the park is as much a part of this ecosystem as is the same bear within its official boundaries. The bear pays little or no attention to our lines on a map.

The same is true of a moose hunter stalking a bull along the park boundary. The shooting of a moose has the same effect on the ecosystem as any other form of predation. A surplus animal has been removed. (Such hunting, by the way, is carefully managed and is responsible not for an overall decrease in the large game species but an increase!)

These are small only examples of our species' effect but consider the broader influences – pollution, logging, tourism, recreation and, to a lesser extent, even wildlife photography. Algonquin exists because of and in many ways in spite of the whims of people.

I could not write this book on photographing Algonquin's ecosystem without including this chapter. Indeed, perhaps it should have been the first one, since everything I've discussed so far has been touched by human hands, whether it's loons or forests.

ELEMENTARY, MY DEAR SAPIENS

Perhaps I chose to place this chapter last because I try to ignore the human element in favour of the wild land. It is a delusion, I know, but it is one that I share with most of you so I'll dispel it last.

Not, mind you, that photographing the effect *Homo sapiens* has had on this place is an unrewarding experience. It is a challenging and satisfying pursuit. Take the park road for example.

Highway 60 is quite photogenic as it winds through the

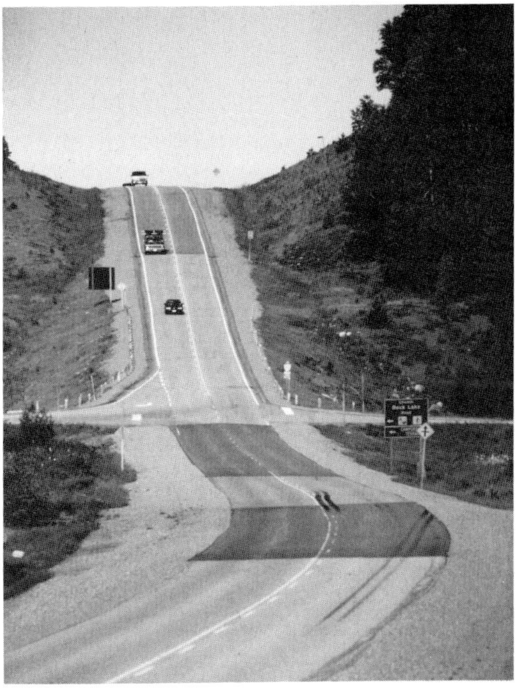

park, especially in the fall when its black ribbon contrasts with the multi-hued forest. I especially like the effect a moderate telephoto lens creates because it tends to compact distances, making this scenic image more spectacular. You've seen this effect used in movies and television commercials, usually where automobiles are being featured.

For a photographer, it is easy to forget the disruption the building of this road must have caused to the ecosystem when it was built in the 1930s. It is just as easy to overlook its benefits, too. In order to maintain a safe highway, it is necessary to keep the forest that borders the road well back from the edge. This is done so that oncoming traffic is visible at a distance.

Highway 60 is always an interesting road to photograph. It is the easiest and generally most productive route in the park for those interested in photographing the park's wildlife. (200mm 2.8L zoom)

For wildlife photographers, this same border provides an open area where animals can be seen. Moose and deer feed here on the young saplings and plants that sprout in the abundant sunlight. It is here that fox hunt mice and voles. Groundhogs dig their dens and, on rare occasions, bears seek berries here.

OTHER PARK ROADS

In the course of doing research for this book, I drove on some of the other park roads, notably the Basin Depot road and the Achray/Barron Canyon road, and while they are of some interest geologically, botanically and historically, they were unattractive places for wildlife photography. Why?

On these roads the forest has been allowed to grow right to the very edge of the highway, a practice that makes for terrible wildlife shooting because all the animal needs to do is take one step off the road and it disappears into thick cover where there is no view and no light!

Highway 60 is the place to work if it is wildlife you wish to capture on film. Their visibility here is thanks to the hand of man. As noted in other chapters, I cannot resist the chance to photograph moose or other wildlife along the highway and often those pictures include the road as well.

Nothing shows off the long lanky legs of a bull moose better than a photograph of one walking across the road. The image is quite startling, because most people do not associate these animals with paved highways. In order to heighten this effect, I've been known to lie down in order to shoot the moose, although just as effective shots can be made by seeking a low angle from the ditches at the side of the road.

I also like to manoeuvre myself into a position from which I can capture both the wild animal and people in the same slide. Including people in shots with wildlife draws an audience's attention and gives them some idea of how close human beings can get to these creatures. A zoom lens is ideal for it allows you to select the composition you want. I've

Moose cross Highway 60 at all times of the day. I try to exercise caution whenever I drive the park road because I've seen moose veer in front of traffic, even during the day, too many times to take these large mammals for granted. (200mm 2.8L zoom)

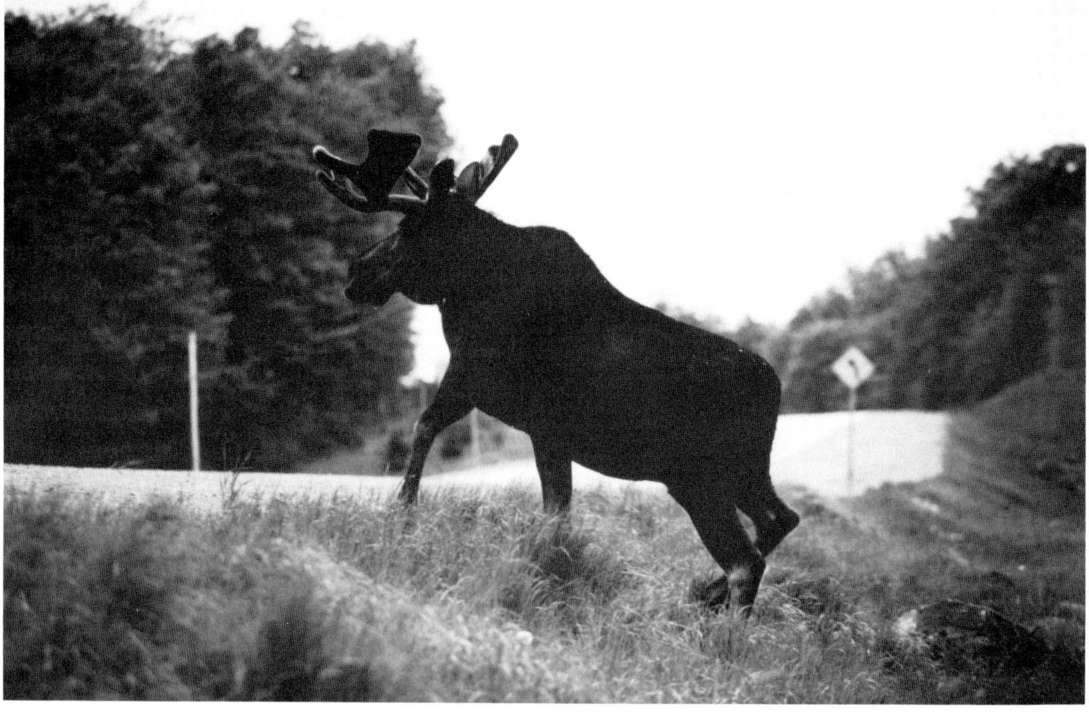

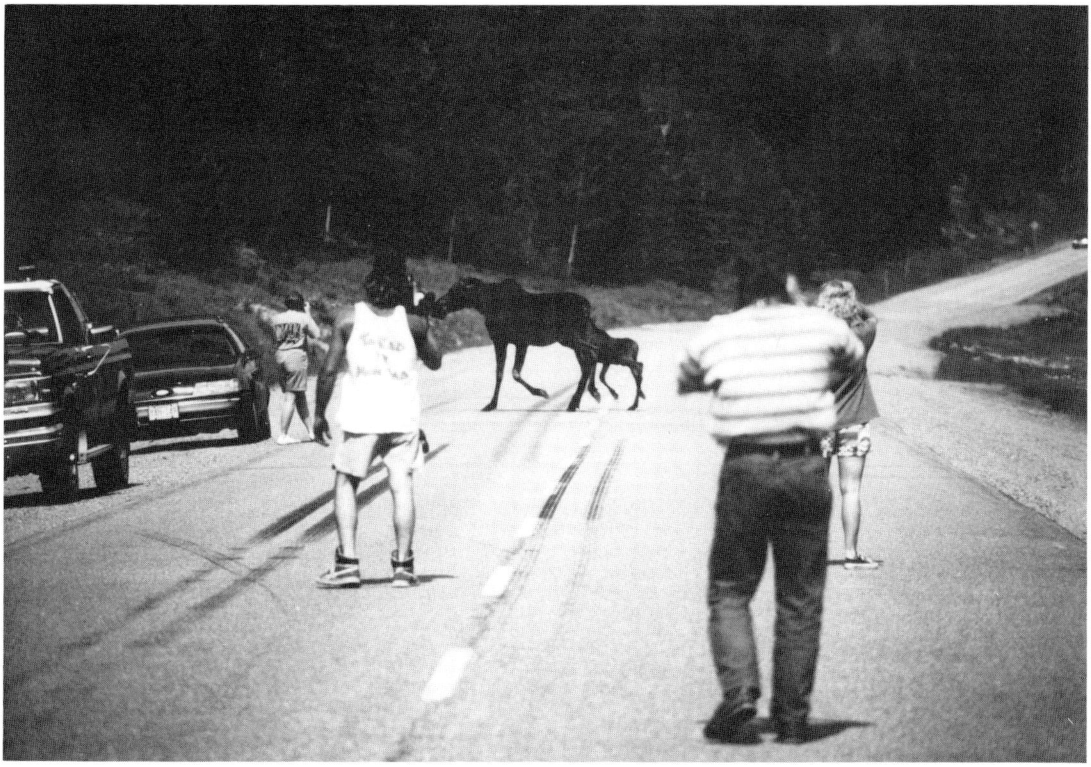

taken portraits of moose in one picture and in the next included onlookers, all without changing position, thanks to the versatility of this type of lens.

Moose jams are a fairly common sight along the road in the spring and summer. The greatest danger here to both people and moose is oncoming traffic. In this case mother and calf crossed safely and so did the people. (200mm 2.8L autofocus zoom)

A TRAGEDY

There is another side to the story of roads, cars and moose. Often it is a tragic one, most often costing the moose its life and sometimes the lives of the people in the car. Moose–auto collisions happen almost every year in the park, so I never drive the road at night without being acutely aware of the danger. Even during the day I've seen a moose run along the road and then veer out right into the path of an oncoming vehicle!

To date I've photographed the results of three of these incidents. Severe damage was done to the cars involved but no one was seriously hurt. Unless you count the moose. In all three cases the moose died. Why would I want to photograph this carnage?

Sometimes a photographer has to move away from recording beauty and instead record "darker" images. I use the pictures of these accidents to illustrate the dangers of driving too fast or too carelessly in moose country. In an ecological sense, these pictures represent a form of mortality in a wild population that can in some places have as much impact on that population as predation or hunting. This is particularly true when applied to deer in the province, for road kills are one of the leading causes of death in that species. Moose road kills, especially in the park, are of only minimal consequence to the population but they still are a loss to the ecosystem. As such, they are a valid subject for my cameras and yours.

At the same time I am conscious of a need not to offend an audience (either in a book or a slide presentation) so I avoid taking photos that are too graphic. A wide-angle lens is the lens I chose here. It allows me to compose an image that tells the story (I can, for example include the dead moose, the meadow, the car and the road in one picture) while it reduces the overall size of the moose and the gorier details.

Some would argue that in a book about Algonquin Park such images, both literal and pictorial, are out of place. This might have been an acceptable attitude twenty-five years

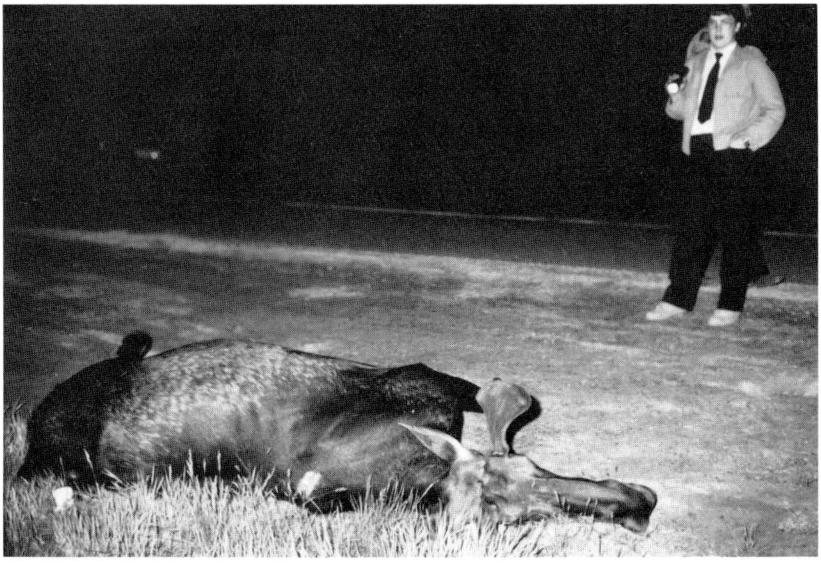

Every year a few moose die in road accidents. Moose are prone to veer onto the road suddenly, even in the daylight. I've come close to hitting one on three different occasions, twice in the park and once in Alaska. Thankfully I was driving slowly and was able to stop in time. (35mm 3.5 flash)

ago but today I feel people want a more honest approach to ecology and the world. No longer is it desirable to view things through rose-coloured glasses (or tinted filters!). It is acceptable to show pictures of predators at a kill. Should it not be just as acceptable to show the impact of humans on the ecosystem as well?

To be honest, a dead moose or two or even the impact of building Highway 60 are minor examples of our effect on the local ecology. Virtually the entire park has been logged and or burned. There are only two stands of four hundred-year-old virgin white pine trees left in the entire park, neither of which is accessible by road. The one hundred year old stand at Achray is the only spot easily visited.

HOW MUCH WOOD WOULD A WOOD CUTTER CHOP?

The logging industry over the past one hundred and fifty-odd years has had a much greater influence on the ecosystem here than the fires which destroyed Yellowstone National Park's forests in 1989. As a photographer-naturalist I cannot ignore that fact, much as I have tried to in earlier chapters.

For, just as the glaciers created the foundation for the park in the last ten thousand years, so has logging created the foundation of the park we now know.

All around us the signs of the massive change wrought on this land by the lumber industry lie quietly awaiting us. Take a walk off the trail almost anywhere in the park and you will find rotting tree stumps busily becoming soil again. They tell of days gone by when great trees covered the land and men arrived in the winter to harvest them. Some remain charred even today from fires in the last fifty years, fires often began by the loggers themselves.

The birch trees, so plentiful on the eastern half of the drive along Highway 60, are recent arrivals taking advantage of the cleared land and the abundant sunlight that the cutting of the pine forests allowed. Even the west side's maple forests are a direct result of the systematic cutting of the white pines.

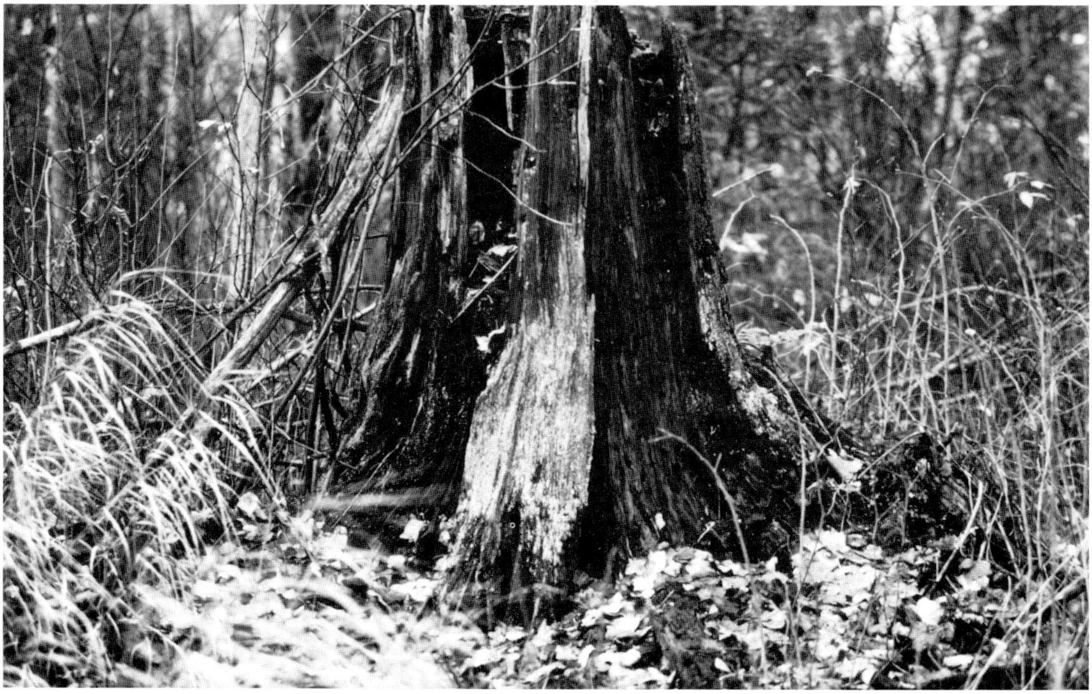

Virtually all of the park has been logged over or burned. Everywhere you look you will find evidence of this in the form of new growth forests, birch trees and old stumps. (28mm 2.8L auto focus)

Many publications produced by the Friends of Algonquin Park tell the story of the logging industry and the changes it brought about. Three of the best are *Booth Rock's Trail*, *Algonquin Logging Museum* and *A Pictorial History of Algonquin Provincial Park*. Also worth a read is *A Chronology of Algonquin Provincial Park*.

After reading these books, I was left with a much greater appreciation for how much this park has changed... and how much better and healthier a park is today's Algonquin than was the park of the 1930s and 1940s. One has only to look at the reproductions in the pictorial history of Algonquin to realize just how much damage and environmental change occurred here during the heyday of logging.

As a youth I imagined that the recent past would have been a wonderful time to be alive. I pictured primeval forests teeming with wildlife, but I know now that was an illusion. The fact is that that imagined Algonquin never really existed, at least not in the recent past.

From the mid-1800s on Algonquin has been reshaped. The

story of much of that handiwork can be captured on film at the park's refurbished logging museum. It presents in words, artifacts and reconstructions a bygone era. I used a combination of a 28mm and an 80-200mm zoom lens to photograph the displays here.

Photographing the creations of man, be it log shanties, alligators (a type of amphibious boat used by loggers), square-cut timbers and log flumes, is not easy. The wide-angle lens was handy for getting the entire structure in the picture but I had to take care to insure that the resulting image didn't look one-dimensional. This often happens when you're photographing buildings unless you take care to include something that gives them some perspective. For example, taking a three quarter view of the structure that includes a view of one of the sides helps a lot. Sometimes shooting from a low angle helps, too.

I used the zoom lens to compact the image, drawing in the forest so that it appears closer and more confining than it actually was. I also used the zoom lens to capture people looking at the objects. The zoom allowed me to take their pictures from a distance so that often they were unaware of the camera's presence and they acted more natural than they might have otherwise.

I must confess that my dedication to recording the logging museum was not strong. A desire to return to the wilder side of the park prevented me from doing a better job on it. Still, I got the images I wanted in order to illustrate the role logging used to play in the park.

Of course, logging is still going on in the park, although all the mills have finally been moved outside its boundaries. If you go on canoe trips back into the interior, you are bound to cross a logging road currently in use or to hear the sounds of logging in the quiet of the evening. The park planners are good about keeping boundaries of forest along the canoe routes thick and wide enough to at least hide most of this work from the traveller.

The most visible sign that most visitors will see of the current logging program is the trucks hauling logs out of the

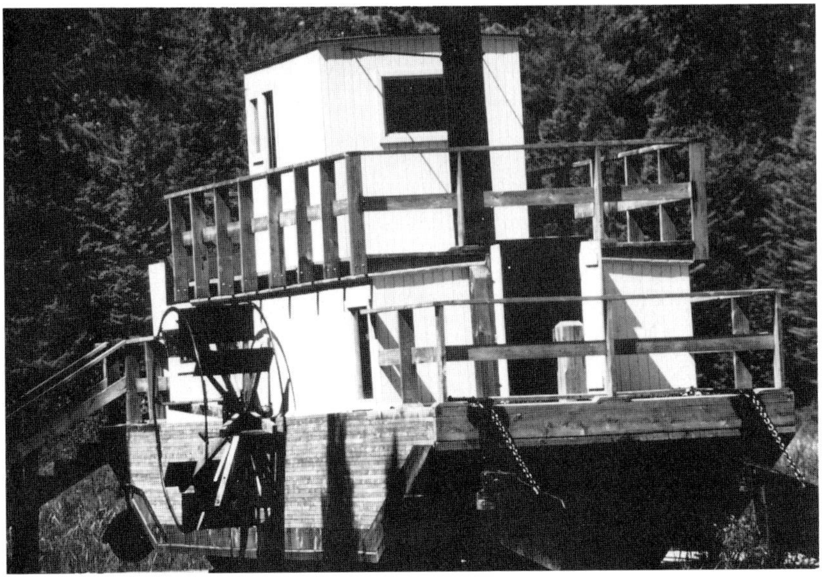

The alligator boat was given this name because loggers were able to haul it overland through a winch and pulley setup. (200mm 2.8L zoom auto-focus)

park along Highway 60. My favourite shots of them are taken in the dead of winter with a long telephoto lens.

I would not wish to leave the impression that I think logging is by its very nature a bad thing. There is an ongoing political dispute about whether continued logging in the park should be permitted. I'll not take sides, for both the lumber interests and the wilderness interests have valid points to make.

Regarding Algonquin's ecology, an argument can be made that logging fills the same role as fire, without the economic loss. A twenty-metre-high forest is of little value to large ungulates because they cannot reach the leaves they need to eat. Fire and logging both create areas where browse can grow within easy reach allowing animal populations to rise.

No matter how one feels about the need for continued logging, it is contributing to the park's ecological balance in one way or another. On the other hand, there is no doubt that some harm is done to the habitat as well. One need only to read about the park in the 1950s and early 1960s to find stories about the tremendous number of deer to be seen along the highway here.

Those deer were a product of Ontario's logging program. Deer were absent from the region until human beings created an environment where they prospered providing lots of browse and few predators. Whitetails were quick to respond and invaded the north, establishing themselves as far as Sudbury in the late 1800s and early 1900s Ironically these northern deer flourished in what was a traditionally poor "deer" area while market hunters virtually wiped out southern Ontario's deer early in the century.

The deer followed the loggers and as they did, they spread brain worm, killing off the resident moose. This is good if you prefer deer to moose in the park. I prefer moose.

WOLVES

Wolves found deer easier prey, and were soon adept at hunting them, especially in winter. People, given their limited understanding of ecology at the time, responded by placing a bounty on the big bad wolf in order to protect the deer herds. Wolves in the park were "removed" (i.e., killed) until 1959 when the practice was stopped so that the animals might be studied.

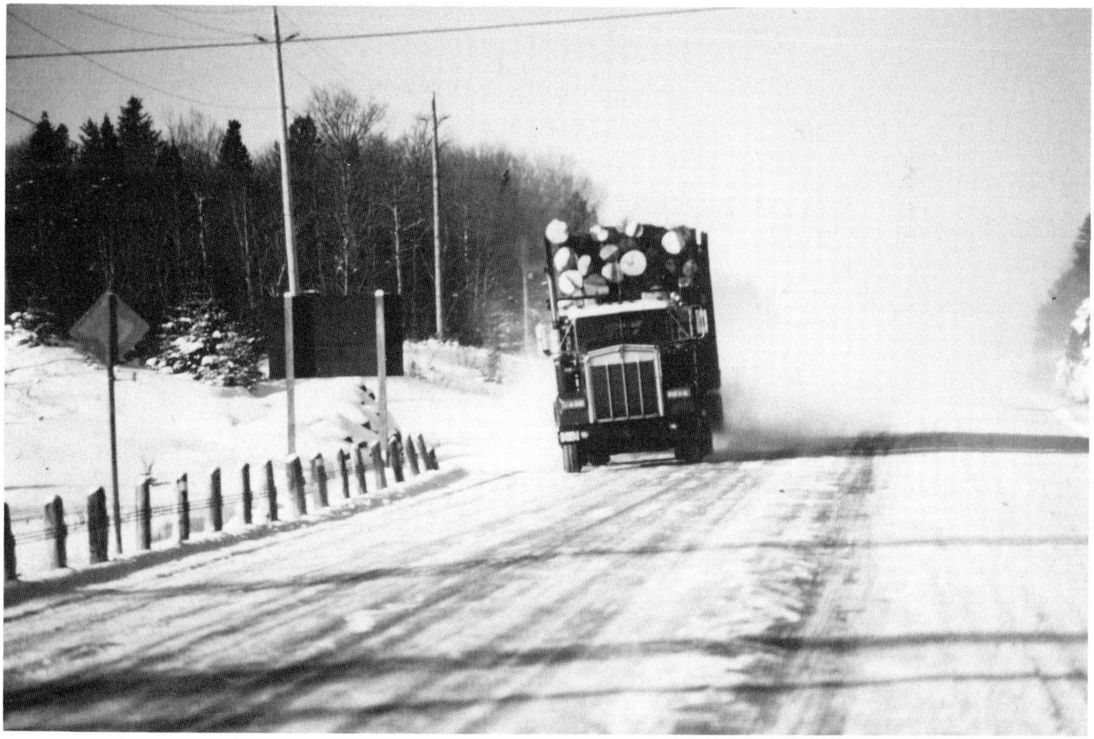

Logging continues in and around the park to this very day. I am especially cautious of the logging trucks in winter and never more so then when I am working one of the park's side roads, such as Rock Lake Road, because the loggers are not really expecting anyone to be using this route but them. (200mm 2.8L auto-focus zoom)

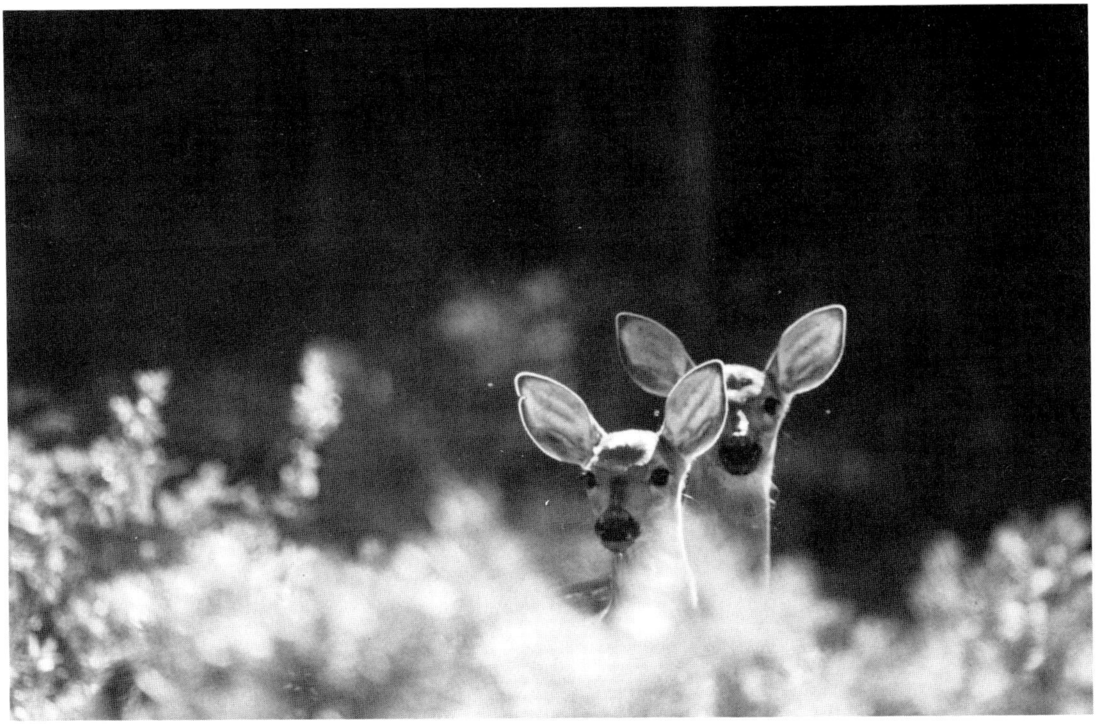

Whitetail deer are making a comeback on the eastern side of the park. These two fawns were orphaned and may have lost their mother to a large cream coloured wolf I saw in the area. (500mm 4.5L)

Enlightenment followed and suddenly the public embraced wolves and an Algonquin tradition was born – the wolf howl. These wolf howl nights are a must for a visitor to the park. The naturalists leading the howl have a good record of coaxing wolves into responding, which is a real thrill. Photography opportunities are limited to pictures of traffic and people, however.

Do not feel that you have to attend the park wolf-howl nights. Go to the museum and listen to the recorded sound of wolves and then try to imitate their howls at night. Drive the road, make frequent stops and give it a shot. You likely won't succeed but you may get lucky, and then you are in for a magical serenade.

Not, mind you that howling is a prerequisite. Several years ago, I was waiting for a ride at the junction of Rock Lake Road and Highway 60. It was nearly midnight and it was dark. I started to sing "The Night Has a Thousand Eyes." Soon wolves interrupted me from a distant hill. I stopped and listened.

When they stopped, I started singing again. Some minutes later so did they. This time they were closer.

I waited until they stopped and then began singing once more. This time when I stopped, I could hear a scratching noise on the highway's pavement. I was surrounded by wolves! They were very close and everything I knew about them and people went right out the window. I was scared!

They soon left, and the next day another ranger and I came back and looked for tracks. There was "sign" of at least two adult wolves and several pups. It is a memory I cherish and an experience I will never forget or duplicate.

WHERE THE DEER WENT

In the late 1960s, the deer began disappearing and every old-timer I met knew the cause – the wolves were killing our deer. It looked like public empathy might turn once more against the wolf. Fortunately, the research done on wolves in the park and elsewhere had finally made the public recognize the important role of predators in the ecosystem, and Algonquin's wolves were spared. The researchers were also able to point out the true culprit that caused the deer population to plummet. An aging forests provide less browse for the deer and this coupled with a few severe winters was enough to dramatically reduce the park's deer herd.

With the decline in the deer herd, the wolf numbers appear to have dropped only slightly. The wolves were apparently unable to adjust their hunting techniques to handle much larger moose in the seventies but they were able to maintain numbers by including a higher percentage of beaver in their diet.

Research like this has come about in part because Algonquin provided an ideal and convenient place for biologists and students to work. I had occasion to visit the research facilities several times when I was writing for *Ontario Out of Doors* magazine about such things as moose numbers or wolves. For the casual visitor, however, such visits are most likely out of the question as they would take researchers away from their tasks.

Still, it is possible to photograph some of their handiwork

and occasionally the researchers themselves. Along Highway 60 you may from time to time find a moose with a radio collar on its neck. A picture of one of these animals makes for an interesting shot that is different enough that a tale can be spun for your audience, like the one told above.

I've also come across marked turtles, basking on logs and any visitors in winter will almost certainly find banded grey jays raiding their camp.

THE PHOTO SCRIPT

Speaking of camps, I find it helpful whenever I set out on a canoe trip to mentally map out a shooting script of the images I will need. Camping and canoeing are major recreational uses of the park and can therefore be considered to be part of the human impact on the ecology. Park rules seek to minimize this impact by restricting the type of food containers used, designating campsites and providing outhouse facilities. I keep these in mind when planning my "camp" shoots.

Camp cooking takes time, patience and talent as my eldest daughter found out. We eat very well on our trips and take care to pack out all garbage. (28mm 3.5 auto-focus)

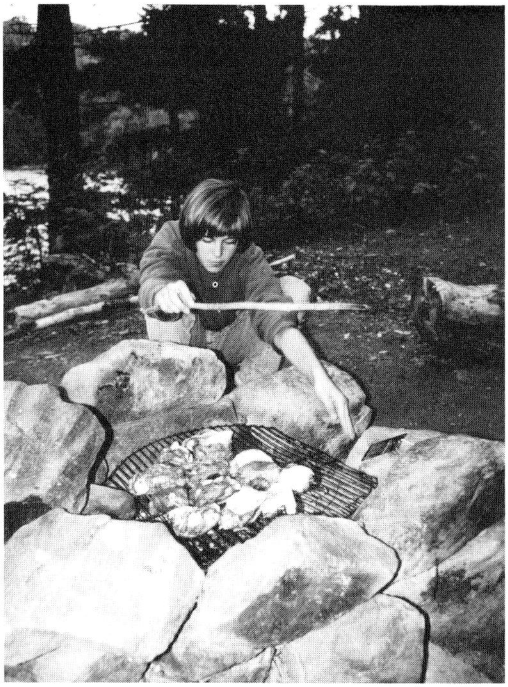

A typical script would include the following:

- pictures of our departure site, including unloading the cars and packing the canoe,
- slides taken from my canoe of the others heading out, as well as shots taken of our journey in,
- pictures of the campsite, including food preparation, tents, campfires, hairwashing, outhouses (with no people using them) and other activities,
- pictures that show what we did, such as having a shot showing campers looking at a feeding moose,
- pictures showing the weather.

You might well ask why I'd bother to take some of those shots, especially of the washrooms. Experience as a speaker over the years has taught me that audi-

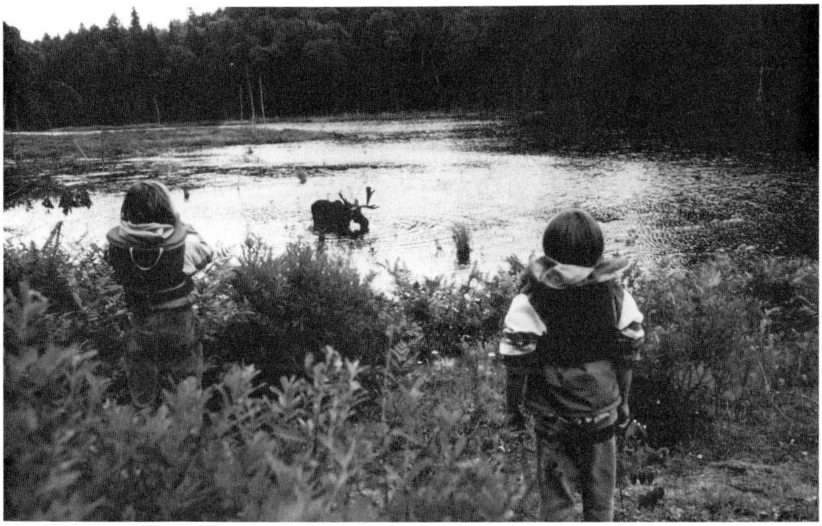

One of the biggest thrills I get is introducing young people to wildlife. This is Kathleen Bowyer's and my daughter Liza's first encounter with the moose. They were nine and seven at the time. I don't know how old the moose was. (35mm 3.5)

ences want to know about the mundane things as well as the spectacular. Sometimes it is those mundane things that audience members can most readily identify with.

I remember a washroom in Kenya's Lake Nakuru National Park that was certainly different. It consisted of a hole in the floor of the outhouse with two large metal handles on either side to help steady the user. I did not take a picture of it but I should have, for it would have truly illustrated my "culture shock" to the audience. Some of Algonquin's backwoods kybos make that one look downright luxurious!

When I shoot pictures of my trips, I do so for at least two reasons. The first is to record for family and friends the experience so that they might share in it. The second is for marketing either to photo agencies, books or magazines. As a photographer, amateur or professional, you will want to consider your "market," too.

Who will be your consumer? Photography is, after all, an art and art is meant to be shared. Perhaps it will be with a spouse, a child or a friend. Perhaps it will be to a wider audience. I think photographers owe them some thought. What would they like to see? What can I tell them through pictures?

At the same time, however, you as the artist must be true to your own vision and shoot for yourself first. Some images

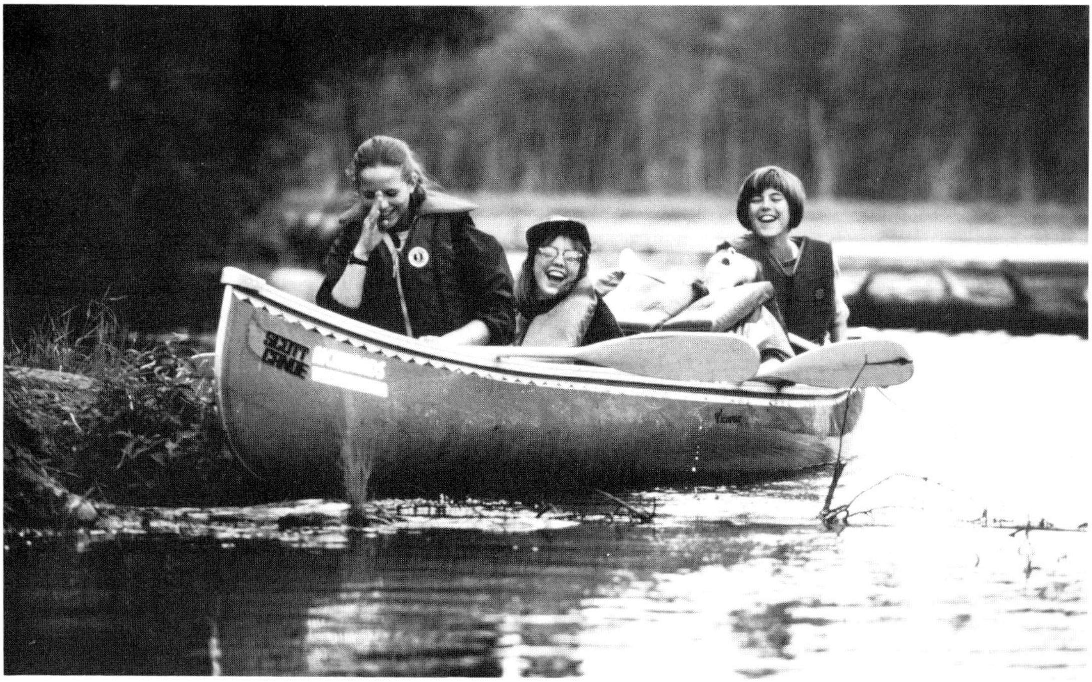

The "Daughters," Heather Watts, Kathleen Bowyer, Heather Stanners and Liza, share a laugh as they fail to navigate over a small (very small) beaver dam. (200mm 2.8L auto-focus zoom)

will work and some won't and every time you share them, you run the risk of having your efforts rejected. You also run the risk of having them accepted even when you don't find them particularly worthy. Learn from both and incorporate what you learn into your next photographic excursion.

One area where I find my photographic awareness has been heightened is my own need to photograph people with animals. There was a time when I went out of my way to avoid including a human being in my wildlife pictures. Now I go out of my way to incorporate them. Why? Because my audiences enjoy them and I have learned to enjoy them, too.

From the ecological perspective, it makes good business sense as well. Animal watching is a fairly non-intrusive way for our species to interact with theirs. It is big business in some places and although there are negatives such as the possibility of disturbing the animal's routine or causing the animal to habituate to people, there are many benefits. The main one is that viewing wildlife encourages people to become involved with these animals and their ecosystems.

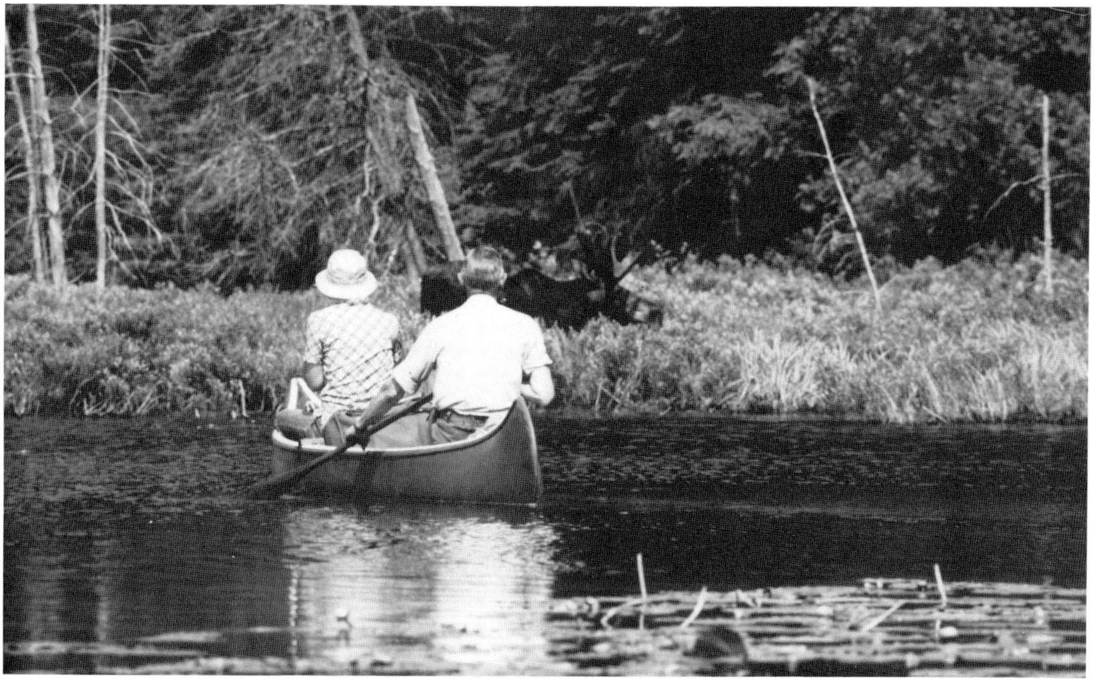

There is nothing like seeing a moose from a canoe. Usually the moose will let you get quite close, probably because it feels confident in its ability to escape – or dunk you! (300mm 4L)

OF MOOSE AND MAN... AND WOMEN, TOO

Photographs of people looking at wildlife can be used to encourage others to try it. I know that safari brochures enticed me to go so that I too could sit in a vehicle next to a lion or see a whale breech. I can't back it up with data, but I'll bet the articles I've written about fish viewing or seeing Algonquin's moose or Rondeau Provincial Park's deer have drawn people to these places. I hope this book does the same.

Photographing our species with theirs is a valid thing to do, but how do you do it? Sometimes a wide-angle lens works but I've found that if you are able to include people and moose in the same frame with this lens, the animal will be small and unimpressive.

A telephoto lens is much better. Often at a "moose jam," I'll quietly manoeuvre into a position where I can shoot the animal while including part or all of one or two human onlookers in the picture.

A zoom lens gives me flexibility in composing the picture. At 80mm I can get the whole body of the person(s) and the moose in the same shot; at 200mm I can isolate the animal with the out-of-focus head and shoulders of the viewer framing the moose.

The easiest shot is to shoot from behind the tourists, but I am always looking for opportunities to shoot so that the animal is in front of the people. It is a different angle from the shots most people take, and that makes it more interesting.

Don't overlook opportunities to show animals crossing roads or with signs in the picture. Think about your angle. Should you be standing, kneeling or lying down? You may wish to consider recording things like the new park museum, nature trails, park signs, entrance gates and park stores. The park museum's displays are among the best I've ever seen and it may be the only place you'll see a wolf or a rutting bull moose.

All in all, recording the human impact on the park's ecosystem, both good and bad, could be a worthwhile challenge on its own.

Algonquin is a special place that will never fail to provide photographic opportunities no matter what your approach to it may be. I've discussed only one approach in this book, but there are many others. Perhaps you are a specialist and want to photograph only birds or mushrooms. Then again underwater-Algonquin or Algonquin's people may call to you. Maybe all you wish to take home are your family's memories.

It is also a good place to begin a photographic study of ecosystems and to come to some understanding of them. Apply what you learn here to other trips and apply what you learn from those to your next visit to the park.

No matter your interest, I'm certain the park will accommodate and test you. Enjoy it.

Excursion 6

Saturday, September 17

As noted earlier in this book, Algonquin can be a stingy or a generous hostess. She was the latter on this trip.

I left home at 5:45 and was in the park by 8:30. Once again I was alone because social engagements prevented my usual companions from joining me. By nine I had spotted cars pulled off to the side of the road. I knew it was a moose but was it a bull or a cow?

It turned out to be both. There was a calf, too. The only problem was they were fifteen metres or so back in the bush, a problem which was compounded by overcast skies. I took a few pictures in the low light with my 300mm f/2.8 and my 80-200mm f/2.8 lenses and then I had to make a decision. Should I leave or should I stay and try to work these three animals in the hopes that I might catch a break with the lighting conditions?

I chose to stay and quietly entered their domain after the last car had driven off. For the next hour and a half, I was alone with these three animals – watching them, photographing them.

I do not suggest such intimacy with moose, for they are big and potentially dangerous animals. I felt reasonably comfortable doing this only from having had years of moose-watching experiences from trips to the park, the Rockies and

Alaska. Even at that, I was very wary and respectful of the animals and never pressed them. Most of the time I stood still and watched, letting them move towards or away from me as they chose. At one point all three came to within less than four or five metres of me. I stood very, very still then.

Finally they moved out into the open and crossed the road, which provided me with the very opportunity I wanted and I got some good shots. Once they crossed the road, I started to follow them into the woods, but the bull made a bluff charge at me and I felt it was time to leave them be. At least for a while.

Down the road I photographed a young falcon which I thought might be a peregrine. It turned out to be a merlin when I looked it up in a bird field guide. I also saw and photographed another hawk.

Around one thirty I photographed a cow moose feeding by the road and a spike horned bull which might have been a yearling. His antlers were the oddest I've ever seen on a moose as they went almost straight up.

I drove on, hoping for more wildlife to see. I was surprised by the lack of fall colours – only about 3% of the trees had turned.

While in the park I made stops at the Opeongo Outfitters store, the Visitor Centre and a few ponds where I thought I might find moose. Nothing.

At Mew Lake I watched a blue heron spear fish and I revisited the falcon, which seemed to have taken a liking to the stretch of highway by Lake of Two Rivers. No moose, though, despite several slow drives through the park.

I decided to try once more for the trio of moose I had last seen three hours ago. I'd noticed there was a well-used trail where the moose had vanished, and I thought I'd give it a hike. It turned out to be a portage route.

I went very quietly along it listening for the cow's call or the bull's. I heard nothing until I got to the end of the portage where the trail crosses a hydro line. I had just passed this opening when I heard a noise. I stopped and turned slowly.

There in the ferns I could see something moving. I knew it was a bear.

I stood very still and slowly raised my camera. The bear paused, unseen, and then stepped out onto the trail a few metres in front of me. I took his picture. He didn't even turn to look at me but rather spun and hightailed it out of there.

The one question that nagged me all day was whether I would have had better luck if I hadn't stayed with the first three moose. I'm always second-guessing myself and usually I never find out, but today I did. When I got back to my car, I met a photographer from the States who had also photographed those first three moose. He chose to leave while I stayed to work them. I asked him if he'd seen any more. He hadn't. In fact, in three days in the park, they were the only moose he'd seen.

I'd made the correct decision.

Can you imagine a better day? I came home higher than a kite.

CHAPTER 6

A Word About "Knowing"

One of the questions I often get when doing a slide presentation is: "How do you know all this stuff?"

As a writer and amateur naturalist, I get my information from three sources: conversations with researchers, from the media and through personal experience.

The most important of these is without a doubt media. A few years ago, that heading would have referred only to books and magazines, but today it has expanded to include video tapes and CD-ROM programs for the computer. No one can know everything about an ecosystem. There is just too much to know and there are too many volumes on any given topic for the researcher to sift through.

The core of my research "facility" is my personal library. It contains about one thousand volumes of books on the subjects that interest me. It also includes material that relates directly to ongoing projects, such as this book. As noted elsewhere I have a bias towards game animals and birds so it was necessary to build up my resources on Algonquin's geology and plant life for this project.

I also tape nature shows for future reference. While I find these helpful, I do not use them as a primary reference unless they are very current.

For current information, I rely more on magazines and

newspaper stories. For this book the magazines I found most useful were *Natural History, National Geographic* and *Discovery.* However, sometimes you get lucky as with the information on the pitcher plant that just happened to appear in the *Toronto Star* the very day I was photographing this species for the chapter on waterways.

Current information is readily available in most cases from the Ministry of Natural Resources and Friends of Algonquin Park. The park publication, *The Raven* was "must" reading for my research.

It also helps to have a friend or two who will discuss and debate points with you. I find that sometimes a fresh point of view can alter my thinking.

Any writer can do this type of research without ever leaving the office but doing it that way has no appeal for me. Over the years, I've had to write articles on assignments about places I've never visited, and these pieces have been the least personally satisfying of all my writing.

Indeed, I find being there with a camera in hand enriches my understanding of the complexities of nature. Such first hand experiences work as a two-way highway to this understanding.

Very often I will photograph something I've never seen before and that will lead me back to the books to find out more. On the other hand, I also find that having done research before I go out taking pictures makes me more aware of the "behaviour" of animals and plants. I find myself looking for certain things that I might have otherwise overlooked.

Being out in the field also raises more questions than it answers. I am constantly amazed about how little we know about nature and how tentative some accepted facts really are.

The books tell you that a pitcher plant is a carnivorous plant but recent research finds that it is not.

Loons in Ontario were believed to be rapidly declining but again, recent findings show that they are stable in numbers.

Mallard males are commonly believed to desert their hens

after the mating season, so why is it that I consistently see males near or with the hen and her brood?

Sitting in a canoe or standing by a roadside observing nature, one is constantly learning things that stretch the limits of one's curiosity and understanding. Capturing those things on film just adds to the experience for me.

ECO-TOURISM

Don't underestimate the importance of travel and eco-tourism. Ecosystems are a global matter and to view one and interpret it well, it is an invaluable aid to have viewed another. I truly believe that having been to Kenya's Masai Mara game reserve makes me a better writer about Algonquin Park. For example, I've seen wild dogs, the wolves of the Mara, hunt and kill gazelles. This gives me a better understanding of the role of Algonquin's wolves in their ecosystem. I "know" how wild canines hunt and kill.

On the other hand, having worked with Algonquin's wildlife for so many years, I've learned a great deal about approaching wildlife and "reading" their behaviour. Practise, practise, practise.

I cannot imagine photographing and interpreting any place without bringing previous experiences into consideration. Nor can I imagine ever "finishing" work on an ecosystem and doing the definitive job. There are always new challenges that you can begin to grasp only if you are out there.

Finally, I try to make it a rule not to write about something I have not had some personal experience with. I'm not always successful in this endeavour but trying to keep to that guideline certainly opens new doors.

PART 2

PHOTOGRAPHIC EQUIPMENT AND RECOMMENDATIONS

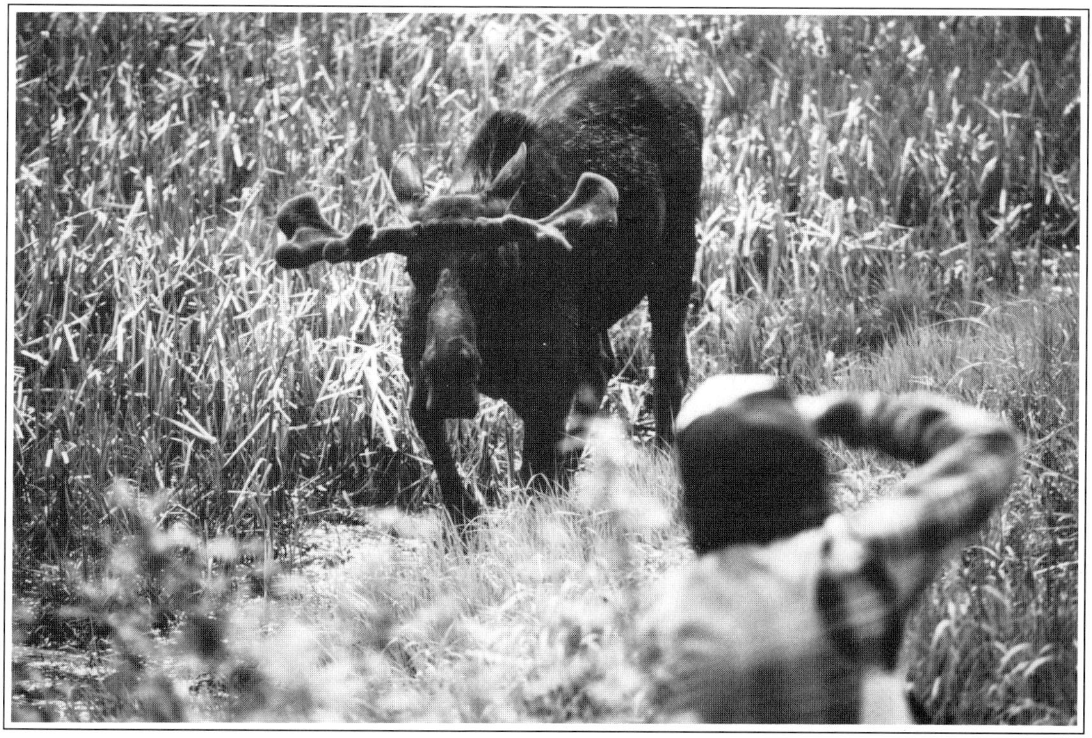

Photographing people photographing moose can be a challenge. I used a zoom lens to compact the distance between Jim Markou and the bull. I don't suggest you get this close. (200mm 2.8L zoom auto-focus)

CHAPTER 7

The Right Camera

Virtually every person who visits the park carries a camera, or at least it seems that way. But which camera should you buy before starting out to photograph Algonquin's ecosystems?

Selecting a camera is not as easy it is may seem. There is no such thing as the perfect camera for all the different things a park visitor might want to use one for. Let's take a look at several different options available. One will probably come close to describing how you see your photographic needs.

Recently a fisherman came up to me and asked my advice about cameras. Before I even started, I turned the conversation back to him. "What do you want a camera to do for you?" I asked.

"Well, it can't be too big. I'm a fly fisherman and I'm usually pretty loaded down with gear. I guess I'd like it to fit in my vest pocket." He went on to say that he really wanted a camera that was simple to operate but still good enough to take pictures of both scenery and the fishing trip itself. He was fortunate because the vast majority of cameras made today are designed to fit his needs.

The cheapest and most common of these cameras are the Instamatics. You may have been given one as a child but they've changed a lot since those days. The really cheap cameras that I remember have been replaced by throwaway cameras that are little more than a roll of film with a cheap lens attached. Both Kodak and Fuji make versions of these, and for the money, they're not a bad buy. When I was in Hawaii recently, I noted that they even have a version that snorkellers can use to a depth of a few metres.

They are limiting in that they take only colour prints (I prefer slides) and you get only what you pay for. *National Geographic* will not likely come after you for their next cover if you use this type of equipment.

A step above are the reusable Instamatics. They take much better pictures and offer a wider range of film choices. The film comes in a cartridge that you drop in and take out. No rewinding or loading problems here. I would suggest, however, that the next type of camera is a better value.

SIZE IS IMPORTANT

Look at a 35mm (that's the size of film they take) "pocket" camera. There are several brands available and all offer a wide variety of options. You should consider the following features.

First, the size. There is quite a range that varies from one brand or model to the next. Many are truly "pocket" size – if you have a fairly large pocket. (Only the 110 Instamatic cameras will actually slip into a normal shirt pocket.) All will fit in a purse or fanny pack. You will have to make certain it fits your own guidelines for "easy carrying." For example, you may not want to carry it in either of the above mentioned places. Perhaps it has to fit in a fishing vest pocket or a backpack. Test fit the camera before you buy it.

Second, lens quality. The quality of the lens is important but until you have used it, it will be difficult to judge. Don't let plastic lenses throw you, however. These days they can be every bit as sharp as glass ones.

Third, the flash. I like a built-in flash and if the price is reasonable I'd go for a "smart" camera that knows when to use a flash and will tell you. I sold cameras for a while in the early 70s and I'd swear most of the sales requests began with "I need a camera any idiot can use." These new 35mm's qualify. The simplest have a wide-angle lens built into them so that virtually everything past arm's length is in focus.

THE SPEED OF FILM

Look for a camera that sets the film speed automatically, and consider how fast a film you will generally use. The typical colour films most people use are rated from 100 to 400 ISO. We'll go into details in the next chapter about speed, but what you need to know here is that the ISO number is a guide to how "fast" the film is. The higher the number, the lower the amount of light needed to expose the film. Therefore 100 ISO-rated film needs more light than 400 does. Cameras are rated to take ISO numbers from 25 up to 2000 and beyond. A normal range for outdoor shooting is anything between 100 and 400. There are occasions when you might want to use the faster films. If you are going to photograph a raccoon raiding your food in the middle of the night, you'll probably need to use ISO 2000 film!

For almost any photography you are likely to do, the ISO ratings between 100 and 1000 will be fine but *not for me.* I shoot 64 ISO slide film for magazines and book reproduction so I have to be picky about the ISO rating on a camera. Many of these less expensive cameras are not rated that slow. Some professionals shoot 25 ISO film to get even greater image sharpness so you should ask yourself if you have any need for large blow ups.

IT'S ALL IN THE REFLEXES

Spend a little more money, and you can move into "pocket" cameras that have zoom lenses, auto wind and rewind, and auto-focus. If you are around water frequently in your travels look at some of the waterproof models.

I own a fairly simple pocket camera but seldom use it any more. I bought it for a horseback trip in the Rockies and it took great pictures but I felt I needed greater versatility.

These cameras run anywhere from $100 up to $400. When you start getting into the high end of this range, though, I'd suggest you look at a 35mm reflex camera. They are a bit bulkier (some are a lot bulkier!) but they do have features which I like.

Reflex cameras allow the photographer to "look" out through the lens. You see exactly what will be in your picture instead of a close proximity, which is what the pocket cameras give you. This is important when doing close up work or when framing is crucial to your subject.

The main benefit of a reflex camera, though, is that it can take other lenses beyond the standard one the camera comes with. In fact, many of these cameras are priced "body only" and the lens is extra. I will discuss lenses in the next chapter.

These cameras are among the most popular on the market. For this book, I used the Canon EOS Elan for all the excursions and for earlier work I used Canon T90's, but other reputable brands include Nikon, Pentax and Minolta. The technology behind these cameras is changing rapidly, so shop around before making a final decision. At this writing the two leading brands among professionals are the Nikon and Canon EOS systems. They are high-quality cameras that, like most of the others above, have built-in flash, auto rewinds, automatic exposure and self-focusing.

SOME PIPE DREAM!

I can remember joking in the early 70s that an auto-focus camera was a pipe dream. How could any camera be smart enough to actually focus itself? How would it know what to focus on? Today I am amazed each time I handle one. Unlike early models, today's auto-focus 35mm can shoot through windows and grass to achieve sharp pictures every time. Canon even has one with a feature called "predictive-focusing." The camera and lenses are capable of judging where a subject will be when you fire the camera. In effect, the camera allows for the split-second difference in time between when your brain orders your finger to fire and when the finger actually releases the shutter.

Purists will argue that such a camera takes all the creativity out of photography. Perhaps they're right – but there have been few times when my creativity has not been equalled by today's technology. Let the purists have their way – I'll go with the competitive edge.

Which of these cameras should you buy? That will be up to you, your pocket book and your aspirations. The auto-focus reflex cameras are perfect for the point-and-shoot type of photographer as well as the serious professional. They are somewhat more intimidating and bulkier than the simpler cameras such as the Instamatics and pocket models we dealt with first. When you add lenses to the reflex camera, it became much more expensive, but it is a more flexible camera. As noted, once you are in the $400 price range you should consider both and buy the one you like best.

I like reflex cameras because of their versatility. If the assignment is to photograph duck hunters in a blind or anglers in a small boat, the reflex camera combined with a wide-angle lens is perfect. But I also have the flexibility to change to a telephoto to shoot wildlife or creative scenics while still using the same camera.

For professionals, there is no other route to go. Clients demand high-quality material, and my back demands a camera of reasonable weight. I could choose a large-format camera but they are expensive, bulky and heavy, especially when you add a telephoto lens to your kit. For most active outdoor people they are a poor choice. The 35mm reflexes are the perfect compromise. They are reasonably sturdy, fairly lightweight and with the right lens they produce sharp photographs. The automatic ones have pretty much eliminated any problems and left the photographer free to concentrate on the image.

What impresses me the most with the cameras I use?

The exposure. Exposure is something you are forever trying to get right, especially in slide film. Black and white film and, to a degree, colour print film have a greater tolerance of dark and light. Colour films may be under- or overexposed several stops and still give an acceptable image,

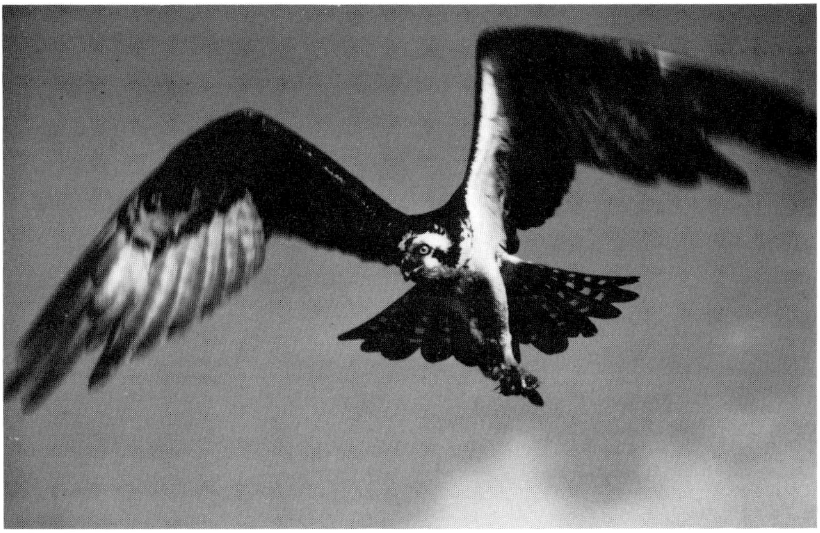

This osprey was photographed with a manual focus lens. Since then I have switched to auto-focus and greatly increased my success rate. (500mm 4.5L)

thanks to latitude that the printing process brings to the equation.

Slide films lack this tolerance. If you are shooting slides of a well-lit subject against a dark ground, a choice must be made. Do you want the detail in the lit subject and therefore lose the detail in the shade or vice versa? (I have read that slide films may be successfully exposed one stop below or above the proper rating. My cameras expose the equivalent of one stop below "normal" as this gives me darker, richer images and a higher shutter speed.)

In the past I was always very conscious of this dilemma, even when using auto-exposure cameras. There were three auto exposure readings available on my old Canon T 90s: averaging, centre-weighted or spot. All worked well once you knew what each would do.

Averaging took a reading of the light and dark areas visible in most of the view finder and then selected the appropriate exposure. This worked well on overcast days or with uniform coloured animals in more or less uniform backgrounds. (It was also perfect for zebras because the black and white stripes balanced out.) Averaging did not work well with black animals such as bears and moose against light backgrounds, light animals against dark (or light) backgrounds and scenics where the main colour was green (the green was usually washed out). Solution? Switch to centre-weighted if the subject was surrounded by a very contrasting background or foreground. If the subject was small or isolated, such as a white bird lit by a ray of sun in an otherwise dark forest, I'd switch to spot metering.

As good as these solutions are they were not perfect. Once when I was photographing a herd of bison and I was shooting on a spot setting to keep the bulls' heads black against a grassy shore (I took the reading off the grass and not the bull's head) when a bald eagle flew by. My spot meter took a reading off the eagle's black body and made it go grey on the film which in turn caused the eagle's head to wash out. I tossed the picture.

(I should explain here that virtually all camera meters are calibrated to what is known as "16% grey." That means they will expose their subject matter so that it balances out. A metered image of white snow will turn the snow grey. A metered image of a black bear will also be grey.)

THE ELAN

Then the Canon EOS Elan came into my life. I knew I had a three-week shoot coming up in Montana and Alberta, and I also knew that I had to produce results. So I decided to give the camera and its lenses the acid test – I'd take them to Florida and shoot nothing but auto-focus and auto exposure placing my trust entirely in the camera's mechanics.

For three weeks in between bouts of Disney World, shopping and beaches with my family, I shot film after film. I shot grey manatees, white egrets, black bears, dolphins and osprey. I shot on grey overcast days, on bright sunny days, in early and late light, in swamps, on beaches, in zoos and anywhere else I found wildlife. I was prepared for an absolute disaster. In fact I backed up a lot of the shooting with my Canon T 90s. I needn't have.

I could not believe the results! All I can say is that the technology in this system is incredible. My white egrets (exposed against blue skies, green jungle and brackish water) turned out wonderfully. The detail is there in the feathers while the background looks perfect. The black bear was black, not grey. The background was, again, bang on. The T 90s, with my expert brain to guide them, did not do as well. Certainly not better.

I knew then that my style of photography was going to change. I was confident that with Canon's auto-focus system I could take on the best and worst the west would offer. My confidence in the exposure capability of the cameras was borne out and was only reinforced doing the work in Algonquin Park.

But these cameras are mainly noted for their auto-focus abilities. I'll discuss lenses in detail in the next chapter, but it is worth noting here that they out performed my manual abilities consistently.

Were their drawbacks to the EOS camera system I used? I found that there were times, especially with grey "round" birds like ruffed grouse and backlit Canada geese, when the camera had difficulty focusing. This was made even more noticeable at certain angles. Was it a serious problem? No, not so far. I suppose it cost me ten or eleven missed opportunities. I didn't lose film because I had set the camera to fire only when it was in focus. (This is one of the options most auto-focus camera have.)

I also worry about the warning the camera instructions carry about not getting wet, which in the Algonquin "rain forest" can be a major concern. I assume that is due to the fine-tuned engineering and electronics in these cameras. So far it has not been a problem but I do take precautions in rain and snow. The Elan is likely not the work horse that the more expensive EOS 1 is but the camera performed to my satisfaction. While working on this book another assignment took me to Alaska where dust became a major concern. Once again, the cameras proved up to the task.

The battery seems to die quickly in cold weather so I carry a spare in my shirt pocket. A quick change and the old one warms up in my pocket while the new one runs down. Then I switch them again. It seems to work. When selecting a camera, you must bear in mind the longevity of your battery. In the EOS system, the bigger telephotos quickly drain batteries and that can be a concern.

The centre-weighted focus on my cameras at times is constricting. It is something you can overcome, either by going to manual focus or a mode where you lock on to the subject before you compose the picture. Still, I find the centre-focusing annoying at times – about once every hundred shots. Some models offer a choice of focusing point, so if this ever becomes a major worry, I know there are ways to solve it.

The other major annoyance is that the programming dial on the Elans does not lock solidly in place except in the "off" position. Sometimes it will get shifted by rubbing against my coat and I'll lose the mode I selected. This problem has caused me to lose a few pictures, so I just try to remember to check the selection dial regularly.

When all is said and done, these are really minor concerns. I like the system and will stick with it. The camera is light weight and exceptionally quiet, perfect for my line of work.

Selecting a camera that is right for you is as personal as buying a car or a suit. Take the time to shop the market. New cameras are coming out all of the time and they are like computers – faster, better and smarter.

CHAPTER 8

The Right Lens

Each person who selects a camera does so with a particular bias. It may be related to cost, size or that person's photographic goals. For some, this latter bias might be the desire to record trip as snapshots, others may wish to do underwater photography, someone else may select a camera that is more suited to nature photography.

The camera, however, is for many only the first of a number of purchases. Next comes the task of selecting the right lens to allow you to achieve your goal. If you selected a camera with a fixed lens (such as an Instamatic or pocket camera) there is little you can do to change it, with the possible exception of adding on close-up filters. Most serious photographers will have opted for a reflex camera with interchangeable lenses because this offers a great deal of flexibility and freedom.

My personal bias is towards lenses that make wildlife photography possible. I am interested in capturing on film a wide variety of mammals, birds and reptiles. Within this spectrum, my focus narrows to a preference for so-called "game animals" and within that field to predators.

This specific need affects my selection of lenses. I want telephoto lenses that allow me a degree of safety and security while still allowing me to record with some intimacy the lives of these animals. I have always had as part of my arsenal of lenses over the years a 400mm or longer length lens which has been the work horse of my equipment.

A 400mm lens magnifies the image eight times more than a standard 50mm lens. With 35mm reflex cameras, the formula for working out the power of a lens is to divide the standard length (50) into the length of the lens. Therefore a 400mm is an eight power, a 500 is a ten and a 300 a six. It works for a wide-angle lens, too. A 28mm wide-angle is roughly a .5, which means it increases the viewing area by about two times making the subject appear smaller relative to the image size.

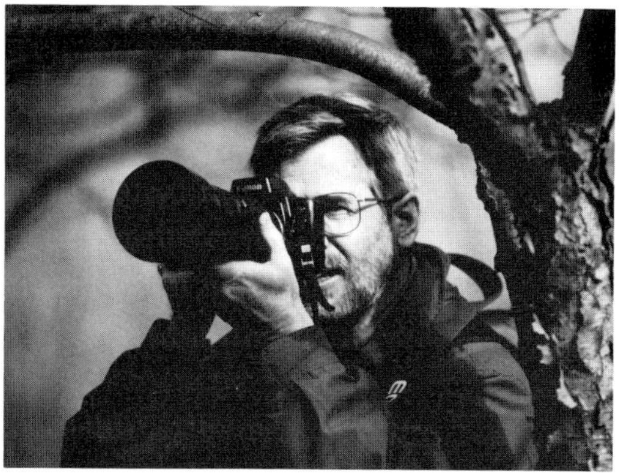

The 80-200mm f2.8L zoom lens is my favorite lens. It is light enough to be hand held and very fast. The quality is excellent. When I hike I always carry it out and ready. (A. Taylor)

I have read many times that a 400mm lens is about the shortest length that should be considered for photographing wild animals. I'm not certain I agree. True, for the past decade, I've used 500mm and 600mm lenses on a regular basis, but during that same time I've found myself drawn to medium-length telephotos. Indeed, most of the wildlife shots taken for this book were done with a 300mm or shorter focal length lens.

THE ANIMAL IN ITS WORLD

I believe the reason for my change stems from a desire to show the animal in its environment. These shorter focal-length lenses allow me to do this. They also allow me greater flexibility in recording animal behaviour. Too often I've felt restricted by the long focal lengths, which take great portrait shots but fail to include enough of the animal's body or surroundings to show what it is the animal is doing.

This is especially true in Algonquin Park, where encounters with wildlife are likely to be along the road or from a canoe. Often, in both these cases, the photographer is fairly close to the subject, and a long telephoto will prove to be too powerful or too constraining.

My advice for photographing the park's wildlife is to purchase a 300mm lens. Choose one that is relatively "fast." This term refers to the lens's largest aperture opening. All lenses are sold by a combination of two numbers – their focal length in millimetres and their aperture opening or f-stop.

Recording an image on film is the product of two things, both of which control the amount of light hitting the film's emulsion and exposing it. The shutter speed of the camera is one of these factors. "Shutter speed" is the measure of time it takes for the camera's shutter screen to open and close. In most of today's cameras, the range is measured from minutes to less than a 2000th of a second. The faster that time is, the less light there is hitting the film. Equally important to remember is that the faster the shutter speed, the less time there is for other things to jigger up your image and blur it (for example, human movement, camera vibration, animal movement, wind, traffic, and so forth).

The second important factor is the lens's f-stop. This is a measure of the diametre of the opening through which the light from your subject passes. If you hold a lens up to the light, you will see the lens's aperture opening. The "faster" or wider it opens the more you can increase the shutter speed of the camera. You can buy a 300mm for the Canon system with f-stops of either 2.8, 4 or 5.6. Other companies offer a similar range of choices. The 2.8 is the "fastest" (which really means largest maximum opening) and therefore offers the greatest flexibility. It is also the most expensive of the three examples. The 5.6 is the slowest (i.e., smallest maximum opening) and cheapest.

What's the difference? On a bright sunny day, all three will work about equally well but let's assume you've come across a moose in late afternoon light. You get set up and are ready to shoot. On a lens with a 2.8 f-stop, the reading is 250th at 2.8. Plenty of light even for a hand-held shot. (As a general rule, the shutter speed should equal or exceed the length of the lens you are using. A 250th of a second is close enough to the 300mm length of our lens that it will work.)

Consider the same situation but with an f-stop of 4. Your shutter speed must slow down to 125th of a second in order to compensate for the decreased amount of light this lens lets in. It is dicey, to say the least, to get away with a hand held-shot although this shutter speed is still sufficient to stop most movement by the moose.

Now try the f5.6. Its shutter speed is a 60th. You can't hand-hold it and even if you could, any movement by the moose would result in a blur.

The obvious choice is the 2.8, isn't it? Yes and no. First there is a question of money. A Canon 300mm f2.8 lists well above $6000.00 while an f4 can be had for around a third of that. For me, though, there is an even greater concern and that is the weight. The glass required to let all that extra light in makes for a very heavy lens, one that demands a tripod. Much of the shooting in Algonquin especially is jump shooting, where your ability to respond quickly often means hand-holding a lens. My first choice is the 300 f4 because it is reasonably fast and lightweight.

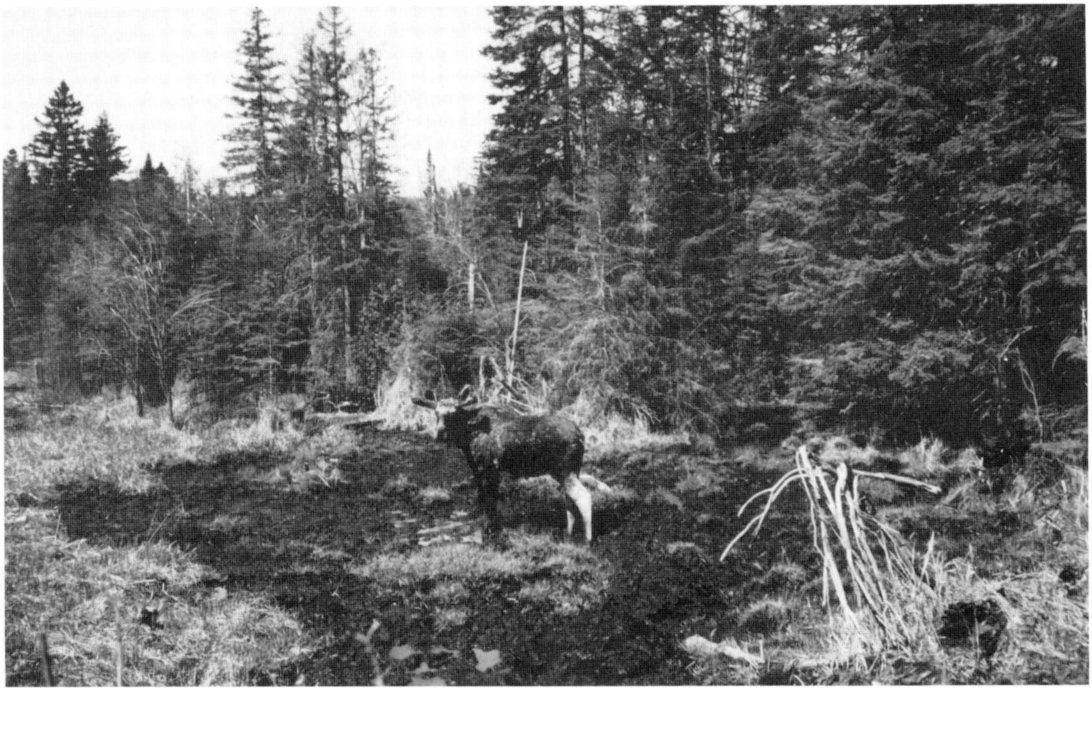

Each spring moose seek out the salty water that collects beside the road. This is the best time to see moose for the muddy salt licks draw them at all times of the day. (28mm 2.8L auto-focus)

TRIPODS AND TELES

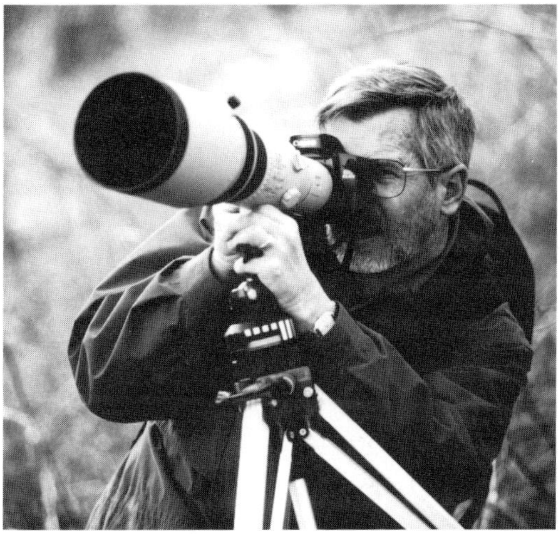

I purchased the 300mm f2.8L for its speed and its quality. It is an excellent lens and can be used with either a 1.4 tele (converts it to 420mm 4L) or a 2 times (converts it to a 600mm 5.6L). All give you great results. (A. Taylor)

I do, however, own and use a 300 f/2.8, which I use mounted on a tripod in low light conditions when it is no longer feasible to hand-hold the 300 f/4 or when there is time to set up the more cumbersome 2.8. My decision to purchase a 2.8 was not based on the f-stops speed alone. I chose this lens because of its versatility when coupled with a tele-converter.

Tele-converters are simply short lenses on which a longer lens may be mounted. Ten years ago they were of poor quality and nobody paid them much attention. Today that has changed. I've used tele-converters for about five years and I have consistently been impressed with the results.

Canon makes two "teles." The first, a 1.4, is usable in the auto-focus mode with both my 300 f/4 and my f/2.8 lenses. It increases the power of each lens by a multiple of 1.4. This makes a 300mm lens into a 420mm lens. The combination of the converter and a 300mm medium telephoto effectively gives you a quality long telephoto lens without the cost.

There is, of course, a drawback. The tele-converter also reduces your effective f stop by the same factor it multiplies your lens' length. Therefore a 300 f 4 becomes a 420 f 5.6 lens while a 300 2.8 becomes a 420 f4 approximately.

The second tele-converter Canon makes is a "two times." It doubles the lens's length and its f-stop. This is where the 2.8 lens becomes worth the extra cash. With the addition of the two times tele-converter it becomes a superb 600mm f/ 5.6. This lens retains all its auto-focus features but the 300 f/ 4 converts to a manual focus at f/8 since the Canon auto-focus lenses work in manual only when coupled with a tele past f/5.6.

The 300 lenses mention above are all "L" series lenses. Other manufacturers use other terms to designate their top colour-corrected lenses, but essentially they correct for changes in the light spectrum. You may or may not need this feature but if you can afford it, buy it.

A LESSON LEARNED AT WOLF HOWL

About fifteen years ago, I had a tremendous opportunity to photograph a bull moose up in Algonquin near Wolf Howl Lake. The sun was rising above the horizon and there was plenty of light. The bull was cooperative and close, and I had time to set up a tripod. I spent almost forty minutes working the animal.

I kept very few pictures. They were all out of focus. What went wrong? It was the early morning light with its orange hue that did me in. The lens I was using was not a colour corrected one. The "L" designation means the lenses are colour corrected for the entire light spectrum. They won't go soft in the orange light of dawn or dusk when the light waves travel at a different frequency than midday light, and therefore the actual point of focus is slightly in front of or behind the normal focal point.

Since the bulk of wildlife photography tends to be done early or late in the day, the "L" series lens which corrects the focal point for all light waves is worth the extra investment.

My favourite lens is a zoom lens, and if you buy no other lens consider this one. It is an 80-200mm f2.8L lens. The maximum length makes it a reasonable medium telephoto while the minimum length approaches a standard 50mm lens. It is fast and lightweight and it is an "L" series lens.

It my favourite because it has tremendous versatility and can be used as a wildlife lens, a portrait lens or a scenic. There was a time when zooms, like tele-converters, were looked down upon by serious photographers but that time has passed with the great strides made by all top lens makers in the last decade.

It is not a perfect lens for a dedicated "large mammal photographer" such as I am. I have increasingly found myself inclined in recent years to record ecosystems. So when I'm in the field, I can usually be seen carrying two camera bodies and two lenses. One of those two lenses is the 80-200 zoom. With it, deciding what goes into a picture becomes a lot easier. For example, I recently was shooting a moose by the road and could, without moving, frame the shot so that only the moose was showing; I could then shorten the lens to include some of the background and draw it back further to include the other people watching with me. My other camera had a long telephoto lens attached so that I was able to cover all the bases from portraits to scenics.

This zoom is especially good for "ecosystem" photographs from a canoe, whether that be a close-up of a water lily or a feeding moose. You can move quickly from the close-up to the environment of your subject without paddling backwards or forwards.

There are times when even an 80mm lens is too much lens for the subject. I own a 50mm 1.8 which, to be honest, I seldom use and a 28mm 2.8 wide-angle which I truly enjoy.

The wide-angle lens was used for a variety of photos in this book and they are not all the obvious scenic shots that one tends to associate with this type of lens.

All the above lenses are auto-focus lenses. For most of my photographic career, I used manual-focus lenses but I've given them up completely. This is not out of some desire to be first on the block with new technology. Indeed, the opposite is more like it. I was likely one of last to move to the new system, believing that my reflexes and abilities were a match for the newer methods.

I was wrong.

When I made the move to auto-focus, I kept my old equipment and tried it out alongside my new "stuff." I won't say the auto-focus systems are perfect but they are a darn sight closer to it than I am. Some of the photographs I've taken recently defy belief, unless of course you are a regular reader of *National Geographic* where such shots are commonplace. Ten years ago if I could have taken the photographs I routinely take now, I would be working for that magazine today.

But, sadly, I am not because I'm not the only one to discover the new technology!

The quality of the auto-focus systems, both camera and lenses, is such that anyone can get *National Geographic* quality pictures.

To succeed as a professional photographer today takes persistence, luck and good equipment. It also takes something the auto-focus cameras can never give you. Talent.

Talent and creativity will always be the most important ingredients of any photographer's equipment. Auto-focus lenses and cameras, no matter how good, are still just the tools of the trade. Whether you wish to purchase and use them is up to you. Many great photographs were taken long before the advent of this technology and many more will be taken by photo-journalists and artists without the aid of these wonders.

Also remember that this book has a decided focus (pardon the pun). It is not my intent to cover the whole range of photographic lenses available. I have not, for example, touched on close-up lenses and macro-photography. Nor have I dealt with super long telephoto lenses or underwater equipment. Just remember that there are lenses available for every interest no matter how specialized or generalized.

Rather than attempt to include all this what I have done is shared with you the equipment I used to create the images used in this book. You must consider the results, the ideas tossed out and then make your own decisions about what is right for you. Like my own decisions, yours will be coloured by your interests, your purpose for taking pictures and your budget.

CHAPTER 9

The Right Film and Other Accessories

The number of types of film on the market grows almost daily. A wide range of film speeds is available in an equally wide range of film types. You can choose from colour print film, black and white film, slides and even a video still picture "film." You can get most of these in speeds from 25 ISO to at least 400 ISO with some rated as high as 2000. There are discounted films, brand name films and bulk films to consider. In Canada, at least, you can buy several films with or without processing included. You can get professional or amateur films, indoor or outdoor... Confused? No wonder!

Before making a decision about which brand or type of film to purchase, let's review some of the basics. Today there are really only three types of film available on the market: colour print, reversal or slide film and black and white. There is a fourth possibility that is not really a film in the technical sense but it is growing slowly in popularity – cameras that take still video discs. This is the one that is called the "film of the future" and once the technology is perfected, it may well take over the market. Today, however, the most preferred choice is colour print film.

If I am shooting a wedding for friends, this is the film I choose. Like slide and black and white films, colour print film comes in a wide range of speeds. I prefer an ISO rating of

400 for many reasons. I find that it has a reasonable grain for most prints and its speed allows me to shoot available light where flash photography is not allowed (such as during a wedding ceremony). When I can use my flash, the higher ISO allows me to reach out for portrait shots with my medium telephoto lens from a much greater distance than a slower film would.

At this point some explanation of the term ISO is needed.

ISO (which in the good old days was also called ASA) is the international code used to indicate a film's speed. The speed of the film is important because it indicates its light sensitivity. A low rating of ISO 25 means the film requires a fairly long exposure while rating of 400 requires much less exposure time. However, because of its greater exposure time, the ISO 25 film will result in a much finer grain and therefore sharper picture than a faster film. This is because the light reaching the camera has longer to saturate the finer grain on the emulsion, resulting in greater detail in the final image.

A colour print film of ISO 400 suits me just fine on those rare occasions when I am shooting print film. None of the images I take with this film will ever be sent to a publisher because they prefer to work with slide film. If your purpose in taking pictures while in Algonquin is to record your trip's memories for personal use, this is the film speed and type I recommend.

Black and white film used to be the cheapest but it has lost much of its popularity due to the public's demand for colour prints and its increased use has brought the cost of developing and printing it below that of black and white.

Black and white continues appeal to dedicated photographers who revel in its shades and tones. It is considered by many to be the "art" film and much of the fun of working with it is in printing your own blow ups. Although I shot many rolls of black and white film to illustrate this book, it is not a film that I recommend unless you own your own dark room.

It is in the dark room that much of the "fun" of black and

white photography happens. With colour slide film, little can be done to enhance an image in the processing unless you go to computerized manipulation. Either you have the image or you don't. With black and white, you have much more control, especially if you learn to "see" in black and white when you are taking the photograph.

As a colour photographer, I have trained myself (or been trained) to see in colour images. When I shot a lot of black and white film I learned to see image in that medium. For example when I took the colour slides of the loon I was picturing the effect the soft early morning light would have on the image. When I turned to my camera, loaded with black and white, my thoughts were about the contrasting greys and how I could manipulate and enhance them in the dark room. The result was two different images, each shot with a different process in mind.

Don't sell black and white short. There is a quality to it that makes it quite worthy of your attention. But you won't see that quality unless you immerse yourself in the darkroom. There, using filters, different papers and techniques, you can create striking images from what at first glance seemed dull pictures.

Don McClement believes that you should view the standard printed photographs you get back from the processing lab as contact sheets from which to work. I think he is right. My experience with both black and white and colour prints has been that the standard prints you get back are printed taking average values. They are a good introduction to your work, but they fall far short of showing off their true qualities. Custom printing of the same images can bring out qualities in your photograph that will amaze you.

The trouble is that for most, the only film that can be developed and printed by the amateur photographer is black and white. (There are very few places around today where you can even get your black and white films developed commercially!)

With slides, the excitement always comes when I open the

box and view the image. With black and white, the excitement never comes until I see the image I create in the darkroom.

If you choose to shoot black and white film, read Ansel Adams' books on the subjects. They are classics by a master of the medium.

NEW TECHNOLOGY AND TRIED WAYS

The newest technology in film and camera types is the video disk camera. Think of these as high quality video cameras that take only stills. I have not owned or even used one of these, and frankly they scare me because I think they could well spell the end of the type of cameras I use. They scare me because they are so darn good! As video resolution increases, the images taken with these cameras equals and surpasses the blow-up capabilities of most films.

Right now this technology is new and relatively expensive to process (if you can find a place to do it) but the future holds promises of vending-type processing machines in every corner drugstore. When these machines become available, you will be able to select your image format: colour print, black and white or slide as well as the image size.

Until that system arrives, however, the preferred film for serious amateurs and professionals alike will no doubt continue to be slide (or reversal) film. They can of course be projected or made into prints. The cost of thirty-six slide images is cheaper than that of thirty six colour prints and slide film continues to be preferred by most book and magazine publishers.

A drawback to slide film is that the film offers very little leeway for mistakes in exposure. Errors in prints can be corrected in the developing but that option is not possible with slide films.

The best advice is to choose one type and stick to it. Too often in the past I have made the mistake of shooting two different types of film only to forget to reset the ISO or, more recently, shooting black and white when I thought I was shooting colour.

I choose Kodachrome 64 slide film. Part of my reason is product loyalty; when I started out twenty-five years ago, Kodak offered reliable processing and consistent results. So far, they have not let me down. I shoot the Kodachrome brand as opposed to Kodak's Ektachrome because I prefer its colour balance over the bluer tones of the latter.

Over the years I have shot Kodachrome films with a variety of ISOs including the ultra-fine 25 and the fast and somewhat grainy 200 speed. On major trips, I still carry a few rolls of the high-speed film but as a general rule I stick with the 64 ISO film. It gives me enough freedom with aperture and shutter speeds to allow me to get the picture under most conditions, while at the same time giving me the sharpness my publishers demand.

I understand from other photographers that Fujichrome 100 is equally good (and some would say superior) but my trust in the Kodak product remains unshakable. Out of the over one hundred thousand slides Kodak has processed for me in the last decade alone, I think two or three may have been damaged by them, and they did everything possible to restore the damaged slide to my satisfaction. That kind of record and service get my loyalty.

I have tried both the professional Kodachrome 64 and 200 speed film and have found them to be excellent but expensive films. I think the value is there for photographers in a position to shoot their films and get them processed quickly. This is necessary since neither professional film has a long shelf life. Heat can be especially damaging to them. I find them impractical for long summer trips and so have stayed away from them.

TRIPODS

I am not the world's greatest expert on tripods. I own a good one but not a top-quality one because a lot of what I enjoy doing in wildlife photography involves stalking and shooting animals the way a hunter would. It is possibly the closest thing I have to a "style."

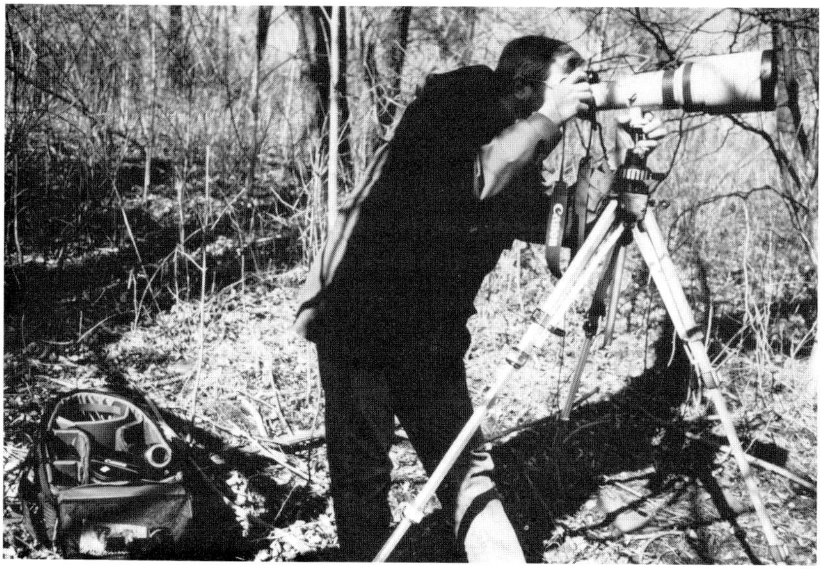

A good tripod is essential. Get one with adjustable legs so that they can accommodate a hillside. A ball and socket head is essential. Stay away from the pan and tilt heads... they are for video and movie camera buffs. On the ground behind me in this shot is my Lowe Pro backpack. It carries my complete outfit and allows me ready access to the equipment. I usually carry my tripod by hand rather then strapping it on to the backpack. (A. Taylor)

Still, about half the photos in this book were taken with a lens mounted on a tripod or monopod. One mistake many photographers make when they buy a tripod is purchasing the wrong type of head mount. Most tripods come with a video or movie camera head known as the "pan and tilt" style. It is easily recognized because the control for this consists of a handle with which you manipulate and guide the camera.

Still, cameras will function in a satisfactory manner on this type of head but wait until you try a ball and socket head! The sheer fluidity of movement possible with this style head is a joy to experience. It seems silly but it reminds of the scene in *Star Wars* where Luke and Han Solo are blasting away at Imperial fighters. The ball and socket's flexibility is similar to the movement you see in the weapons the film's heroes manipulate in this sequence.

Imagine having that capability of movement when following a fast-flying duck or loon! The "ball and socket" head allows you exactly that. At the same time, this head may be locked up to hold a camera or heavy large lens in place to allow for maximum sharpness. My advice is to buy one for your tripod and get rid of the pan-head.

I use a tripod for two purposes. The first and most obvious is to hold steady the longer lenses. Many professionals will shoot all their images using a tripod no matter what length of lens they use and there is no question it pays off in sharper, better composed photographs. You will have to decide how you feel about using one. I'm about the middle of the spectrum when it comes to tripod use – not too heavy into it but I do use one frequently.

The other use I find for tripods is when taking longer exposures. As discussed earlier in the book, I set the camera up and take long exposures. These allow the moving water or animals to blur and often create a pleasing image that shows motion.

There are several alternatives to tripods. The monopod is one. They are lighter and easier to carry, especially on long hikes or when portaging. I do not use a ball and socket head on a monopod (although I do have a spare) but instead mount the lens on the pod's mounting screw. I find little advantage to that head on a monopod as the pod itself is quite easy to tilt, swivel and turn.

The problem with a monopod is quite basic. You can't walk away and leave it standing. It falls down – and if you lean it against something, the chances are pretty good somebody's leg will hook and knock it over.

As a result, when I use a monopod, I generally restrict myself to one camera and lens combination at a time. When I use a tripod I always have two cameras on the go. One, usually with a long lens, is mounted on the tripod while the other has a shorter telephoto that I hand hold while shooting.

When driving the road in Algonquin, I will often use a car window as a support for my longer lenses. Make certain you turn off the motor to avoid vibrations.

In a pinch I have been known to use the guard rails at the side of the road to support a lens but only when things are happening too fast for me to take the time to set up a tripod.

FLASH

Because I have done a fair amount of wedding photography, you would think that I would have got used to a flash. I haven't. I generally dislike the effect of flash photography when used to enhance wildlife shots taken during the day, although I have done it. I have never tried setting up a photo electronic eye to trigger my flash and cameras to capture bats or owls, although I do admire the results of those intrepid individuals who manage this feat of magic. This book's bibliography contains some titles that are written by people who have a much greater knowledge than I do on this subject.

That having been said I do strongly advise you to carry a flash. The one I use has a telephoto feature that allows it to be set for a wide-angle, a normal and a short telephoto lens depending which you are using. I've found that it works reasonably well with the 80-200 zoom lens I use throughout the lens's range. When I use it at night I find it handy to have along a strong flashlight (and someone to aim) to aid in focusing the camera.

The Elan camera, in common with many of the new models, comes with a built-in flash that is really quite good when used with shorter length lenses. I used it for some of the people shots and quite a few of the pictures I took to illustrate the ecology of the forest floor.

When all is said and done, however, there is something artificial about flash photography when it comes to nature. I think we have come to accept its use with people, but it still strikes a jarring note when used with animals. A diffuser in front of the flash sometimes helps (for example; Kleenex tissue over the flash or the opaque plastic that comes with your outfit). Tilting the flash upwards and bouncing the light off a piece of cardboard also helps.

For all my discomfort with using a flash, I still carry one as part of my basic equipment. There have been times on assignments when the flash has provided the only workable source of light. In a forest setting or in overcast weather the flash may be the only tool you have that allows you to photograph an animal or plant.

The other thing about flash photography is that it is fun to play around with. It will stop the action, especially at night, and I've been known to have friends run up and down the road for the sole purpose of stopping them in mid-stride with a burst of light. I've also used the flash to "paint" a campsite with light. You do this by mounting your camera on a tripod and then tripping the shutter so that it stays open for thirty seconds or so. Once the camera has been fired, use the flash to fire beams of light at the areas you want exposed. Try it.

And of course there is no better way on a black night in a black dump to photograph a black bear.

CAMERA BAGS AND SUCH

The choice of a camera bag will largely be determined by the amount of equipment you want to carry. For canoe trips and visits to dusty countries (like Kenya), I prefer a hard-sided, air- and watertight case. Most will float should you tip (or worse, your plane crashes) and that makes them well worth the extra room they take up.

I recently added a Lowepro backpack camera bag to my equipment list. While it will not provide the level of protection the hard-sided case does, it allows me to carry my cameras and lenses on my back. This case is a lot easier to hike with and will likely take over the carrying work on more and more trips as time goes by.

No matter what style of case you buy, it has to protect your investments. It should be padded and have sturdy straps for carrying the heavy equipment. There should be space for spare batteries, films, cleaning equipment and instruction books. (Some of the new cameras are so complicated you will want to carry an instruction book at all times ... trust me on this.)

Good bags will cost you a few dollars but they are worth the investment.

Acknowledgements

As with any book, it falls upon the author to acknowledge those people who helped him either directly or indirectly with the project. It is with great pleasure that I perform this task as the very writing of their names recalls memories of campfires, moose, stories and adventures.

First, I must thank my wife, Anne, who supported this project wholeheartedly and understood that writing and photography (even if they are fun to do) are in fact work. My daughters, Liza and Ashley, also went out of their way to make it easier for me to write and were willing company on many trips to the park. Jim Markou is a friend, a brother-in-law, an advisor and a competitor, whose company and experience I truly benefited from. Thanks.

Everyone needs someone to bounce ideas off and to advise on more technical matters. While I had many sources, the one who took the greatest interest and care is Don McClement. Don was always willing to make suggestions to make the manuscript better and search out answers. He is one of the finest naturalists I know and a good friend.

Many people accompanied me on trips into the park while I was working on this book. Besides the ones listed above, they include the "Dads and Daughters" group: Bob and Kathleen Bowyer, Bob and Heather Watts, Ian and Heather Stanners, who joined me on our traditional father daughter canoe trip for several years now. Ben and Brendan McClement, who one early spring day met a moose close up and personal.

My parents Wes and Edna, sisters Susan, Nancy and Donna, who were there during my first visits to the park back in the 1960s. It was my parents' willingness to give up cottage life for South Tea Lake Annex to which I owe my Algonquin roots. As a family, we shared many great times and the closing of that campsite still remains a loss for us.

Thanks too to Jim and Pat Allinson and Jan and Kathy Porszt, along with friends and relatives Sonny Allinson and Wayne Hollingshead, Betty and Kay Irvine, Ed Jessop, Don Caswell, Jim Hollet, Jack Putterall, Ken McRae, Kenny and Barb Taylor, Ann and Jane Weller and especially Richard and Bernice Stevens and their mother Bernice who first told us about the park's wonders. They made my summers in the park so much fun. Thanks for the memories.

I appreciate, too, the help Ron Tozer has been over the years. I haven't seen much of him since I worked for him as a park naturalist but whenever I had a question he always kindly answered it and pointed me in the right direction.

Thanks are owed to Burt Myers, Mike Bolton, John Kerr and Yukio Yamada at *Ontario Out of Doors* Magazine. It was here I got my start as a writer and many of my assignments took me to the park. Thanks go to the many biologists that I interviewed in the course of my years as a freelance writer. I also acknowledge a debt to those many whose books and articles enriched my pool of knowledge.

I acknowledge the support and advice I received from Canon, Canada. As noted in the text, I use Kodak film and I greatly appreciate their support too. Anne and Lil and the others always take good care of my film when I bring in it to them for processing.

Thank you as well to my publisher, Barry Penhale, for his interest and advice.

Of course, any errors in the text are mine alone and I take full responsibility.

Bibliography

Attenborough, David. *The Living Planet.* Boston, Mass.: Little Brown & Company, 1984.

Bauer, Erwin. *Erwin Bauer's Deer In Their World* . New York: Outdoor Life Books, 1983.

Bennet, Doug & Tim Tiner. *Up North: A Guide to Ontario's Wilderness.* Markham: Reed Books, 1993.

Benyus, Janine M. *The Field Guide to Wildlife Habitats of the Eastern United States.* New York: Fireside, 1989.

Benyus, Janine M. *Northwoods Wildlife: A Watcher's Guide to Habitats.* Minoqua: Northword Press, 1989.

Dickinson, Mary B. *The Curious Naturalist.* Washington D.C.: National Geographic Society, 1991.

Editors of Eastman Kodak Company. *The Joy of Photography.* Rochester: Addison Wesley/ Eastman Kodak, 1979.

Editors of Eastman Kodak Company. *More Joy of Photography.* Rochester: Addison Wesley/Eastman Kodak, 1981.

Editors of Time Life Books. *Photographing Nature.* Alexandria: Revised Edition. Time Life Books, 1981.

Ehrlich, Paul R., David Dobkin and Darryl Wheye. *The Birder's Handbook: A Field Guide to the Natural History of Birds.* New York: Simon and Schuster, 1988.

Fitzharris, Tim. *The Audubon Society Guide to Nature Photography.* Toronto: Stoddart Publishing, 1990.

Freeman, Michael. *How To Take Great Nature & Wildlife Photos.* Tucson: HPBooks Publishing, 1981.

Guillet. G.R. *Geological Guide to Highway 60 Algonquin Provincial Park.* Toronto: Ontario Dept. of Mines, 1972.

Guiness, Alma E., Editor. *The Joy of Nature.* Pleasantville: Reader's Digest Inc., 1977

Information Officer. *Fishing in Algonquin Provincial Park.* Toronto: Ministry of Natural Resources, 1978.
Information Officer. *Reptiles and Amphibians of Algonquin Provincial Park.* Toronto: Ministry of Natural Resources, 1976.
Information Officer. *Mammals of Algonquin Provincial Park.* Toronto: Ministry of Natural Resources, 1976.
Information Officer. *Birds of Algonquin Provincial Park.* Toronto: Ministry of Natural Resources, 1977.
Information Officer. *Wildflowers of Algonquin Provincial Park.* Toronto: Ministry of Natural Resources, 1978.
Information Officer. *A Pictorial History of Algonquin Provincial Park.* Toronto: Ministry of Natural Resources, 1978.
Information Officer. *Spruce Bog Board Walk.*Toronto: Ministry of Natural Resources, 1980.
Johnson, Bob. *Familiar Amphibians & Reptiles of Ontario.* Toronto: Natural Heritage, 1989.
Lee Rue, Leonard III. *How I Photograph Wildlife And Nature.* New York: W.W. Norton & Company, 1984.
MacKay, Rory. *A Chronology of Algonquin Provincial Park.* Whitney: Friends of Algonquin Park, 1988.
McDonald, Joe. *The Complete Guide to Wildlife Photography.* New York: Amphoto, 1992.
Reader, John and Harvey Croze. *Pyramids of Life: Illuminations of Nature's Fearful Symmetry.* New York: J.P. Lippincott Company, 1978.
Runtz, Michael W.P. *The Explorer's Guide to Algonquin Park.* Toronto: Stoddart, 1993.
Runtz, Michael W.P. *Algonquin Seasons.* Toronto: Stoddart, 1992.
Runtz, Michael W.P. *Moose Country.* Toronto: Stoddart, 1991.
Simons, Paul. "Meateating vegetables not so weird after all." Toronto: *The Toronto Star,* Sunday July 4, 1993.
Stirling, Ian, Editor. *Bears. Majestic Creatures of the Wild.* Emmanus: Rodale Press Inc., 1993.
Strickland, Dan. *Wolf Howling in Algonquin Park.* Whitney: The Friends of Algonquin Park, 1992.
Strickland, Dan. *Trees of Algonquin Provincial Park.* Whitney: The Friends of Algonquin Park, 1989.
Strickland, Dan. *Acid Rain in Algonquin Provincial Park.* Whitney: Friends of Algonquin Park, 1988.
Strickland, Dan. *Algonquin Logging Museum.* Whitney: Friends of Algonquin Park, 1993.
Strickland, Dan and Russ Rutter. *The Best of the Raven.* Whitney: Friends of Algonquin Park, 1993.
Taylor, Dave. *Safari: Journey to the End.* Erin : Boston Mills Press, 1990.
Taylor, Dave. *Ontario's Wildlife.* Erin: Boston Mills, 1988.
Taylor, J. David. *Game Animals of North America.* Toronto: Key Porter (Discovery), 1987.

Theberge, John. *Legacy. The Natural History of Ontario.* Toronto: McClelland and Stewart, 1988.

Theberge, John and Mary. *Wolves & Wolf Research in Algonquin Park.* Toronto: Faculty of Environmental Studies, 1990.

Thorn, Greg R. *Mushrooms of Algonquin Provincial Park.* Whitney: The Friends of Algonquin Park, 1991.

Tozer, Ron. *Checklist & Seasonal Status of the Birds of Algonquin Provincial Park.* Whitney: Friends of Algonquin Park, 1990.

Wolfe, Art and Martha Hill. *The ART of Photographing Nature.* New York: Crown Trade Paperbacks, Crown Pub., 1993.

Index

Page numbers in italics refer to photographs.